COMMENTARY ON
PETER & JUDE

COMMENTARY ON
PETER & JUDE

MARTIN LUTHER

kregel
CLASSICS

Grand Rapids, MI 49501

Commentary on Peter and Jude by Martin Luther

Published in 1990 by Kregel Classics, an imprint of Kregel Publications, P.O. Box 2607, Grand Rapids, MI 49501. Kregel Classics provides trusted, time-proven publications for Christian life and ministry. Your comments and suggestions are valued.

For more information about Kregel Publications, visit our web page at http://www.kregel.com.

Chapter Outlines by J. G. Walsh
Edited by John N. Lenker

Library of Congress Cataloging-in-Publication Data
Luther, Martin, 1483–1546.
    Commentary on Peter and Jude / Martin Luther.
      p.   cm.
    Translation of: *Enarrationes in epistolas Divi Petri duas at Iudae unam.*
    Reprint. Originally published: The Epistles of St. Peter and St. Jude. Minneapolis, Minn.: Lutherans in All Lands Co., 1904.
    1. Bible. N.T. Peter—Commentaries—Early works to 1800. 2. Bible. N.T. Jude—Early works to 1800. I. Title.
BS2795.L8713   1990   227'.9207—dc20   90-30216
                                                        CIP

ISBN 0-8254-3147-6

Printed in the United States of America

4 5 6 / 03 02 01 00 99 98 97

CONTENTS

PUBLISHER'S PREFACE

"A sword which was wielded by a giant." This is what has been said of this work by that stalwart of the faith, Martin Luther. What a giant he was!

This commentary on the epistles of Peter and Jude, first published in German in 1523 is, as "the prince of preachers" Charles H. Spurgeon called it, "one of his best productions."

Second Peter and Jude are often neglected portions of the New Testament, but Luther — even though writing more than four and a half centuries ago — brings to the surface the important message these epistles have for the church today.

Written in his pungent, simple, and clear style, this study amplifies the variety of themes recorded in these epistles. Luther deals hard with sin, but he shows forth in a precise manner the way of salvation through Christ. His emphasis on the Christian life is full of practical advice for deep, spiritual growth. In a definite and stirring way, the author presents the eternal hope of the believer with a reminder that he is but a pilgrim and stranger here on his way to an eternal rest with the Lord. As is expected in a work of this caliber, Luther carefully defines the relationship of faith to works.

This new edition combines into one volume the earlier editions of 1523 and 1539, which were translated into English and edited by John Nichols Lenker in 1904. It retains the 1539 supplementary notes of George Roerer and the outlines of each chapter by J.G. Walsh.

The cry of the past is the cry of today: "Read Luther!" It is the publisher's hope that the reading of this work, written by this giant in the faith, will penetrate your soul and bring you to a deeper and more thorough knowledge of God's Word.

THE PUBLISHERS

INTRODUCTION TO FIRST PETER

Before we enter upon the explanation of the epistle of Peter, it is necessary that we give a brief introduction or a few words of instruction so that we may know in what esteem this epistle is to be held and so that we may grasp the right understanding of it.

In the first place we must remember that all the apostles advocated one and the same doctrine; and it is not correct that we count or speak of four evangelists and four gospels, for all that the apostles have written is one gospel. But gospel means nothing more nor less than a sermon or proclamation of the grace and mercy of God, merited and acquired through our Lord Jesus Christ by his death. And properly speaking, it is not that which is contained in books and comprehended in the letter, but rather an oral sermon, a living word, a voice which sounds and resounds through the whole world and is proclaimed publicly so that it is heard everywhere. Hence it is furthermore not a lawbook that contains many good doctrines, which have hitherto been held. For it does not bid us to do certain works by which we become pious. Instead, it makes known to us the grace of God, bestowed gratuitously and without any merit on our part. Also it tells how Christ has taken our place and made satisfaction for our sins and canceled them and through His own works justifies and saves us.

Now, whoever proclaims this by preaching or writing teaches the pure gospel, as all the apostles did, especially Paul and Peter in their epistles. Therefore it is all one and the same gospel that we preach concerning Christ, although one pursues a different method and speaks in different words from another. For it may indeed be a short or a long discourse, and a brief or an extensive writing. But whenever it touches the point that Christ is our Savior and that we are justified and saved through faith in him without our works, then it is the same Word and the one gospel; just as there is also only one faith and one baptism in universal Christendom (Eph. 4:5).

Thus one apostle has written precisely what is found in the epistles of other apostles; but those who have advocated the most frequently and the most intensively that faith in Christ alone justifies, they are the best evangelists. Therefore the epistles of Paul are more a gospel than Matthew, Mark, and Luke. For these latter set forth more the history of the works and miracles of Christ. But the grace we have through Christ none paints forth so valiantly and so fully as Paul, especially in his epistle to the Romans.

Since far more depends upon the words of Christ than upon his works and deeds, if we must be deprived of one, it were better for us to be deprived of his works and history than of his words and doctrines. Therefore those books are justly praised the highest which treat most of the doctrines and words of our Lord Jesus Christ. For if the miracles of Christ had never been performed, or if we had no knowledge of them, we would still have sufficient in his word, without which we could not have life.

Consequently this epistle of Peter is one of the grandest of the New Testament, and it is the true, pure gospel. For Peter does also the very same thing as Paul and all the evangelists do in that he inculcates the true doctrine of faith,—how Christ has been given to us, who takes away our sins and saves us, as we shall hear.

From this you can now judge of all books and doctrines, what is gospel and what is not. For whatever is not proclaimed in sermons and writings in harmony with the above, you may freely pass judgment upon it that it is false, however good it may appear to be. This ability and power to judge is something all Christians have,—not the Pope and Councils, who boast how they alone possess the power to pass judgment on doctrine.

Peter wrote this, his first epistle, to the converted heathen and exhorted them to continue steadfast in their faith and to grow in it under all kinds of suffering and in every good work.

In the first chapter he strengthens their faith by the divine promise and power of their future salvation, and he shows that it was not merited by us; but that it was first proclaimed through the prophets. Therefore they should now live righteously in the new man and forget the old, as those who are born anew through the living, eternal Word of God.

In the second chapter he teaches them to know Christ the head and cornerstone, as true priests to offer themselves unto God, and as Christ offered himself. Then he begins to instruct men in all the various callings of life. In the first place, he teaches them in general to be subject to the civil government, and then in particular he tells the servants to be obedient to their masters and if necessary, suffer unjustly from them for the sake of Christ, who also suffered unjustly for us.

In the third chapter the apostle teaches wives to be in subjection to their husbands—even if they are unbelievers—and adorn themselves in holiness of character. Likewise the husbands are admonished to be patient and forbearing toward their wives; and then in general to be humble, forbearing and kind in their relations to one another, as Christ was to us sinners.

In the fourth chapter he teaches us to bring the flesh into subjection by fasting, watchfulness, temperance, and prayer; then he comforts and strengthens us with the sufferings of Christ. Next he instructs the spiritual government, how it should confine itself to the administration of the word and work of God alone each is to help the other with their gifts, and not to be surprised, but be joyful, if compelled to suffer for the sake of the name of Christ.

In the fifth chapter the apostle Peter admonishes the bishops and priests how to live and shepherd the people, and he warns us that Satan is seeking our destruction everywhere without tiring.

THE FIRST EPISTLE OF PETER

1 Peter 1

The Superscription, Subscription and Greeting of Peter; The Doctrine of Faith; and The Twofold Exhortation.

Outline

I. The Superscription, Subscription and Greeting of Peter, vv. 1-2.
 A. The superscription includes:
  1. The character of those to whom the epistle is written. Teachers of work righteousness are no apostles of Christ.
  2. The character of those to whom this letter is addressed.
   a. Their outward character, v. 1.
   b. Their inner character, v. 2. In what true sanctification consists. Of the spiritual and of the Levitical cleansing and sprinkling.
 B. The subscription.
  1. Its nature.
  2. All doctrines not in harmony with this subscription must be suppressed.
 C. The greeting. v. 2b.

II. The Doctrine of Faith , vv. 3-12.
 A. The author, origin, and foundation of faith, v. 3. In the work of salvation, the mercy of God alone is to be praised. All believers have the same treasure and blessing.
 B. What faith is and with what it has to do. Comparison of the eternal and temporal blessings, v. 4.
 C. Faith, the work and power of God, v. 5.
 D. Faith is accompanied by good works.
 E. Faith gives the right and clear understanding of things

pertaining to salvation. Of the source of work righteousness. Of the heavenly inheritance of believers.

F. Of the trial of proof of faith, vv. 6-9.
    1. The ground and cause of this proof, v. 6.
    2. To what the Christian should give heed in this trial.
    3. The nature of this trial, v. 7. Of the true character of the Christian life. Comparison of the joy of the world and of believers, vv. 8-9.

G. The conception and the promise of faith as set forth in the holy Scriptures, vv. 10-12.
    1. In General. Of the books of the Old Testament.
        a. If the books of the Old Testament are necessary for Christians.
        b. Of the difference in the writings of the Old Testament.
        c. In how far the books of the Old Testament are no longer in force and in how far they are in force.
    2. In Particular, v. 10. How and why we should not believe the Pope and Councils, when they deal with us without the word of God. Of the sufferings of Christ and of His believers, v. 11b. Of the Scriptures of the Old Testament. How and why the gospel must be apprehended by faith.

III. A Double Exhortation, vv. 13-25.
    A. The first exhortation pertains to faith, vv. 13-16.
        1. The true sense and understanding of this exhortation. The nature of the hypocrite. The character of true faith.
        2. The precaution to be observed in this exhortation. What is to be held as to fastings. The form of true faith.
        3. The motives which are attached to this exhortation.
            a. The first motive, v. 13a.
            b. The second motive v. 13b. In what way we become partakers of Christ.
            c. The third motive, v. 14. Where the knowledge of Christ is not, there blindness and error reign.
            d. The fourth motive, vv. 15-16.
                (1) Its nature.
                (2) How to preserve the same against the false interpretations of the papists. A short repetition of the above.
    B. The second exhortation pertains to the Christian life, vv. 17-25.
        1. The true sense and understanding of this admonition.
        2. The objection to the exhortation, and the answer. The

character of the true fear of God. The life of the
Christian is only a sojourning for the night.
3. The motives attached to this exhortation, vv. 18-25.
   a. The first motive, vv. 18-20.
      (1) Its nature.
      (2) Its use. Human righteousness is the greatest
         sin.
      (3) How and why Peter in this motive leads us
         into the Scriptures. "The last time" and "the
         last hour."
   b. The second motive, vv. 21-22. Of chastity.
      (1) How it is a fruit of faith.
      (2) How it must be constituted.
      (3) In what way it is to be promoted.
      (4) To what should it serve. Of the brotherhood of
         Christians.
   c. The third motive, vv. 23-25.
      (1) The foundation of this.
      (2) The explanation of this foundation. Of the
         power of the divine word. Conclusion of the
         exposition of the first chapter.

I. Superscription, Subscription, and Greeting (vv. 1, 2)

vv. 1,2. *Peter, an apostle of Jesus Christ, to the elect who are
sojourners of the Dispersion in Pontus, Galatia, Cappadocia, Asia,
Bithynia, according to the foreknowledge of God the Father in
sanctification of the Spirit, unto obedience and sprinkling of the
blood of Jesus Christ.*

This is the superscription and the subscription of the epistle.
Here at once you perceive the theme is the gospel. The writer
says he is an apostle, which means, "one sent to declare a
message" (Mundbote). Therefore it is correctly translated into
German, a *messenger*, or a *twelfth-messenger* (*zwoelfbote*), being
one of twelve messengers. But since it is now understood what
the Greek word *apostle* means, I have not rendered it in German. But its real meaning is, "one who bears a message by
word of mouth; not one who delivers letters, but a more ca-
pable person who presents and advocates a cause by the word
of his mouth, who in Latin is called an *orator*."

Observe here how all who preach the doctrines of men are at once excluded. For he only is a messenger of Jesus Christ, who advocates what Christ commanded him. Does he preach anything different, then he is no messenger of Christ, and therefore he is not worthy to be heard. But if he does as Christ commissioned him to do, then it is just as if you heard Christ Himself in person.

v. 1a. *Peter, an apostle of Jesus Christ.*

This is the subscription, the signature, of the epistle before us. In it Peter highly extols and praises his office. He says he is an apostle, an ambassador not of an earthly king or emperor, but of Jesus Christ, who is Lord over all (Acts 10).

He does not, however, bear this glorious title for the sake of his own person. He does it first of all because he will show by it that he has not been inducted into this high office by his own choice or presumption nor by human counsel, but that he has been promoted and called to it—without using any means on his part—by Christ, the Lord himself. Second, he carries this title so that we might be assured that his preaching and teaching, like the preaching and teaching of other apostles, was the Word of God, and whoever hears him and believes his testimony, hears the one whose messenger and ambassador he is, and will be saved; and whoever despises him, despises the one who sent him (Matt. 10).

Thus now with these few words, "Peter, an apostle of Jesus Christ," he testifies that he has been commissioned to fill an office in order that there might be preached to all the world the forgiveness of sins, deliverance from death, righteousness, life and salvation. This comes not through the law of Moses, much less through human laws, works, righteousness, merit; but alone through Jesus Christ, who was ordained thereto from eternity, and preached by all the prophets in order that he might bruise the head of the serpent and release all generations from the curse. He thus also at once in this subscription condemns all doctrines that lead one astray from this Savior and point to another way to become righteous before God and be saved. He also intimates that all who teach thus are not

Christians, but the apostles of Satan, no matter who they may be.

v. 1b. *To the elect who are sojourners of the Dispersion in Pontus, Galatia, Cappadocia, Asia, Bithynia.*

This is the superscription designating the people to whom Peter wrote this epistle, namely, to the heathen who lived in the countries he here mentions by name, who had been converted to the Christian faith by the preaching of the gospel. Otherwise he would not have written to them, nor admonished them to continue in their faith and grow.

Today these lands are in the possession of the Turks, and instead of Christ the cursed Mohammed is preached and worshiped. Yet, there may be some Christians still there. Pontus is a great and broad country by the sea; Cappadocia is near and borders on it. Galatia lies on this side of them, and Asia and Bithynia join them on the west, Bithynia bordering on the sea. They all are in the East and are large countries. Paul preached in Galatia and Asia, but whether he preached also in Bithynia I do not know. In the other two countries he never preached.

Here we observe that the apostles were sent especially to the heathen, just as the prophets were to the Jews. This is proved by the fact that the apostles wrote all their epistles to the heathen except the epistle to the Hebrews and that of James. Yes, you say, but Paul teaches (in Gal. 2:7) that he had been entrusted with the gospel to the Jews. However that argues nothing; for Peter preached also among the heathen or Gentiles, as recorded in Acts 10, and also wrote to them, as this superscription and the whole epistle prove. Therefore he is the apostle of the Gentiles as well as of the Jews, just as also Paul is called the Apostle of the Gentiles, yet he preached Christ unto them. But where they would not hear him nor accept his testimony, he turned to the Gentiles, as we see in the Acts. Hence even Christ calls him his chosen vessel, who should bear his name not only unto the Gentiles, but also unto the children of Israel (Acts 9:15).

Therefore Paul speaks in Galatians 2 of the condition of things at that time, when Peter was preaching to the Jews and he to the Gentiles. For Paul soon had a call and commission to go among the Gentiles and preach the gospel to them, yet he preached, as I said, also to the Jews. However Peter, along with others, had a commission to go to the lost sheep of the house of Israel, to whom Christ had been promised. After they visited them and had converted to the faith the little company, as Paul was accustomed to call the remnant, and the great mass remained hardened and even persecuted the apostles in the severest manner and ensnared them; they received the commission from Christ: "Go ye in all the world," and they turned to the Gentiles.

Therefore the apostles are really the fathers and teachers of the heathen, and it matters not that certain leading apostles remained for a time among the Jews. For if they all at times through their entire lives had preached only to the Jewish people in their own land, which was not the case, what would that argue over against the fact that their epistles were written to and had been delivered to, not only one people in a little corner of the world, as the Jews were, but to all the Gentiles, or heathen in the whole wide world? They preached through these epistles to the believers among them from that time until the present and will continue thus to preach to the end of the world? The evangelists also serve us heathen with their writings, for they teach and bear witness of him who has come as the Savior of the whole world and who fulfilled what was proclaimed concerning him in the Scriptures. Namely, that he should redeem the human race, that the Jews should be rejected, and that the heathen would be received as the people of God, just as has come to pass.

"Sojourners" are those we call foreigners. He calls them sojourners however they had been heathen. But since they had been converted to faith, he does not call them common sojourners, but elect sojourners; just as if he should say: You, while you were heathen and strangers who did not know God and had no hope, have never been but are now citizens with the saints and members of the family of God (Eph. 2); or as he here says, the elect who are sojourners, partakers of all the heavenly riches in Christ; just as he will explain in the following suggestive and glorious words:

v. 2a. *According to the foreknowledge of God the Father.*

Peter says, they are elected. How? Not by themselves, but according to the order or purpose of God. For we will not be able to raise ourselves to heaven nor create faith in ourselves. God will not permit all persons to enter heaven; he will very definitely identify his own. Here the human doctrine of free will and of our own ability avails nothing any longer. It does not depend upon our will but upon the will and election of God.

This means that you are chosen. You have not obtained it through your own strength, work, or merit, for the treasure is too great, and all the holiness and righteousness of mankind far too worthless to obtain it. Moreover, you were heathen, knew nothing of God, you had no hope, and you served dumb idols. Therefore, without any assistance on your part, out of pure grace you have come to such inexpressible glory, namely, only in the way that God the Father appointed you to it from eternity. Thus he presents the foreknowledge of God in a very beautiful and comforting light, as if he should have said: You are chosen and you will indeed remain so, for God who foreknew you is sufficiently strong and certain that his foreknowledge cannot fail him, nevertheless so far as you believe his promise and esteem him as the true God.

From this we can in brief draw the teaching that this foreknowledge does not rest upon our worthiness and merit, as the sophists hold, for then Satan could every moment make it doubtful and overthrow it. But it rests in the hand of God and is founded upon his mercy, which is unchangeable and eternal; consequently, it is called the foreknowledge of God. Therefore it is certain and cannot fail. Hence if your sins and unworthiness trouble you, and you begin to think you were not included in the foreknowledge of God or that the number of the elect is small and the company of the godless large, or if you are terrified by the awful examples of divine wrath and judgment, dispute not long why God made this or that so, and not differently, when he could have easily done so. Be not so bold as to try to explore the depths of the divine foreknowledge with the human reason, for thus you will certainly

go astray, you will either begin to doubt or be thrown over-
board to take your chances. Instead hold firmly to the promises of the gospel, which teaches you that Christ, the Son of
God, came into the world to bless all people upon the earth;
that is, that he might redeem them from sin and death, make
them righteous and happy, and that he did this according to
the command and gracious will of God, the heavenly Father,
who so loved the world that he gave his only begotten Son
that whosoever believeth on him should not perish, but have
eternal life (John 3:16). Dost thou follow this counsel, namely,
dost thou acknowledge that thou by nature art a child of wrath,
worthy of eternal death and condemnation, from which no
creature, neither human nor angelic, can save you? And dost
thou accordingly grasp the promise of God and believest thou
that he is the merciful, true God, who faithfully keeps, moved
by pure grace without our work and merit, what he has spoken, and has therefore sent Christ, his only Son, in order to
make satisfaction for thy sins and impute unto thee his innocence and righteousness, to redeem you finally from all need
and from death? Then doubt not, thou dost belong to the
company of the elect. If we consider the foreknowledge of
God in the manner Paul is accustomed to do, then it is comforting beyond measure. Whoever considers it differently, to
him it is something horrible.

v. 2b. *In sanctification of the Spirit.*

God has foreknown us, that we should be holy, and moreover that we should become spiritually holy. The precious
words *holy* and *spiritual* have also been perverted by the glut-
tonous preachers, in that they have called their state—that is,
the state of priests and monks —holy and spiritual. Thus they
have scandalously robbed us of these noble, precious words,
as also of the word *church*, since with them the pope and the
bishops are the church; while they do whatever they please,
saying the church has commanded it. Holiness does not consist in being monks, priests, and nuns, and in wearing the
tonsure and cowl. It is a spiritual word meaning that we are
inwardly from the heart holy in our spirit before God. And

this Peter has said for the purpose of showing that nothing is holy, except the holiness God works in us. For the Jews had in their day much outward or ceremonial holiness; it was, however, no genuine holiness. Peter will now say, God has foreknown you to the end that you should be truly holy; as Paul also says in Ephesians 4:24: "In righteousness and holiness of truth," that is, in genuine and well-founded holiness, for the outward holiness as the Jews had, avails nothing before God.

The Scriptures thus call us holy, while we still live here on the earth, if we believe. But the papists have robbed Protestants of this name, and say, "We are not to be holy, the saints in heaven only are holy." Hence we are compelled to reclaim this noble name. You must be holy; but you are to so govern yourself that you do not think you are holy of yourself or through your own merit; but you are holy because you have the Word of God, because heaven is yours, and because you are truly righteous and have become holy through Christ. This you must confess if you would be a Christian. For it would be the greatest dishonor and blasphemy of the name of Christ, if we took from the honor due to Christ's blood, in that it is this that washes away our sins, or from the faith that this blood sanctifies us. Therefore you must believe and confess that you are holy; but through this blood, not through your own excellence, to the extent that for it you would be willing to give up life and all you possess, and be ready for whatever may meet you.

God, the Father, the apostle says, ordained you that you should be his chosen children and be sanctified, but not by the outward, bodily sanctification of the law, which has never yet with all its sanctity been able to make a single person perfect in his conscience (Heb. 7:19; 9:13-14; Phil. 3:9). Much less however through your heathen customs and idolatrous worship. Through what means then? Through the sanctification of the Spirit, for your hearts are sanctified and cleansed through faith from the filthiness of idolatry. Unto what?

v. 2c. *Unto obedience and sprinkling of the blood of Jesus Christ.*

By this, he says, we are made holy, if we are obedient, if we believe the word of Christ, and if we are sprinkled with his blood. Here Peter speaks in a different manner from Paul. But it is in substance the same as when Paul says that we are saved through faith in Christ; for faith makes us obedient and submissive to Christ and his Word. For to obey the word of God and the word of Christ is the same thing, and to be "sprinkled by his blood" is the same as to believe. For it is hard for human nature, hostile to it and exceedingly humiliating, to submit to Christ, give up all its own possessions, and account them contemptible and sinful. But yet it must be brought into subjection.

Of sprinkling, Psalm "Miserere Domine," 51:7 also speaks: "Lord, sprinkle [or purify] me with hyssop, and I shall be clean." It refers to the law of Moses, from which Peter has taken it, and he discloses Moses to our view (2 Cor. 3:14), and leads us into the Scriptures. When Moses built the tabernacle, he took the blood of bullocks and sprinkled the tent and all the people (Ex. 24:8a; Heb. 9:19). But this sprinkling sanctifies not in the spirit, but only outwardly; therefore there must be a spiritual purification (Heb. 9:13-14). That was an outward holiness, one that pertains to the flesh, and is of no avail before God. And so God, by this sprinkling, has typified the spiritual sprinkling. Hence Peter said that the Jews in their holiness that was outward were held by the people as righteous, and persons of a pure life. But you are reputed to be base, being Gentiles, yet you have a better sprinkling. You are sprinkled in the Spirit, that you may be pure from within. The Jews were sprinkled outwardly with the blood of bullocks, but we are sprinkled inwardly in the conscience, so that the heart is made pure and joyful.

Thus the Gentiles are Gentiles no longer, the righteous Jews with their sprinkling are no more righteous, but all is reversed. There must be a sprinkling which converts us and makes us spiritually minded. But this sprinkling is to preach that Christ has shed his blood, has ascended to his Father, and intercedes, saying, "Beloved Father; behold my blood which I have shed for these sinners." If you believe this, you are sprinkled. Thus you see the right method of preaching. If all the popes, monks, and priests were to fuse all the material of their preaching into one mass, they would not even then teach and present as much as Peter does in these few words.

Thus you have the subscription of the epistle, in which he indicates his office and what he preaches, as you have now heard. For this alone is the gospel, and all else that does not accord with it is to be trodden under foot, and all other books are to be avoided in which you find some fine pretense of works and prayers and indulgence that does not teach the same doctrine, and is not confessedly grounded on it. All papal books have not a letter of this obedience, of this blood and sprinkling.

You are chosen of God and now sanctified. Peter says, not to the end that you should continue and remain in the sins of your former heathen and vain ways, but that henceforth you should be obedient to and believe the gospel of Jesus Christ, which is preached to you. No longer should you be sprinkled with the blood of calves and rams (Ex. 24:6-8, Heb. 9:19), nor with the sprinkling water of the ashes of the red heifer (Num. 19:9), as the Jewish people were sprinkled according to the law of Moses. By that sprinkling they were sanctified only to an outward and bodily holiness (Heb. 9:13), but by a far, far better and more costly sprinkling water, namely, with the precious blood of Jesus Christ, the innocent and spotless Lamb of God, through whom you are inwardly cleansed and sanctified in your spirit and conscience from all sin, so that now you are true servants of God, and pure and holy both in your soul and in your body.

And this sprinkling is accomplished when the gospel of Christ is preached, that he is the true Easter Lamb, who has offered himself for the sins of the whole world, gave and sacrificed his body and blood for us all. Whoever is obedient to his preaching and believes is sprinkled by the true high priest so that the destroyer can cause him neither suffering nor harm. Psalm 51:7 speaks also of a sprinkling: "purify me with hyssop, and I shall be clean: wash me and I shall be whiter than snow." It is as if he had said, "sprinkling and washing, commanded in the law, will never make my heart clean and snow white, so that I may be delivered from my sin, have a good and a joyful conscience before thee, and become righteous on

earth and saved in heaven. Lord, then thyself must here become the washer and the bather, and you must wash and
sprinkle me with another water and another blood than that
used by the Levitical high priest; otherwise, I will remain forever black, leprous and filthy, although I now sprinkle and
wash all my sins."

Here you see that not only the apostle Peter, but also the
holy prophet David, enlightened by the Holy Spirit long before and at the very time the reign of the law had reached its
height and was the most glorious, shows that the law with all
its beautiful and glorious worship and ceremonies, which were
many, as sacrifices, offerings, incense, washing and sprinkling,
were not able to make the heart and soul of the sinner clean.
All of that was only a type and figure of the true offering and
sprinkling of blood, which the true high priest himself had to
accomplish.

v. 2d. *Grace to you and peace be multiplied.*

Peter adopts here the mode of greeting of the apostle Paul,
although not fully, and it is as if he had said, "ye have now
peace and grace, but yet not in perfection; therefore ye must
continue to increase in them till the old Adam die." *Grace* is
God's favor, which now begins in us, but which must continue to work and grow even till death. Whoever confesses
and believes that he has a gracious God, possesses him, while
his heart gains peace also, and he fears neither the world nor
the devil; for he knows that God, who controls all things, is
his friend, and will deliver him from death, hell, and all evil;
therefore his conscience has peace and joy. Such is the desire
of Peter for those that believed, and it is a true Christian greeting with which all Christians might well greet one another.

"Grace to you and peace be multiplied." That is the greeting. You are now, he will say, obedient to Christ, with whose
blood you are sprinkled and through whom you are cleansed
from your sins. You believe on him, for whose sake you are
righteous and holy before your heavenly Father by grace. Since
you know and believe this, you have a joyful and peaceful
conscience. But Satan and the world will inflict upon you all

kinds of suffering because of this knowledge and faith, the latter by fear and the former by persecution. Therefore I wish from the depth of my heart that God, the merciful Father, would give you abundant grace and peace, so that, although Satan may attack thee hard with his fiery darts and make bold to overthrow your faith, for he sleeps not, but goes about like a roaring lion, and the world persecutes, reviles and condemns you as a heretic, that you let not such things trouble you. But comfort yourselves always in the face of these horrible experiences and trials with the thought that God in heaven is gracious unto you for the sake of Christ, in which you have a good conscience and constant peace. As long as he only is gracious to me, then let Satan and the world terrify, rage, and persecute as much as they wish.

Thus we have the superscription, with the greeting. Now he begins the epistle, and says:

II.   Doctrine of Faith (vv. 3-12)

vv. 3-9. *Blessed be the God and Father of our Lord Jesus Christ, who according to his great mercy begat us again unto a living hope by the resurrection of Jesus Christ from the dead, unto an inheritance incorruptible, and undefiled, and that fadeth not away, reserved in heaven for you, who by the power of God are guarded through faith unto a salvation ready to be revealed in the last time. Wherein ye greatly rejoice, though now for a little while, if need be, ye have been put to grief in manifold trials, that the proof of your faith, being more precious than gold that perisheth though it is proved by fire, may be found unto praise and glory and honor at the revelation of Jesus Christ: whom not having seen ye love; on whom, though now ye see him not, yet believing, ye rejoice greatly with joy unspeakable and full of glory: receiving the end of your faith, even the salvation of your souls.*

In this preface you perceive a truly apostolic address and introduction to the matter in hand, and as I have said already (in the Introduction, pp. 9-11), this is the model of a noble epistle. For he has already exhibited and made manifest what Christ is, and what we have attained through him, when he

says that God hath begotten us again unto a living hope
through the resurrection of Christ. He also said that all good
things are bestowed upon us by the Father, not for any merit
of ours, but from pure mercy. These are true gospel words
that are to be preached. But how little, God save us, of this
kind of preaching is to be met with in all sorts of books, even
those that must be considered the best—even those written by
St. Jerome and St. Augustine. How little agreement is there
with this passage! We must preach Jesus Christ, that he died
and rose again, and why he died and rose again, that through
such preaching men might believe on him and be saved. That
is preaching the true gospel. Whatever is not preached in this
manner is not the Gospel, and it matters not who does it.

This is now the grand summary of these words: Christ,
through his resurrection, has brought us to the Father; and so
also Peter would with them bring us to the Father by the Lord
Christ, and he sets him forth as Mediator between God and
us. Hitherto we have been taught to call upon the saints; that
they are our intercessors with God, while moreover we have
had recourse to our dear Virgin, and have set her up as Me-
diatress, and have let Christ go as an angry judge. This the
Scripture does not do; it goes further and exalts Christ, teaching that he is our Mediator, by whom we come to the Father.
Oh! it is a blessing infinitely vast, bestowed upon us through
Christ, that we may go into the presence of the Father and
claim the inheritance of which Peter here speaks.

These words also well exhibit the feelings the apostle had
as he began with the deepest reverence to praise the Father.
He would have us adore and bless him for the sake of the
infinite riches he has bestowed upon us, in that he has begotten us again, and this too, before we had desired or sought it.
So nothing is to be praised but pure mercy. Hence we cannot
make our boast of any works, but we confess that we hold all
that we have of God's compassion. There is no longer the law
and vengeance before us, as heretofore, when he terrified the
Jews so that they were forced to flee, but dared not go toward
the mount (Gen. 19:19). He vexes and chastises us no more,
but shows us the greatest friendship, creates us anew, and
appoints us, not to do some work or works, but produces

within us an entirely new birth and new being, that we should be something different from what we were before, when we were Adam's children. Namely, we are transplanted from Adam's heritage into the heritage of God so that God is our Father, we are his children, and thus also heirs of all the good he possesses.

Observe how valiantly the Scriptures present this matter. It is all a living, not a vain, matter in which we are concerned. Since we are thus begotten again, the children and heirs of God, we are equal in honor and dignity with Paul, Peter, our blessed Virgin, and all the saints. For we have the treasure and all good things from God just as richly as they, for it was just as necessary for them to be begotten again as for us. Therefore they have nothing more than all other Christians.

v. 3. *Blessed be the God and Father of our Lord Jesus Christ, who according to his great mercy begot us again unto a living hope by the resurrection of Jesus Christ from the dead.*

Satan has through the fall of Adam brought the human race into such awful ruin and misery that all men are conceived and born in sin. Consequently they must be subject to the power of Satan. Therefore the physical birth from their father and mother can bring them and give them nothing more than this temporal and transient life, which is not only full of toil and trouble, but is moreover very short and uncertain. In life we are not insured against death for a single moment; and if it would at once destroy us, there would still be no end to the misery; indeed our real distress and torment would then truly first begin. For since we all by nature are the children of wrath and the enemies of God, we have merited, besides temporal death, also eternal death and condemnation. Into this dreadful and inexpressible misfortune all the children of Adam have sunk and there they stick. All, there is no one excepted.

The question arises, what can we do to free ourselves from this misery, find the right path, become pious and be saved? Here everyone wishes to be an expert and thinks he knows best how to put all in order again. Ask the Jew, and he gives you this answer: if he is circumcised and keeps the law, then he will become righteous and be saved. A monk says, if he conducts himself according to the rules of his order. A Turk says, if he does what stands written in the Koran. The sum of the whole matter is that every person, even if he be of a different opinion, cherishes by nature the thought that he will and can, through his own strength, free will, good works, and merit, or indeed especially through the laws of Moses, not only atone for his sins and still the wrath of God, but also merit the grace of God and acquire eternal salvation, and thus heal and abolish this deadly disease. Higher the human reason cannot rise, and therefore neither can it think, speak, and teach otherwise than has been said, as we have indeed sorely experienced in the papacy.

The holy Scriptures speak quite differently of this subject. It says that we can never by what we do nor by what we do not do be free from sin, escape death, obtain righteousness and salvation; that is come to the first original innocence and righteousness, which Adam lost through the Fall, and we all in him, unless we become really new creatures, are born again and in another way, not of father and mother, but of water and of the spirit (John 3:5; Tit. 3:5).

This is what Peter also teaches here when he says, "You are elected according to the foreknowledge of God, the Father, sanctified and sprinkled with the blood of our Lord Jesus Christ. To this you have come, not by your doing or not doing, but by the pure love and grace of our God and the Father of our Lord Jesus Christ. He has begotten you unto a living hope, who were without faith and hope in him, according to his great mercy, not because of your work or merit, much less for the sake of your sins. In that living hope you can surely expect the eternal, heavenly inheritance, which neither moth nor rust can devour and no thief can steal, for it is reserved for you in heaven. Now he who did the work has also the glory and the praise, and to him be honor and blessing through eternity, Amen."

But how or by what means does this new birth take place? "By the resurrection," Peter says, "of Jesus Christ from the dead;" as if he should say, God, the Father, has begotten us, not of corruptible (as he himself will explain later) but of incorruptible seed, namely, of the word of truth, which is the power of God. It begets new life and makes all alive and blessed who believe in it (Rom. 1:16). What kind of a word then is that? Even that which is preached among you concerning Jesus Christ, that he died for your sins and the sins of the whole world, and arose again on the third day that he might make satisfaction by his death for the sins of the whole world and by his resurrection bring us righteousness, life, and salvation. Whoever now believes this preaching, namely, that Christ died and rose again for his benefit, upon him the resurrection of Christ has proved its power. He is born again, that is, created anew after the image of God, receives the Holy Spirit, knows God's gracious will, has a heart, mind, courage, will and thoughts, which no work-righteous person or hypocrite has. Namely, it is not through the works of the law, much less through his own righteousness, but through the suffering and resurrection of Christ, he is righteous and a saved person.

This is what may be called true apostolic preaching. For the office of a true apostle is that he preaches not of the righteousness of man nor of the sanctity, but of the unspeakable grace and mercy of God, who spared not his only Son, but offered him for us all, that he might die the ignominious death of the cross and arise again for our righteousness. The apostles faithfully and powerfully advocated this doctrine. Whoever reads through their epistles, especially those of Paul, and reads their sermons in the Acts from beginning to end, will find that their discourses and words tend to show that Christ the Lord was rejected and crucified by his own people, to whom he was promised, although indeed he gave strong proof by deeds, miracles, and signs that he was the true Lord and Messiah; that God raised him again from the dead and made him to be Lord and Christ; that all who believe on him should in his name receive the forgiveness of their sins, which they could not secure through the works of the law (Acts 13:38, 39); that there is salvation in no other, as there is no other name given among men by which we shall be saved; and likewise that all we lost in Adam has been restored better than we enjoyed in Paradise. In brief, that all who believe on him will not only

become righteous and be saved through him, but also become
the children and heirs of God, will be brothers of Christ and
co-heirs with him, and like him will be raised again and placed
in our heavenly state (Eph. 2:6).

This is the blessed, comforting preaching Christ commissioned his apostles to herald forth in all the world for the
consolation of poor and troubled consciences. The Gospel, he
himself said in Matthew 11:5, is preached to the poor, that is,
to those who feel their sins, are terrified by death, earnestly
fear the wrath and judgment of God, and sigh for help and
comfort. Such persons can hear nothing more lovely and comforting than that Jesus Christ, the innocent and spotless Lamb
of God, has taken upon himself our sins, death, and all the
misfortunes that distress and oppress us here in this life and
torment and torture us forever in the life to come. He suffered
the law to condemn him as an evildoer, and he allowed death
to take his life. But since he himself was the eternal righteousness and the life, sin and death with all their power could not
hold him. Therefore he is the almighty Lord and God, who
had to lay down his life; but who had power to take it again
(John 10:18). He arose again from the dead, triumphed over
all these adversaries and led them captive, not for the sake of
his own person—for he never had any need of that—but for
the benefit of us poor, condemned sinners. We believe on him,
in order that those adversaries could not henceforth through
all eternity do us any harm or condemn us, although they at
times while we still live here terrify and torment us.

v. 3b. *Unto a living hope.*

The reason we Christians continue to live on the earth is
that we, after becoming believers, should proclaim abroad the
virtue of him who called us out of darkness into his marvelous light, that others might through us come to the same
knowledge and faith, just as we received it through brethren.
Otherwise it would be best if God would permit us to die as
soon as we are baptized and commence to believe. But as long
as we are upon the earth, we must live in hope. For although
we are indeed assured that through faith we possess all the

treasures of God (for faith certainly brings with it a new birth, adoption as a child of the heavenly family, and the inheritance), we do not yet possess them according to the senses, but we expect them through hope, which Peter, according to a Hebrew idiom, calls the hope of life. According to our manner of speaking, we call it a living hope or that in which we confidently hope and have the assurance of eternal life. The treasure, however, is still hidden, and a curtain is drawn before it, so that we cannot see it. It can now be apprehended only by the heart and through faith. Therefore we must in the meanwhile comfort ourselves with the hope, which is certain and will not let us be put to shame, until that day when we shall see what we now hope for. We call it "a living hope;" that is, one in which we certainly expect, and may be assured of, eternal life. But it is concealed, and a veil is drawn over it, that we see it not. It can only be apprehended in the heart and by faith, as John writes in his epistle, 1 John 3:2: "Now are we the children of God, and it doth not yet appear what we shall be; but we know that, when he shall appear we shall be like him, for we shall behold him as he is."

For this life, and the life to come, cannot be commingled, cannot consist with one another, so that we should eat, drink, sleep, watch, and do other works of the flesh which this life renders necessary, and at the same time enjoy our full salvation. Therefore we can never arrive at eternal life unless we die, and this present life passes away. Thus, as long as we are here we must stand in hope, until it be God's pleasure that we should behold the blessings that are ours.

But how do we attain to this living hope? "By the resurrection of Christ from the dead," he says. I have often asserted that no one can believe on God except through a mediation, since none of us can plead for ourselves before God, inasmuch as we are all children of wrath (Eph. 2:3); but we must have another through whom we may come before God, who shall intercede for us and reconcile us to God. But there is no other mediator than the Lord Christ, who is the Son of God. Therefore, that is not a true faith which is held by the Turks and Jews, namely, "I believe that God created heaven and earth." Just so do also the devils believe, but it does not help them

(James 2:19). For they venture to present themselves before God without having Christ as their mediator.

So Paul speaks in the fifth chapter of Romans, "We have access to God by faith," not through ourselves, but "through Christ," (vv. 1-2). Therefore we must bring Christ with us, must come with him, must satisfy God with him and do all we have to transact with God through him, and in his name. That is the thought implied here by Peter, and he would also say, we surely expect this life, although we are still on earth. But all comes in no other way than through the resurrection of Christ, since he has arisen and ascended to heaven, and is seated at the right hand of God. For this purpose he ascended, namely, in order to bestow upon us his Spirit, that we might be born again and now through him come to the Father and say, "Behold, I come before thee and pray, not because I rely on my own request, but because my Lord Christ has gone before me and is become my intercessor." These are all glowing words wherever there is a heart to believe them; where there is not, all is cold and unimpressive.

But by this, one may judge what is truly Christian doctrine or Christian preaching. For if we wish to preach the gospel, then in short the preaching must be about the resurrection of Jesus Christ. Whoever does not preach that, is no true apostle. For that is the chief article of our faith. Hence one can indeed feel that the epistle of James is no true apostolic epistle, for it contains scarcely a letter on these things. [See Luther's Preface to the Epistles of St. Peter.] The greatest force or importance lies in this article of faith. For were there no resurrection, then we would have no consolation and no hope, and all the rest that Christ did and suffered would have been in vain (1 Cor. 15:17).

Therefore one should teach after this manner: You perceive that Christ has died for you, has taken upon himself sin, death and hell, humbled himself under them, and in no respect were they able to crush him, for he was too strong for them. But he has risen from beneath them and has vanquished all, and he has brought them in subjection to himself: to this end, that you might be made free from them and made to triumph over them. If you believe this, then you possess it. All these things we could not effect by our own power; hence it was necessary that Christ should do it. Otherwise there would never have been any need for him to come down from heaven. Therefore it cannot be otherwise. If one preaches human works, then his preaching will find no entrance and it cannot be understood. Oh, so thoroughly as we Christians should know this, so clear should this epistle be to us!

By this sermon Peter will first of all forcibly dash to the ground all the glory of human power, of free will, of good works, of your own righteousness, yea, also of the righteousness of the law of Moses. For if it were possible for us to prepare ourselves for grace and secure eternal life through our own work and merit, as the pope and his sophists and canonists have shamelessly taught and written and wish still to defend the same as right; what need was there that God should have mercy upon us out of pure grace, permit his only son to become man to die on the cross for our sins, and to preach in his name repentance and the forgiveness of sins among all nations? Then, do I indeed hear that we dare do nothing that is good? Yea, we are born again in Christ Jesus just to that end, that we shall not only do good and are now for the first time able to do good, but must also suffer evil for all our good works, of which I will say more later.

Second, Peter here further shows, that we come to grace and are reconciled to God the Father through Christ alone as our only Mediator between God and man; for he says in plain words that God has begotten us again through the resurrection of Jesus Christ. Hence what has heretofore been taught in Christendom concerning praying to the saints, as if they were our mediators and intercessors who represent us before God and intercede in our behalf and could make us partakers of their merits, that is all false and a mere human invention. We have no authority for that in the Scriptures; moreover, the honor would thus be given to the saints, which belongs to Christ alone. This cannot under any circumstances be tolerated.

The same doctrine Paul also here and there teaches in his epistles. In Romans 5:1 he says, "Now being justified through faith, we have peace with God," not through our own selves, but "through our Lord Jesus Christ." Hence we must bring Christ with us, come with him, pay our debts with him, and do all through him and in his name that we wish to transact with God. Likewise does Peter here now say, we certainly are waiting for the eternal life, although we are still upon the earth; but in no other way than that Christ arose from the dead, ascended to heaven and sitteth at the right hand of God. For he ascended on high to the end that he might give us his Spirit, in order that we may be born again and now through him appear before the Father with a thirsting desire and say: "I come and pray before thee, heavenly Father, not that I depend upon my prayer for merit; but I come and pray in the name of Jesus Christ, my Lord, who arose from the dead and now sits at the right hand and is my advocate."

Now whoever is not placed in a contented frame of mind by this comforting doctrine of the Gospel and has not gained through Christ a joyful conscience and a strong refuge in God the Father through it, he will not certainly secure them through the law of Moses, much less through the commandments of men. For if he cannot be comforted by the facts that Jesus came into the world for the sake of sinners, died for them, shed his blood for them; a thousand times less can he be comforted by his orders, his own righteousness and the like for what is the holiness of all the angels and the suffering and merit of all the saints compared to the precious blood of God's Lamb? Hence the work-righteous people almost deserve that they permit their hearts through their entire lives to become as we say soured. They do great and heavy work, and yet have nothing from it except in time mere worry and labor and never a cheerful conscience, and in eternity condemnation and the torments of hell. If they would believe the gospel and permit Christ to become the Savior of the world, they would not dare to do so. But the world will not take any counsel; it is and will remain the devil's own possession. Therefore it hates the light and loves the darkness (John 3:20).

v. 4a. *Unto an inheritance incorruptible, and undefiled, and that fadeth not away.*

That is, we hope not for a blessing or an inheritance that is far off. But we live in the hope of an inheritance that is just at hand, and that is imperishable as well as undefiled and unfading. This blessing is ours henceforth and forever, although we do not now behold it. These are powerful and excellent words. Into whosoever mind they enter, he will, I imagine, not be greatly anxious about worldly goods and pleasures. How can it be possible that one who assuredly believes this should yet cleave to perishable possessions and lusts?

For if worldly goods are presented in contrast with this, it is at once seen how all passes away and endures but for a time; but this alone lasts forever and will never change. Besides, that is all impure and defiles us, for there is no man so devout that worldly prosperity will not soil him. But this inheritance alone is pure; whoever has it is ever undefiled; it will not fade; it will not wither and rot. All that is on earth, be it as hard as stone and iron, is yet changeable and has no permanence. As soon as man grows old, he becomes deformed and ugly. But this inheritance does not change, it abides forever, fresh and green. On earth there is no pleasure that will not at length become irksome, as we see man grow weary of all things; but with this blessing such is not the case. All this we possess only in Christ, through the mercy of God, if we believe, and it is freely bestowed upon us. For how is it possible that we poor wretches should be able to deserve through our own works such good, which no human reason or sense can grasp?

The apostle will thus say, God has begotten us again through the resurrection of Christ; not that we should here upon the earth be rich, powerful, and great lords, which natural birth brings with it unto those whom God favors, but he has begotten us to a heavenly inheritance compared with which all the riches, honor, and power of the whole world is merely nothing. For what the world offers, be it so costly, firm, beautiful, and lovely as it possibly can be, it is only transient and very uncertain. Therefore, a person is not secure for a single moment, and it is moreover corrupt, for people misuse it to their own ruin and condemnation; and besides one is also soon weary and tired of it. But our inheritance, which the new birth brings us is first incorruptible and eternal. We need not be concerned about any danger that it be injured or that it will have an end.

In the second place, this inheritance is undefiled. That is, it is very fair and beautiful, and it can never defile us or make us unclean, like our temporal possessions are so apt to do. In the third place, it fadeth not away. That is, it will neither wither nor decay, it does not decrease, as all kinds of worldly treasures do, but it continues fresh and green forever. Consequently, we will never become satiated and tired of it. We do not yet actually possess such an inheritance, but we have a sure hope of it.

These are indeed admirable and comforting words, which rightly cheer our hearts. However, since this our inheritance and treasure, of which Peter here speaks, are still hidden and cannot be apprehended by any of the senses, there are hence no poorer and more unworthy people upon the earth than those who wait for this inheritance in hope and must experience the terror of Satan in their hearts and suffer that the world is their bitter enemy, that it hates them, and that it persecutes and condemns them as the worst villains who are the cause of all evil. This makes them appear and feel as if they were not only forsaken by the whole world, but also by God himself. It does not seem that they are the children of God who are waiting for a better and more glorious inheritance in heaven than the riches and glory of all the kings of the world; yea, the world considers them mere beggars and fools. This horrible and terrifying view is a hindrance also to their faith and joy, and it is the cause that they of course often experience the opposite and think that God is angry at them and wishes to cast them to the abyss of hell and condemn them.

However, let all that disappear from your view and cling firmly to the words of Peter when he says, "God, the Father, hath by the resurrection of Jesus Christ begotten us to an inheritance incorruptible, undefiled and that fadeth not away; who do not yet possess it visibly, but with a sure hope expect it in due time." Although Satan will not now grant you this honor, and therefore, makes this life bitter and the world attacks you, do not let that worry you. It will not continue forever. We tarry here in his realm for but a short time, and since he receives and holds us only for evil, we ought to consider it for the best. Be patient and remain steadfast. We shall be repaid indeed and that richly for the small damage he can do us. After this little poverty, this small contempt, and this short-lived sorrow shall follow the eternal heavenly riches, glory and unspeakable joy and blessedness, compared with which all the suffering and evil that oppress us are not worthy to be mentioned. As the children of the world endure great perils and necessities with the hope of acquiring something temporal, why should we not much more have such a glorious, divine promise concerning this heavenly and eternal inheritance?

v. 4b. *Reserved in heaven for you.*

It is certain that this imperishable, undefiled, and unfading inheritance is ours. It is only for a little while concealed from us until we close our eyes and are buried, when we shall surely find and behold it if we believe.

Your heavenly inheritance, the apostle Peter says, is most certain, although you do not see it with the eye and do not at present possess it, it will be reserved and kept for you, where it is safe and where it will remain so, namely, in heaven, where no one can rob or steal it. There is left only a short time yet, and then you will not only see it, but also secure it as your own and possess it forever in glorious and unspeakable joy. When will this take place? At the last time, namely, when Christ shall appear in his glory and raise us from the dead. We think that is a long time yet in the future, but with God a thousand years are as one day, yea, as a watch in the night. So will it be with us when we are raised from the dead and have been a thousand years or more under the ground, we will think it is a short time that we slept in the grave. Moreover our present life passes so rapidly, it fairly flies (Ps. 90:10), and death overtakes us before we prepare for it.

v. 5a. *Who by the power of God are guarded [kept] through faith unto salvation.*

We wait for this priceless inheritance, he says, in the hope to which we have attained through faith. For this is their order of succession: From the word follows faith, from faith the new birth, from the new birth we pass to hope, so that we certainly expect and are assured of the blessing. Therefore Peter has here asserted in a truly Christian manner that it must take place by faith, not by our own works.

Moreover Peter significantly says here, "Ye are guarded by the power of God, unto salvation." But there are many people who, if they hear the gospel, namely, that faith alone, irrespective of works, justifies, rush plump forward at once and say, "Yes! I believe too!" They think the thoughts that they themselves conceive as faith. Yet we have also been taught from Scripture that we cannot do the least without God's Spirit; how then should we be able by our own power to do the highest work, namely, believe? Wherefore such thoughts are nothing else but a dream and a fiction. God's power must be present and work in us, in order that we may believe; as Paul also says, "God give unto you a spirit of wisdom to know what is the exceeding greatness of his power to us-ward who believe, according to that working of his mighty power" (Eph. 1:17, 19). Not only is it God's will, but a power of God, so that he lets it cost him much. For if God produces faith in men, it is certainly as great a work as his creation of heaven and earth.

Therefore those fools know not what they say, who ask, How can faith alone do it, seeing many believe who yet perform no good work? For they imagine their own vain dream is faith, and what faith may exist without good works? But we say, just as Peter says, faith is a divine power. When God produces faith, man must be born in another way and become a new creature; good works flowing from a purified nature must follow faith. So that we dare not say to a Christian who has faith, Do this or that work, for he performs of himself and unbidden nothing but good works. But this must be said to him, that he is not to deceive himself with a false, imaginary faith. Wherefore away with those rag-tag babblers (Lumpenwaescher), who say a great deal on the subject that is nothing after all but mere froth and vain prating. Of them Paul also speaks in 1 Corinthians 4:19-20, "I will come to you shortly and will know not the word of them that are puffed up, but the power; for the kingdom of God is not in word, but in power." Wherever this power of God is wanting, there is neither genuine faith nor good works. So they are mere liars, who pride themselves on their Christian name and faith and yet lead a wicked life. For if it were God's power, they would certainly be otherwise.

But what does Peter mean when he says, "Ye are guarded by the power of God unto salvation?" This is his meaning: So tender and precious is that which pertains to the faith that the power of God, that is with us and fills us, produces in us, that he gives us a correct, clear understanding of all things that pertain unto salvation. This allows us to judge all that is on the earth, and say, this doctrine is true, that is false; this conduct is right, that is not; this work is good and acceptable, that is evil. And whatever such a person resolves, is just and true, for he cannot be deceived; for he will be guarded, and preserved, and will remain a judge of everything that is taught and preached.

Again wherever faith and this power of God are wanting, there is nothing but error and blindness; there reason suffers itself to be led hither and thither, from one work to another, for it would gladly reach heaven by its own works, and is ever imagining thus, "Yes! this work will bring you to heaven: do it and you shall be saved." Hence there are so many chapters, cloisters, altars, priests, monks, and nuns in the world. Into such blindness does God permit the unbelieving to fall. But he keeps us, who believe, in a sound mind and in the true knowledge, so that we fall not into condemnation, but attain unto salvation.

v. 5b. *Ready to be revealed in the last time.*

That is, the inheritance appointed for them was long ago acquired, and it was prepared from the foundation of the world. But now it is hidden, as yet covered, reserved and sealed. But this is only for a little while, when in a moment it shall be opened and revealed, so that we shall behold it.

That is to say, it is impossible for you to endure the fierce wrath, poison, and cunning of Satan, and bear the bitter enmity, calumny, and persecution of the world. But you have a strong rear-guard and helper, whose name is God, the Father of our Lord Jesus Christ. He has begun a good work in you, and he must also complete it or all is lost. He will guard you through his divine almighty strength and power that you may continue steadfast in the faith of his word and await the salvation in the living hope through patience prepared for you from the foundation of the world, lying yet hidden and mantled, reserved and sealed, so that it remains indeed invulnerable and sure. However in due time it will, in the twinkling of an eye, be opened and uncovered so that you may view it forever and possess it as your joy.

The papists scoff at us because we so faithfully propagate the doctrine of faith, exalt it so highly, and make it so important that no one can readily apprehend and retain it. They say we can do nothing but teach about faith. Christians know beforehand what to believe, and faith should be preached to the Turks and heathen and the like. Also among us there are many who, when they hear that faith alone justifies without any works, form the delusion: Behold, what you hear and read in and out of the Scriptures, that you hold to be right and true, therefore you have faith. They think the delusion or dream, which they themselves create in their hearts, is faith.

But Peter constantly teaches here that faith is not an opinion or a simple illusion, which man creates for himself, but God's power must be there and work in us faith, and through faith we must be guarded and kept unto eternal salvation. In the same manner Paul speaks in Ephesians 1:17-20 concerning faith: "The God of our Lord Jesus Christ, the Father of glory, give you the spirit of wisdom and revelation...that you may know what is the exceeding greatness of his power to usward who believe, (not out of our own power or free will, but) according to that working of the strength of his might, which he wrought in Christ, when he raised him from the dead." Thus he would say that we believe in Christ and through him have an affectionate refuge to God as to our loving Father, which is accomplished through his exceedingly great power and mighty strength, by which he raised Christ from the dead. By the same, he creates and works in us such faith. From this, one readily sees that the apostle did not esteem faith as a small and mean art to be acquired by human power and to be learned so easily and quickly as the work righteous persons imagine. Paul constantly prayed for the Christian congregations to whom he wrote, that God would strengthen and keep them in the faith, and he wished that they might increase in the knowledge and faith of Christ, that they might have a perfect hope. As for himself, he confesses that he counts all things as loss compared with the excellency of the knowledge of Christ Jesus. Yet he says soon afterward that he has not yet apprehended, and is also not yet perfect. He strives for it, presses toward the mark and treasure (Phil. 3). Peter also does the same. He expresses to the believer his desire that God would richly give and increase his grace and peace unto them. Also, he wishes that they might grow in the grace and knowledge of Jesus Christ; and he prays that the God of all grace, who called them to his eternal glory in Christ Jesus, would prepare, strengthen, confirm, and establish them.

Consequently, when the poor papists represent that every Christian knows very well how or what he is to believe, they give sufficient evidence that they neither understand nor have experienced what faith is. Also the secure and false Christians, who are always more than the true believers, have no correct information concerning faith, for they think if they straightway fall into and continue in sin—yet they only believe—then there is no danger, for faith alone justifies without any good works. In that, they rest. They do nothing good, yea, only evil, and for all that, they wish to be Christians. But they are worse than the heathen. However, we heard above that faith begets new men and makes all things new in the heart, mind, and senses. These new men then as a good tree, bear good fruit, and lead a holy life. Where this is not the case, there is no true faith.

In brief the doctrine concerning faith is unknown to the world, and hence its judgment cannot be different, for the world thinks it is either a mere inferior art or an error and heresy. Those who confess and accept it are corrupters and enemies of the church. But Peter teaches here that faith is a precious and noble treasure with which nothing can be compared, for he gives a true, clear understanding, so as to judge rightly and firmly in all things. For whoever is informed and persuaded concerning faith from the Scriptures, and through faith has laid hold of the fact that Christ is the only Savior of the world (without whom and outside of whom no one will be redeemed from sin and death nor obtain salvation), he can readily pass judgment as to which doctrines are divine and wholesome and which are misleading and satanic. Only he can tell which is the true and which the false faith, which works are good and which are hypocritical, and which rests are holy and spiritual, and which are sinful and damnable. And he makes no mistake, for God's Word, according to which he judges, does not permit him to err. Again, where such knowledge and faith are not, there is nothing but blindness and error. Therefore the natural man cannot rightly judge of spiritual matters. He calls black white, darkness light, and again white black (Isa. 5:20). Hence it happens that man accepts now this and then another good work to atone for his sins and obtain God's grace. Therefore we have so many institutions, monasteries, and false modes of worship. That is all in vain, for Christ alone is the way, the truth, and the life; whom he does not enlighten through his word must go astray, accept lies for the truth, die in their sins, and be condemned.

v. 6. *Wherein ye greatly rejoice, though now for a little while, if need be, ye have been put to grief in manifold trials [temptations].*

Are you a Christian, and do you look for this inheritance or this salvation? Then you must cleave to this alone, despise all that is upon earth, and confess that all worldly reason, wisdom, and righteousness are nothing. This the world will not be able to bear. Therefore you are to expect that men shall condemn you and persecute you. Thus Peter joins faith, hope, and the holy cross together, for one follows upon the other.

And here the apostle gives us a source of consolation in case we suffer and are persecuted. This grief shall last but a little while; afterward ye shall be exceeding glad, for this salvation is already prepared for you. Wherefore be patient under your sufferings. This is moreover a truly Christian consolation, not such comfort as human doctrines give, which attempt nothing more than to find relief from outward ill. I speak not of bodily comfort, he seems to say; it is no real injury that ye have to endure outward ill, only go forward vigorously and be steadfast; inquire not how you may be free from the trouble, but think with yourself: "My inheritance is prepared and held out to me; it is only a short time before my suffering must cease." Thus we should lay aside temporal consolations, and over against them we should place the eternal consolation we have in God.

Moreover it is also well to observe here that the apostle adds "If need be." Just as he will also say later in 1 Peter 3:17: "If the will of God should so will." There are many people who would storm heaven and enter at once, hence they impose a cross upon themselves for their own fancied good; for reason will do nothing but propose forever its own works. It is not God's pleasure that we should select our own works, but wait for whatever God imposes upon us and ordains for us, that we may go and follow wherever he leads us. Hence, you are not to run after your own pleasure. In case it should be by God's appointment that you are to suffer, accept it and comfort yourself with the salvation that is not temporal but eternal.

Here the apostle sets forth how the Christians fare in the world. Before God in heaven they are the beloved children of the eternal, heavenly inheritance,—assured of their salvation, as has been said. But upon earth they are not only sorrowful, cast down, and forsaken, but they must also suffer many temptations from the devil and from the wicked world. How have they merited this? Their greatest sin was that they believed in Christ and published, commended, and praised before all the world the unspeakable goodness of God in him. They proclaimed that he alone can deliver us from sin and death, and justify and save us; that human reason through their free will, power and good works cannot prepare them for grace, much less merit eternal life. But with all their planning and doing—and it may sound and glitter as beautifully as it may—it will not reconcile God, but only kindle his wrath the more. They undertake all such things without, yea, even against his word and precept, ignore and despise what he has promised and commanded, and choose out of their own meditations and imaginations something special instead. Then the fire begins to blaze, for the world will not and cannot suffer its good intentions, meditations, holiness, and costly works to be rebuked and condemned, in that they will avail nothing before God. It then rushes ahead, persecutes, and destroys those who speak thus as the greatest blasphemers of God and even revolutionists. In all this they think they do God a service. Hence faith is not a sleepy thought in the heart, but whoever has faith speaks and testifies as one who really experiences it in his heart. Moreover when he then meets misfortune, he laments like the prophet in Psalm 116:10: "I believe, for I will speak: I was greatly afflicted." But prophet-like, we also will be greatly afflicted in this life. Hence Peter says that those of you who are sorrowful now for a short time lay hold of faith, hope, and holy Cross all together, for the one naturally follows from the other.

The apostle however does not stop here. He does not only say how they will become sad and sorrowful and will have to suffer various opposition, but at the same time he comforts them by saying it will last only a short time here on the earth, and then these sorrows and tribulations will most surely be followed by their eternal salvation, in which they will rejoice forever. That is real, true consolation; the very consolation the apostle is anxious to impart. He says nothing of the temporal peace, rest, and favor of the world, but the contrary, namely, that the Christians should ponder it well and freely, that they will not have it better than all the saints that ever lived, and the Lord himself had, the head of all the saints. What shall they then have? Tribulations, unrest, sorrow, anxiety, trouble, and the like. So then the consolation of the Christians does not consist in visible, present things, which however costly and glorious they may be, are nevertheless perishable and uncertain; but it consists in the invisible and future things, which are certain and eternal treasures.

Moreover it is to be observed that the apostle does not add in vain where it shall be, as he does in 3:17, when he says, "It is better, if the will of God should so will, that ye suffer for well-doing than for evil-doing." For there are many people who lay crosses upon themselves without any need of doing so, as the manner of work-righteous persons is. They go along, as Paul says, according to their own choice, in humility and in the spirituality of angels, have the appearance of possessing great wisdom and sanctity through their own self-chosen spirituality and humility, and in that they do not take care of their body nor give the flesh its honor by providing for its needs (Col. 2:23). The papacy has developed a great army of such. It should not be so, for it is not the will of God that you should select out of your own contemplations and mystical speculations your suffering and cross. If however you do, then you are the martyrs of the devil and not of Christ, and it will be harder for you thus to merit hell than for one who suffers for the sake of God, to merit heaven. But whenever it shall be, that is, if God so orders that you must submit to such things for the sake of confessing your faith, then accept it and comfort yourself with what Peter here says, that your sorrow shall last only a short time, but the salvation and blessedness, in which you should rejoice, shall last forever.

v. 7. *That the proof [trial] of your faith, being more precious than gold that perishes though it is proved by fire, may be found unto praise and glory and honor at the revelation of Jesus Christ.*

Peter cites in clear words the use of the Cross and the fruits of such persecution, which overtake believers both from tyrants and from the rabble, when he says: they serve to the end that faith thereby may be preserved and be found approved and more precious than perishable gold purified and tried by fire. For just as the fire does no harm to the gold, devours it not, neither diminishes it, but only serves it, for it takes from it all dross so that it becomes indeed pure and genuine, just so does the fire and heat of persecution and of all opposition indeed grieve us and cause the old Adam pain beyond measure, so that those exercised thereby become sad and for a time impatient; yet their faith will thereby become pure and genuine, like refined gold or silver.

The very nature of the Christian life is that it constantly increases and becomes holier and purer. We come to faith first through the preaching of the gospel, and through faith moreover we are justified and sanctified before God. But as long as we still live in the flesh, which is not without sin, it bestirs itself continually and pulls us back and hinders us from becoming as perfectly holy and pure as we indeed should become. Therefore God casts us into the very midst of the fire of opposition, suffering, and tribulation, by which we are cleansed and proved until the end of our lives; so that also in us not only is sin the more crucified the longer we live, but our faith also is preserved and increased. As a result, from day to day we become more assured of our calling, we grow in the understanding of the divine wisdom and knowledge, and the Scriptures become ever easier and clearer. This allows us to admonish more powerfully with wholesome doctrines those committed to us, and to punish the gainsayer. Had not the devil here of late years both with force and cunning attacked us so strongly, we would never have come to this certainty in our doctrine; neither would the articles of faith on the righteousness of the Christian and the doctrine of faith be developed as fully as they are. Hence, Paul says in 1 Corinthians 11:19: "There must be also factions among you, that they that are approved may be made manifest among you", and Christ says, Matthew 18:7: "It must needs be that occasions of stumbling or offences come, etc."

May we not also rejoice and even laugh when we see that the enemies of the divine truth have their will and desire realized in everything. That they have here every pleasure and joy, are wealthy, esteemed and influential, and that there is no limit or end to their daring and boasting. At the same time, we are poor, miserable and despised. But Peter seems to be saying, When things go thus, then is it well with us, for our faith must be proved to be genuine through various temptations, and we are strengthened and comforted in the face of such offenses, so that we are not provoked because of the godless. We pity them, and think what would it all amount to if they were even twice as rich and merry and had in addition the glory and power of the whole world? How long could they retain it? They are not assured of it for a single moment. Yea, before they expect it there is a change, so that with the rich man they perish forever and cannot have a drop of water, and in place of their short pleasure they must receive eternal suffering and sorrow.

Again, although we now suffer anxiety and tribulation here for a brief period, yet we have peace in Christ. We have it because we possess the true treasure, which is better and more precious than the glory and riches of the whole world, namely, his beloved word, which preaches to us concerning the eternal, heavenly treasures that Peter says are reserved in heaven for us. Here we and all the elect may suffer for a short time, nevertheless take up your cross and follow Christ. In company with him endure abuse and in patience wait for his blessed and comforting revelation and appearance, since he is to appear gloriously with his saints and wonderfully with all believers. Then we will receive our honor, praise, and glory, which God will give. But also will come the tribulations, since we know that tribulation worketh patience (Rom. 5:3).

To this end should the Cross and all kinds of reverses serve—to distinguish between false and true faith. God lays his hand upon us therefore, to try our faith and reveal it to the world, that others may be induced to believe, and we also be praised and honored. For just as we exalt God, so will he in return exalt, esteem, and honor us, insomuch that the false hypocrites, who do not go to heaven in the right way, shall be put to shame.

All Scripture likens temptation to fire. Thus Peter here compares the gold that is tried by fire to the trial of faith by temptation and suffering. The fire does not take from the gold, but makes it pure and bright, so all dross is removed. Hence God has imposed the Cross upon all Christians, that they might thereby be purified. And it has been well said, let faith remain pure as the word is pure so that we depend on the word alone and trust to nothing else. For we need such a fire and cross as this daily, because of the old corrupt Adam.

This is done for the good of the Christian life that it may continually grow and become more holy; for if we are led to faith through the preaching of the gospel, then shall we be justified and grow in holiness; but while we remain in the flesh we can never be fully purified. Therefore God throws us into the midst of the fire, that is, into suffering, shame, and calamity, so that we may become more and more purified until we die. To this we cannot attain by any works of our own. For how can an outward work make the heart inwardly clean? Moreover if faith is to be tried or purified, all that is additional and false must be separated and removed. Thence will follow glorious honors, praise, and thanksgiving when Christ shall be revealed. Therefore it follows:

v. 8a. *Whom not having seen ye love; in whom, though now ye see him not, yet believing, etc.*

Here he praises his readers and bears them the grand testimony that they love Christ and believe on him, although they had never seen him but had only heard of him. Their redemption stands ready and complete. For whoever believes in earnest that he is justified of his sins through the death and resurrection of Christ, and is delivered from death, will surely love Christ. Does he love him? Then the Father also will love him (John 16:27). It must however not be a false, painted love as the hypocrites have. They serve Christ in a different way than he taught and commanded, namely, according to their own good opinion and devotion, and they pose as if they did it in honor of Christ out of the pure love they have to him. Such love he does not desire; yea, he considers it the greatest ignominy and dishonor. Therefore the apostle adds: you believe on him, and this is the true honor, by which one knows that he loves him, namely, by believing his word. Therefore all is in vain that is done to the honor of Christ aside from believing on him.

Peter briefly shows by these words that the righteousness of the Christian is to believe on him, though he has never seen him, as he himself said in John 16:8-10: "The Holy Spirit will convict the world in respect of righteousness, because I go to the Father, and ye behold me no more." Further the Christian is to believe that Christ is true God, because this believing and trusting are becoming God alone. Now we believe on Christ.

We believe he can comfort and help us, he can rescue us from emergency, and he can justify and sanctify us. Also, although we do not now see him, yet we know for a certainty and believe that he is with us and in us (Matt. 28:20), and that he worketh all things in us. Finally, what kind of faith is it by which we are justified before God and sanctified. Namely, it is the faith in Christ, that he is our Savior and Mediator. By this all the innumerable kinds of unbelief are excluded.

vv. 8b, 9. *Ye rejoice greatly with joy unspeakable and full of glory; receiving the end of your faith, even the salvation of your souls.*

Peter speaks here so plainly of the approaching joy in the life beyond that I scarcely know if anywhere in the Scriptures it is treated with such plain and clear words, and yet it cannot then be fully expressed. Although he says your glory, joy, and salvation are wrested from you for a time, and you now still live here upon the earth in disgrace, sorrow, and tribulation because of the envy and malice of Satan and of the world, that will not harm you. Have patience, it will soon be different. When you now fall asleep in Christ and are buried, it will be only an hour or a very little time, as you will experience on that day, and then your joy will begin. It will be so great and glorious, he says, that no heart can reflect upon it sufficiently, much less will any mouth be able to express it. Therefore compared with it, all the joy that has ever been on the earth and yet may be is to be reckoned as mere child's play. For there is as yet no earthly joy so great and glorious that is not impure and mingled with suffering, or where suffering does not soon follow. Therefore Solomon said in Proverbs 14:13: "Even in laughter the heart is sorrowful; and the end of mirth is heaviness." Hence it cannot have any continuance; for it is not only obstructed without intermission by all kinds of misery and torture, but bodily death finally comes and ends it. Where there is no faith in Christ, this short, miserable, beggarly joy is followed by eternal death and condemnation.

However here it is the reverse. Sorrow and suffering are changed to joy, which is not only glorious and inexpressible, but in it we will also live forever and be saved. Therefore remain steadfast in the love and faith of Christ, but for whom you have not yet seen here in time, suffer, just as the devil and the wicked world may mete it out to you. Since you will be richly repaid and rewarded, for the end of your faith will be eternal salvation. That cannot be expressed in words, but it must and will be believed by the heart. Moreover should we not multiply words; it would still be useless. It cannot be expressed.

An unspeakably glorious joy shall it be, says Peter, and in addition to the joy we have honor and praise. The world has a kind of joy from which it receives nothing but disgrace, and of which we are compelled to be ashamed. Here Peter has evidently spoken of future joy, and there is scarcely so clear a passage of Scripture on the subject of the future joy as this one, and still he finds himself unable to express it. This is one point of the introduction, in which the apostle has shown what faith in Christ is, and how it must be tried and purified by reverses and sufferings when God appoints them for us. Now follows further how this faith is constituted and promised in the Scriptures.

vv. 10-12. *Concerning that salvation the prophets sought and searched diligently. They prophesied of the grace that should come unto you: searching what time or what manner of time the Spirit of Christ who was in them did point unto, when it testified beforehand the sufferings of Christ and the glories that should follow them. To whom it was revealed, that not unto themselves, but unto you, did they minister these things, which now have been announced unto you through them that preached the gospel unto you by the Holy Spirit sent forth from heaven. These things angels desire to look into.*

The salvation of which I speak and you will receive is sure because the holy prophets have born witness to it.

Peter refers us here back into the holy Scriptures, to see how God keeps what he has promised, not because of any merit on our part, but out of pure grace alone. For the whole Scriptures aim at this one thing, namely, to tear us away from our own works and bring us to faith. Therefore it is necessary that we study the Scriptures in order to be certain and clear as to faith. Likewise Paul also leads us into the Scriptures when he said in Romans 1:2 that God promised afore the gospel through his prophets in the holy Scriptures; and Romans 3:21, "The righteousness that comes through faith in Jesus Christ and avails before God, hath been manifested, being witnessed by the law and the prophets."

Thus also in Acts 17:2 and following we read that Paul preached faith in Christ to the Jews at Thessalonica and later at Berea. He reasoned with them from the Scriptures, opening and alleging that it behooved the Christ to suffer, etc. And when they had heard this, they examined the Scriptures daily to see if they held the same doctrine they were taught by Paul. We also therefore should search the Scriptures, for it is they that testify of Christ, as he himself says in John 5:39. It is also written in verse 46: "If ye believed Moses, ye would believe me, for he wrote of me." And thus we learn to confirm and establish the New Testament out of the Old Testament, and never give our confidence to the useless babblers, who despise the Old Testament and say it is no longer necessary. Thus we must establish the foundation of our faith out of the Old Testament and from no other source, for God sent the prophets for the purpose to the Jews, that they should bear witness of the future Christ. Hence the Apostles everywhere convinced and overwhelmed the Jews with proofs from their own writings that this Jesus whom they preached unto them was Christ.

Thus the books of Moses and of the prophets are also gospel, since they afore proclaimed and described Christ, whom the apostles later preached and described. Yet there is a difference between them. For, although both according to the letter are written on paper, yet the gospel or the New Testament, was not, properly speaking, written, but was formed from the living voice which sounded forth then and was heard in all the world. That it was however also written was the result from the superabundance or overflow of the preaching. On the other hand, the Old Testament was formed or composed only in writing. Hence it is also called "the letter," and the apostles designate it the Scripture or the writing, for it only pointed to the future Christ. The gospel however is the living sermon or preaching about Christ, who has now come.

Further there is a difference in the books of the Old Testament. First, the five books of Moses are the principal part of the Scripture and are properly called the Old Testament. After them come narratives and historical books, in which are described various examples of those who kept and of those who did not keep the law of Moses. In the third place, come the prophets who are grounded upon Moses. What he had written they picture forth and explain more fully and in clearer words. But the consensus of the prophets and of Moses is the same.

Concerning the saying that the Old Testament is abolished, here is what that means. First, the difference between the New Testament and the Old Testament is, as we have just said, that the Old Testament pointed forward to Christ, while the New Testament gives us now that which was promised in the Old and was there set forth in figures or types. Hence the figures are now abolished, for they served the purpose that what was promised in them is now finished, completed and fulfilled. Hence under the New Testament there shall now be no longer any difference or distinction in things such as meats, clothing, places, and times, for in Christ nothing avails anymore except a new creature. Even the Jews, who were obligated by their law to observe the distinctions in meats, places and the like, were not saved by such observance, and neither were they commanded to observe them for the purpose that they should thereby become righteous before God, but in order that under such discipline and under the burden of the law, they might long and pant for Christ who would bring an end to all that.

Further, it is to be observed that God in the Old Testament administered two kinds of government, through which he himself undertook to rule the people, both inwardly in their heart and outwardly as to their body and their possessions. Hence he gave them so many different laws, all mingled together. To the temporal government belong the laws that teach how to rule children, servants, and the home; also, how they should plant, build, borrow, cast lots, and fight. To the spiritual government belong all laws that give information about the outward forms of worship, but especially those dealing with faith and love, namely, that we should fear, believe, and love God with our whole heart and love our neighbors as ourselves. But now in the New Testament he reigns in us spiritually through Christ, while he executes the temporal or outward government through the worldly authorities. Therefore since Christ has come, the outward government is abolished. Hence God no longer appoints for us outward persons, times, and places, but governs us spiritually through the Word, so that we are lords over all that is outward and temporal, and we are bound by nothing corporal. However, that which pertains to the spiritual government is not abolished. It still stands and will stand, as do the laws of Moses concerning the love of God and the love of your neighbor. These laws God will have observed. Therefore he gives to his believing children the Holy Ghost, that they may be able to keep them.

Moreover, the figures remain also spiritually, that is, whatever is set forth spiritually by the figures; although the outward is abolished. For example, that a man should be divorced from his wife and let her go her away because of her adultery, is a figure and sign, which is now also spiritually fulfilled. For thus God rejected the Jews because they would not believe in Christ, and He chose and received the heathen or Gentiles. Also, he does the same now. If one will not walk in his faith, he permits him to be excommunicated from the Christian congregation, in order that he may reform. Similar it is also that a wife, after the death of her husband, had to take the brother of her husband and with him rear children, and he had to consent to be called by his name and to take possession of his estate. Although this has gone out of use, it is a figure that pointed to Christ; for he is our brother, has died for us and ascended into heaven, and has commanded us that we cause souls to be pregnant and fruitful through the Gospel; and in this we retain his name, are called after him and enter into his estate. Consequently I dare not glory in myself, that I have converted the people, but must ascribe all to the Lord. So it is with all the other figures of the Old Testament, which would require too much time to relate.

Thus all that is not outward or external in the Old Testament is still in force. For example, there are all the sayings of the prophets concerning faith and love. Consequently they even confirm faith and love, as is stated in Matthew 7:12: "All things therefore whatsoever ye would that men should do unto you, even so do ye also unto them; for this is the law and the prophets." Thus Moses and the prophets are witnesses of the future Christ. For example, when I wish to preach concerning Christ, that he is the only Savior, through whom everyone must be saved, may I not take the saying in Genesis 22:18: "In thy seed shall all the nations of the earth be blessed." Out of it I create a living voice and say, through Christ, who is the seed of Abraham, must all mankind be blessed. Therefore it is necessary that we believe on that Seed if we wish to escape condemnation. By the use of such sayings, we must lay the foundation for our faith, and we should let them remain in force, that we may see in them how they bear witness concerning Christ, in order that our faith thereby may be strengthened. This is what Peter will now do in the following words:

v. 10. *Concerning which salvation the prophets sought and searched diligently, who prophesied of the grace that should come unto you.*

Here we see that the beloved prophets had a longing in their hearts for the grace and salvation that was promised in Christ, and that is now offered and ministered to us and the whole world through the Gospel, which we confidently wait for in hope through patience. They would have gladly lived in the day it was revealed, and have seen and heard what we see and hear, as Christ said in Luke 10:24, but it was not possible for them to experience it. However, this they did do, namely, they sighed for it with a deep longing of their hearts, and they sought and searched for it with the greatest earnestness and diligence and with a delight and joy in the promises given unto the patriarchs, and served they us by explaining and developing those promises more richly and fully. Nevertheless they were comforted by the same grace and salvation, and they died in the faith of the future Christ. This is the meaning of Peter, when he says here: "Concerning which salvation the prophets sought and searched diligently...."

In like manner Paul said in Romans 16:25-26: "According to the revelation of the mystery which hath been kept in silence through times eternal, but now is manifested, and by the Scriptures of the prophets is made known." Thus you find many sayings in the New Testament taken out of the prophets. With these saying the apostles proved that everything has come to pass just as the prophets prophesied. Thus Christ himself proved from the prophet Isaiah that the Messiah was at hand when he said in Matthew 11:5: "The blind receive their sight and the lame walk, and the poor have good tidings preached to them," as if to say, just as it was written there, so is it taking place now. Also, we read in Acts 9:22 and 17:2 and following of Paul and in Acts 18:26 of Apollos, how they cornered the Jews and proved by the Scriptures that this Jesus, whom they preached unto them, was the true Messiah. For what the prophets had published, that had now all taken place in Christ. Also, in Acts 15 (or 13:46), the apostles prove how the Gospel must be preached to the heathen, that they might believe. All of that has thus run its course and was thus at the time in motion, so that the Jews were convinced, and they had to confess that it then happened even as the Scriptures long before had foretold.

v. 11a. *Searching what time or what manner of time the Spirit of Christ which was in them did point unto.*

Thus Peter will say in effect: although the prophets did not, properly speaking, know a certain and appointed time, yet they gave in general all the circumstances of the time and place:—How Christ would suffer. What death he would die. And how the Gentiles would believe on him. Also they foretold that one would unmistakably know by the signs when the time had come. They had also the sure prophecy of Jacob, the patriarch, that the kingdom of the Jews would first cease, before Christ came; but the day and the exact time when that should take place was not appointed, for it was sufficient that when the time came they could then know for a certainty by these times that Christ was near. Thus the prophet Joel, also prophesied of the time when the Holy Spirit should come, saying: "And it shall come to pass afterward, that I will pour out my Spirit upon all flesh" (2:28), which saying Peter cited in Acts 2:17, proving that he spake of the time and appointed persons.

It seems to me that Peter had reference especially to the prophet Daniel when he said, "Searching what time or what manner of time the Spirit of Christ did point unto...." *What time* means that he surely measured and appointed the time, how long and how many years should pass. *What manner of time* means that he beautifully pointed forth the condition and tendency of the world at that time: who would have the greatest government or where the empire would be; so that Daniel thus declared not only the time, but also the tendency, appearance and character of that time.

From all this you see how the apostles have everywhere with great diligence cited the ground and the confirmation of their preaching and doctrine from the prophets. At present the pope rushes ahead and will deal with us without the Scriptures and commands us—by virtue of the obedience of the church and of the ban—that we believe him. The apostles were full of the Holy Spirit, and they were sure that they were sent of Christ and that they preached the pure Gospel; yet they cast themselves under its power and wished that no one should believe them if they could not by Scripture confirm that it was as they said, in order that the mouth of the unbeliever might be stopped and that they could not raise any objections. And shall we believe these coarse, untaught blockheads, who do not preach the Word of God? The only thing they can do is continually to cry: It was impossible for the fathers to err. The church has now taught and believed for centuries the same as we do; therefore we dare not be called to give an account.

We can indeed prove from the Scriptures that no one will be saved unless he believes on Christ. Further, they can say nothing against this, but with their idle talk they will never convince us from the Scriptures that he will be condemned who does not fast on this or that day. Therefore we will not and should not believe them. Now Peter says further:

v. 11b. *When it testified beforehand the sufferings of Christ, and the glories that should follow them.*

One may understand this as referring to both kinds of suffering, that of Christ and that of his followers; since Paul calls the suffering of all Christians the suffering of Christ. For as the faith, the name, the word, and the work of Christ are ours because we believe on him; so is his suffering also ours, and ours his, because we suffer for his sake. Thus will the suffering of Christ be fulfilled daily in Christians until the end of the world.

This then is now our comfort in all our suffering. That which is laid upon us for Christ's sake he reckons for his own suffering, for in Acts 9:4 he said, "Saul, Saul, why persecutest thou me?" Yet Saul did not persecute him, for he was now seated too high for that, but he persecuted the Christians, Also, Zechariah 2:8, "For he that toucheth you [the believers], toucheth the apple of his eye," We are sure that eternal glory will follow this suffering. But as Christ our Lord and Savior had to suffer before he came to glory, so we must follow him, first take upon us our cross and bear it after him, and expect thereafter eternal glory and joy.

Hence he says, God's Spirit, who was in them, bore witness through them that whosoever believed in Christ and confessed him shall without fail calculate that he must suffer much first, according to the example of his Lord, before he comes to glory. With this Peter comforts all believers to take no offense when they are compelled to suffer in the world all kinds of anxiety and need, abuse and disgrace for the sake of the name of Christ, and not through impatience, despair, and doubt, as if nothing would come of it all in the end. But remember, all the prophets proclaimed by the revelation of the Holy Spirit that the Cross would precede, and then would certainly follow the glory; for God makes us poor and then rich, bruises and slays, and then heals and restores to life. The devil does just the opposite.

The reason however we now understand the prophets so little may be that their language is unknown to us; but they have in other respects spoken plainly enough. Therefore persons acquainted with their language who have the Spirit of God (and all believers have), for them they are not hard to understand, since they know that the whole Scriptures tend in the direction to teach us concerning faith, hope, love, and pa-

tience, in temptations and tribulations. Whoever does not know
and understand this, and has not the Spirit of God, to him the
writings of the prophets are of course unknown and in a for-
eign language. However, if we must be deficient in one, better
have the Spirit without the language, than the language without the Spirit. If now indeed they have a special manner of
speaking, yet remember it is the apostles who preach, for they
have said much both concerning the suffering and the glory of
Christ and of those who believe on him: as when David spoke
concerning Christ in Psalm 22:6, "I am a worm and no man."
By that he showed how low he was cast down and humiliated
in his suffering. Likewise he writes concerning the Christians
in Psalm 44 that they complain how they are persecuted and
destroyed by the enemies of the truth, and say, "Yea, for thy
sake are we killed all the day long; we are accounted as sheep
for the slaughter" (44:22).

v. 12a. *To whom it was revealed, that not unto themselves, but unto
you, did they minister these things, which now have been announced
unto you through them that preached the Gospel unto you by the
Holy Ghost sent forth from heaven.*

That is, the prophets would have gladly lived in the blessed
time of grace and been present to hear Christ preach and see
him work his miracles, as he himself says in Matthew 13:17:
"Many prophets and righteous men desired to see the things
which ye see...." But as that was impossible, they were satisfied in that they saw and knew from afar the grace and salvation that should be experienced by the whole world through
Christ, and they also comforted themselves with it. But in
doing that they left behind them their writings; they did it in
service and love to us, were thereby our servants and ministered unto us in order that we might go to them to school and
learn also the same lesson. How has grace come to us?
"Through those who have preached the Gospel of Christ unto
you," they had a good and faithful teacher, who taught it to
them, namely, the Holy Spirit, whom Christ sent from heaven.
He opened their minds to understand the holy Scriptures and
to be able to minister to others through sermons and the Scrip-

tures. Hence we have indeed a strong foundation for our faith, so that we can indeed arm and defend ourselves against all false doctrines.

v. 12b. *Which things angels desire to look into.*

So great is that which the apostles have declared unto us through the Holy Spirit coming upon them from heaven, that even the angels have pleasure in looking into it. Here Peter asks us to open our eyes and behold what the Gospel is, that we may have our pleasure and delight in it. Other pleasures and treasures present themselves to us than the riches and pomp of the whole world, namely, how we are rescued from the power of the devil, freed from sin and death, and become the children and heirs of God through Christ. This we cannot yet see with the natural eyes, but must believe it; that we are the partakers and co-partners of the righteousness, truth, salvation, and all the heavenly treasures which God has, for since he delivers up for us all Christ, his only Son, the highest good, how shall he not with him also freely give us all things (Romans 8:32), namely, grace, righteousness, eternal life, and salvation, in which the angels in heaven have extreme pleasure and delight. All this is offered to us in the Gospel. If we believe it, then we will also have like pleasure and delight from it. But our joy and pleasure cannot be as perfect as that of the angels, as long as we live upon the earth in the kingdom of the devil. Here indeed it begins in us and we receive some of it through faith; but in heaven the joy is so great that no human heart can contain it, and when we arrive there we will also experience it.

Thus far Peter has shown what kind of doctrine the Gospel is, namely, that which witnesseth of Christ that we are born again through his death and resurrection to an incorruptible inheritance. And as it was aforetime proclaimed by the prophets, so it should come to pass and be preached. He teaches us in the Scriptures that we may receive from them comfort and the strengthening of our faith and that we shall arm and fortify ourselves with them against all the fiery darts of the devil, the temptations of the world, the melancholy and the sadness of heart. Now he takes a step in advance and admonishes us to hold to the same preaching of the Gospel in faith and imitate it in love.

III.   A Double Exhortation (vv. 13-25)

A. An Exhortation to Christian Faith (vv. 13-16)

vv. 13-16. *Wherefore girding up the loins of your mind, be sober and set your hope perfectly on the grace that is to be brought unto you at the revelation of Jesus Christ; as children of obedience, not fashioning yourselves according to your former lusts in the time of your ignorance: but like as he who called you is holy, be ye yourselves also holy in all manner of living; because it is written, ye shall be holy; for I am holy.*

v. 13 a. *Wherefore girding up the loins of your mind.*

This is an exhortation to faith and the meaning is, inasmuch as such an unspeakable treasure is published and offered through the Gospel, that the angels in heaven have their pleasure and delight in looking into it. Hold fast to it now and place thy trust in it with all thy affections, so that yours may be a true faith and not a painted or devised fancy and dream.

Peter does not here speak of a bodily girding, as a man girds his sword about his loins, but of a spiritual girding of the mind, which is also referred to in Luke 12:35, where we read: "Let your loins be girded about." In some passages of Scripture *loins* mean "bodily unchastity," and according to this sense, *girding the loins* means "to suppress unchastity and live chaste lives." The Scriptures also call loins the natural birth that comes from the father. Thus we read of Jacob in Genesis 35:11 that God promised him that kings should come out of his loins. And Acts 2:30 teaches that David knew that the fruit of his loins should sit upon his throne.

But the spiritual girding, of which the apostle here speaks, means this: as a virgin is bodily pure and chaste, so is the soul chaste through faith, by virtue of which it is the bride of Christ. But when it falls from faith into false doctrine, then it comes to shame. Wherefore the Scriptures everywhere call idolatry and unbelief adultery and fornication, that is, when the soul holds to the doctrines of men and renounces thus faith and Christ. This Peter now forbids here in that he enjoins us to gird the loins of our mind, as if he should say, you have now heard the Gospel and have entered into faith; therefore take heed that you continue in it and become not unchaste through false doctrine, that ye waver not nor run hither and thither with your good works.

And here he continues to speak in a special way when he says, the loins of your mind. By *mind* he means "that which we call 'to be disposed,'" as when I say, I think that is right; and as Paul says, thus we hold, thus are we minded. With these words he, properly speaking, touches upon faith and will say to them, you have created a right mind in that we must be justified before God through faith. In that mind continue, gird it well, hold firmly to it, let nothing tear you from it, and then it will be well with thee. For many false teachers will arise and spread the doctrines of men to pervert your mind and unloosen the girdle of your faith; therefore be warned and take it well to heart. The hypocrites, who rest upon their own works and go about in an honorable, fine life, are also of the mind that God must establish them in heaven because of their good works. They are puffed up, they walk about with high heads, they stand firm in their mind and darkness like the pharisees (Luke 18:11f.), to whom Mary also refers in the "Magnificat." They need even the little words that are found here in Peter. He scatters those who are proud in the imagination of their heart.

v. 13b. *Be sober.*

To be sober is helpful to the outward body and is the chief part of faith. For when man through faith becomes at once justified, he is not yet entirely free of evil desires. Faith has indeed commenced to bring the flesh into subjection; but nevertheless it still continually bestirs itself and rages at times in all kinds of lust, which would gladly again be experienced and act according to their own will. Therefore the Spirit has to work daily to bridle and suppress lust, to slay it thus without intermission, and to give attention to the flesh, lest it casts aside faith altogether. Therefore they deceive themselves who say they have faith and think that is enough and there is no danger, though at the time they are fulfilling the lusts of the flesh. Wherever faith is true and pure, it must attack the body and hold it, as it were, with a bridle, so that it does not do according to its lusts. Therefore Peter says that we shall be sober.

Yet it is not his idea that we should ruin the body or weaken it too much, as do those who have fasted to madness and martyred themselves to death. St. Bernard was for a time given to this folly, although otherwise he was a holy man. He denied his body so much that his breath was offensive, and he could not associate in society. Yet later he rescued himself out of this state, and he then prohibited his brethren from torturing their bodies. For he saw that he had made himself incapable of serving his brethren. Hence Peter requires no more than that we be temperate, that is, deny the body so much that we feel it is still too wanton. Here he appoints no certain time, how long one shall fast, as the pope has done. Instead He places it before each one as a private, personal matter, that he fast so that he continues temperate, and not burden the body with gluttony, to the end that he continue in his reason and common sense and determine to what extent it is necessary for him to chastise the body. For it is of no use at all that a command on this subject be given to a whole company of persons or to the public at large, since we are so unlike one another, one strong and another weak as to the body, so that one must deny himself much, another little, in order that the body may at the same time remain healthy and prepared to do good service.

That the rough element of society falls upon this teaching and hence wishes to live so that they need not fast and dare eat flesh, is not right. For these do not grasp the Gospel, and are of no use, just as well as the others. For the only thing they do is disregard the pope's command, and will nevertheless not gird their mind and soul, as Peter says, but let the body to its wantoness, that they may continue lazy and fat. Good it is that one should fast, that is, fast rightly, that one gives the body no more food than is necessary to retain good health. And let each labor and watch that the old donkey not become too wanton and go dancing on the ice and break a bone; but go in the bridle and follow the Spirit. They should not respond like those do who, when they fast, fill themselves with fish and the best wine so full at the same time that their bellies are puffed out. Hence Peter says here be sober, and adds now further:

v. 13c. *And set your hope perfectly in the grace that is to be brought unto you.*

The Christian faith is of such a nature that it places itself unfettered upon the Word of God with all confidence; it weighs itself upon it as upon a pair of scales and cheerfully lives in that Word. Hence Peter says, then are the loins of your mind girded and your faith pure and upright when you weigh all with the Word, be on it what may, possessions, honor, body or life. Thus with these words he describes very beautifully an upright, unfeigned faith. It must not be a lazy and sleepy faith or dream, but a living and active thing, so that we enter into faith with our whole heart and cling to the Word. God grant that we may press through fortune and misfortune with our faith, go as it will with us. For example, when I shall come to die, then I must turn all my power fresh upon Christ, freely stretch forth my neck and comfort myself with the Word of God, which cannot lie to me. At this time faith must go straight through, let nothing mislead it, and cast everything out of sight that it sees, hears and feels. Such a faith Peter requires, which does not consist in thoughts and words, but in the power to do this.

Peter says further, set your hope upon the grace that is being brought unto you, which means that you have not merited this marvelous grace; but it is purely gratuitously brought to you. For the Gospel which reveals this grace, we have not invented or discovered; but the Holy Spirit has sent it down from heaven into the world. What is it then that is brought to us? That which we have above heard; whoever believes on Christ and clings to his Word, he possesses Christ with all his riches, so that he becomes Lord over sin, death, Satan, and hell and has the assurance of eternal life. This treasure is brought to us before our very door and laid in our bosom without any effort or merit on our part, yea, unlooked for and without us knowing it or thinking about it. Therefore the apostle desires that we cheerfully exercise ourselves in it. For God, who has offered unto us such grace, will surely not lie to us.

v. 13d. *At the revelation of Jesus Christ.*

God does not permit his grace to be brought to anyone except through Christ. Therefore no human being shall venture to appear before him without this mediator, as we have also heretofore sufficiently heard. For he will hear no one unless he brings with him Christ, his beloved Son, whom alone he beholds and for his sake also those who cling to him. Hence it is the Father's will that we know the Son, how we have been reconciled unto the Father by his blood, so that we dare now appear before him. For to this end has the Lord Christ come to the world, taken upon himself flesh and blood, and attached himself to us, that he might acquire for us such grace with the Father. For the same purpose were all the prophets and patriarchs likewise kept through such faith in Christ and were saved; for they all had to believe on the saying God spake to Abraham, "In thy seed shall all the nations of the earth be blessed." Therefore, as we have said, the faith of the Jews and of the Turks avails nothing, and neither does the faith of those who rest upon their own works and try to enter heaven through them. Peter speaks thus: The grace will be brought to you, but through the revelation of Jesus Christ; or to put it in our vernacular still more plainly, because Jesus Christ is revealed unto you.

Through the Gospel it is made known unto us what Christ is. Here we learn to know him and to know him in the sense that he is our Savior, that he takes from us sin and death, that he helps us out of all misfortunes, that he reconciles us to the Father, and that he without our own works sanctifies and saves us. Now whoever does not know Christ thus must fail.

For though you already know that he is the Son of God, and that he died and arose again and sits at the right hand of the Father, you have nevertheless not yet known Christ rightly, and that will not help you. You must know and believe that he has done all this for your sake, to help you. Therefore that which has heretofore been preached and taught in the high schools was trifling and useless, for they knew nothing of this knowledge, and they had not come farther than that they considered how greatly the Lord Christ suffered and how he leisurely sits above in heaven and has joy with himself. Their hearts remain thus only dry and withered, in which faith cannot become a living power.

The Lord and Savior should not be represented as though he did all this for himself, but be so preached that we know he is ours. For otherwise what was the need that he should come upon the earth and shed his blood? But since he was sent into the world for the purpose, as he says in John 3:17, that the world through him should be saved, so then he must have accomplished that at least for which he was sent by the Father. For the sending by and the going out from the Father one should understand not only as referring to his divine nature, but to his human nature and his office. As soon as he had been baptized, he commenced, and he accomplished that for which he was sent into the world, namely, that he preached the truth and enlisted us, so that all who believe on him should be saved. Thus he revealed himself and gave the opportunity to know him and he himself brought us grace.

v. 14a. *As children of obedience.*

That is, conduct yourselves as obedient children. Obedience in the Scriptures is called faith. But that little word the pope has also twisted to pieces for us with his high schools and monasteries and whatever stood in the Scriptures about this obedience they cited to support their nonsense and lies, as for example the saying, to obey is better than sacrifice in 1 Samuel 15:22. For since they see that obedience is highly praised in the Scriptures, they have twisted it to their advantage to blindfold the people so that one would think that obedience to them was that of which the Scriptures speak. In this way they have misled us from the Word of God into their lies and the obedience of the devil. Whoever hears the Word of God and believes it, is an obedient son of God. Therefore whatever is not the Word of God, tread under your feet and turn from it.

v. 14b. *Not fashioning yourselves according to your former lusts in the time of your ignorance.*

That is, do not carry the bearing in your manner of life as before. Then you were idolatrous, you lived in unbelief, unchastity, gluttony, drinking, avarice, wrath, jealousy and hatred; that was a wicked, heathenish state from which you have departed. Like the blind, you did not know what you did. These evil lusts now put away.

Here you see how he attributes the blame to their ignorance, that all misfortune comes from that. For where there is no faith and knowledge of Christ, there is nothing but error and blindness, so that we do not know what is right and what is wrong, and hence the people fall then into all kinds of vice. So has it actually gone in the past. Whenever Christ was supplanted and obscured, error began, and the question broke forth in the whole world: How could men be saved? And this question itself is evidence sufficient of blindness and ignorance, that the right conception of faith was lost and no one knew anything about it any longer. Hence it is that the world is so full of various sects and all is divided into schisms; for every person wishes to enter heaven in his own way. Because of this calamity, we must continually fall the deeper in blindness, since we are not able to help ourselves. Hence Peter says that you have made fools of yourselves long enough. Therefore cease now from that course, because you had been instructed and had received the true knowledge.

vv. 15, 16. *But like as he who called you is holy, be ye yourselves also holy in all manner of living; because it is written, Ye shall be holy; for I am holy.*

Peter cites here a passage from the Old Testament, Leviticus 19:2, where God says, "Ye shall be holy; for I, Jehovah, your God, am holy"; that is, since I am your Lord and your God, and you are my people, so you should be as I am. For a true Lord makes his people like himself, and they walk in obedience and conduct themselves in harmony with the will of their Lord. And now as God, our Lord, is holy, his people are also holy. Therefore we all are holy, if we walk in faith.

The Scriptures do not speak much about the saints who have died, but of those who still live upon the earth. Thus the prophet David glories in Psalm 86:2: "Lord, preserve my soul, for I am holy [godly]." But here our learned leaders again pervert the passage and say the prophet had a special revelation, that he called himself holy. By this they confess they lack faith and have not the revelation of Christ; otherwise they would have experienced it. For whoever is a Christian feels such a revelation; but those who do not feel it are not Christians. For whoever is a Christian enters with his Lord Christ into the fellowship of all his riches. Now, since Christ is holy, so he must also be holy, or lie that Christ is holy. Are you baptized? Then you have put on the robe of holiness, which is Christ, as Paul says in Galatians 3:27.

The little word *holy* means "that which is God's own and is due to him alone," which we in German call *geweihet* (in English *consecrated, dedicated*). Thus Peter says now: You have given yourselves to God as his own; therefore take heed that you do not allow yourselves to be led again into worldly lusts; but let God alone reign, live and work in you; then you are holy, as he is holy.

Thus far the apostle has described the grace that has been brought unto us, the Gospel and preaching of Christ, and taught us how we are to conduct ourselves toward it, namely, that we continue in the pure, fixed meaning of faith, so as to know that no work we can do or think avails before God. When we preach thus, reason falls in and says: Oh, if that be true, then we are not allowed to do any good work. Rough persons and blockheads also stumble and turn the very essence of Christianity into the liberty of the flesh—thinking they may do whatever they wish. Such Peter meets here, stands before them, and teaches how we must use our Christian liberty only in relation to God. For here there is nothing more necessary than faith, that I give God his honor and hold him as my God. That he is just, true, and merciful. This makes us free from sin and all evil. When I now have given God this, what I then live, I live for the good of my neighbor, to serve and help him. The greatest work that follows faith is that I confess Christ with my mouth, bear witness, also with my blood, and spend my life where I may do the most good. However God is not in need of such work; but I do it in order that thereby my faith may be confirmed and published, so that others may be brought to faith. The other works follow, all of which must be directed to the end that I thereby serve my neighbors, all which God must work in us. Therefore it is of no use that we wish to live after the flesh and do whatever we lust after. Hence Peter now adds:

B. An Exhortation to Christian Life (vv. 17-25)

vv. 17-21. *And if ye call on him as Father, who without respect of persons judgeth according to each man's work, pass the time of your sojourning in fear: knowing that ye were redeemed, not with corruptible things, with silver or gold, from your vain manner of life handed down from your fathers; but with precious blood, as of a lamb without blemish and without spot, even the blood of Christ: who was foreknown indeed before the foundation of the world, but was manifested at the end of the times for your sake, who through him are believers in God, that raised him from the dead, and gave him glory; so that your faith and hope might be in God.*

Thus Peter says: You have not through faith come to this, that you are the children of God and he is your Father, and you have obtained an incorruptible inheritance in heaven, as he above said; so that nothing more remains than that the veil be removed, and the treasure now hidden be uncovered. For this however you must wait until you shall see it. Although you have now come into the state that you may cheerfully call God your Father, yet he is so just that he will reward each one according to his works, and respect not the person.

Therefore you dare not think, because you bear already the great name and are called a Christian or a son of God, that he

will on that account spare your work, if you live without fear
and presume it is enough that you glory in possessing merely
the name. The world judgeth according to the person, so that
it does not punish all equally and spares those who are be-
friended, rich, beautiful, learned, wise, and influential, but God
has no respect for any of these, all are alike before him, be the
person as great as he may. Hence he slew in Egypt the first
born son of King Pharaoh just as well as the first born son of
the poorest man. Therefore it is the will of the apostle that we
expect such a judgment of God and stand in fear, so that we
do not glory in being called Christians and rely upon it that he
will be more lenient to us than to other persons. For this was
the very thing that aforetimes misled the Jews, who gloried in
being of the seed of Abraham and the people of God. The
Scriptures make no distinction as to the flesh, but as to the
spirit. True, he had promised that Christ should be born of
Abraham and a holy people would spring from him; but it
does not therefore follow that all who are Abraham's descendants are children of God. He has also promised that the heathen should be saved; but he did not say that he would save
all the heathen.

Here now a question arises. Since we say God saves us
alone through faith without respect to our works, why then
does Peter say God judges not with respect to the person, but
according to the works? Answer: What we have learned as to
how faith alone justifies us before God, is without the least
doubt true, since it is so clear from the Scriptures that no one
can deny it. And now the apostle says here that God judges
according to each man's works; this that is also true; but we
should certainly rather hold where there is no faith, there the
good works that God commands cannot possibly be; and on
the contrary, where no good works are, there is no faith. Hence
faith and good works are yoked together, so that the sum total
of the whole Christian life consists in these two parts; not that
good works contribute anything to our justification before God,
but that faith without good works does not exist, or it is not
true faith. Therefore, although God does indeed judge us according to our works, it remains true that the works are only
the fruits of faith, by which one sees where faith is and where

unbelief is. Therefore God will pass judgment upon you and
convince you that you have believed or not believed. Likewise, we cannot determine and judge one to be a liar except
from his words, yet it is manifest that he did not become a liar
through his words, but he had become a liar before he spoke a
lie, for the lie must come out of the heart into the mouth.

Therefore I understand this passage only in the most simple
manner thus: good works are the fruits and signs of faith, and
God judges people according to such fruits, which must indeed here follow, in order that we may publicly see where
faith or unfaith in the heart really is. God will not judge according to whether you are called a Christian or are baptized,
but he will ask you: Are you a Christian? Then tell me where
are the good works by which you can prove your faith."

Therefore Peter now says: Since you have such a Father,
who judges not according to the person, conduct your manner
of life, as long as you sojourn here, in fear; that is, exercise fear
toward thy Father, not because of pain and punishment, as
un-Christians and the devil fear, but that he forsakes thee not
and withdraws his hand; as a pious child fears lest he provokes his father and does something that may not be pleasing
to him. It is just such a fear God that wishes us to have, in
order to keep ourselves from sin and serve our neighbor while
we live here upon the earth.

A Christian, if he truly believes, has Christ with all his
treasures as his own possession, and is God's son, as we have
heard. But the time he yet lives is only a pilgrimage, for his
spirit is already in heaven through faith, by virtue of which he
is Lord over all things. But God permits him still to live in the
flesh and his body to move upon the earth, to the end that he
may help others and bring them also to heaven. Therefore we
must use all these things upon earth in no other way than as a
guest who travels through the land and comes to a hotel where
he must lodge overnight. He takes only food and lodging from
the host, and he says not that the property of the host belongs
to him. Just so should we also treat our temporal possessions,
as if they were not ours, and enjoy only so much of them as
we need to nourish the body and then help our neighbors
with the balance. Thus the life of the Christian is only a lodg-

ing for the night, since we have here no continuing city, but must journey on to heaven, where the Father is. Therefore we should not live here in rioting, but stand in fear, as Peter says.

vv. 18, 19a. *Knowing that ye were redeemed, not with corruptible things, with silver or gold, from your vain manner of life handed down from your fathers; but with the precious blood of Christ.*

That ought to stir you, he will say, to the fear of God in which you should stand, so that you realize how much has been accomplished to redeem you. Heretofore you have been citizens of the world, sitting among devils, but now God has rescued you out of this state, and placed you in another where you are citizens of heaven, but pilgrims and guests on earth. Therefore pass the time of your sojourning in fear; and see to it that you do not despise this and lose the noble, precious treasure God has bestowed upon you, through which you are bought with a price; and come to glory by virtue of your being now the children of God. What then is the treasure with which we are redeemed? Not corruptible gold or silver, but the precious blood of Christ, the Son of God. The treasure is so costly and precious that the mind and heart of man cannot contain it; so precious that a little drop of this innocent blood would have been sufficient for the sin of the whole world; yet it was the good pleasure of the Father to pour out his grace so richly and to let it cost him so much that he permitted his only Son, Christ, to shed all his blood, and gives us this treasure entirely gratuitously. Therefore it is his will that we cast not such rich grace to the wind or lightly esteem it; but let it move us to live in fear that this treasure be not taken from us.

And here it is well to note that Peter says: You are redeemed from the vain manner of life practiced and handed down from your fathers; for by these words he casts to the ground all the commandments upon which we stand, when we think our cause must be right because it was preserved thus from ancient times to the present, and all our forefathers held the same, among whom were also wise and pious people. For he thus says: All that our fathers ordered and did was evil; what you learned from them about worship was also evil, hence it cost the Son of God his blood to redeem the people from it. And now whatever is not washed by that blood is all poisoned and cursed by the flesh. From this it now follows that the more a man tries to make himself righteous, yet possesses not Christ, the more is he only in his own way and the deeper he falls into blindness and wickedness, and condemns himself by virtue of this precious blood.

The outward, coarse sins against the second table are small in comparison with the sin, that man teaches how he ought to become righteous through his own works and merit, and establishes a worship according to his own reason, which is a sin against the first table, by which this innocent blood is degraded and blasphemed in the highest degree. In like manner have the heathen committed much greater sin in that they worshiped the sun and moon and their idols, which they held to be the true worship, more than in any other. Therefore human godliness is mere blasphemy of the true God and is the greatest of all sins a person can commit. Such is also the very essence of that with which the world haunts us, namely, that which it holds to be worship and godliness is before God worse than any other sin, as for example the offices of the priests and monks; and what appears good in the eyes of the world, and is yet without faith. Therefore whoever will not receive grace from God through the blood of Christ, it is better for him that he never again appears before the eyes of God, for he only thereby provokes his majesty more and more.

v. 19b. *As of a lamb without blemish and without spot.*

Here Peter expounds the Scriptures for this a powerful, rich epistle, although it is short. After speaking of their vain manner of life handed down from the fathers, he makes use of a number of passages in the prophets, as in Jeremiah 16:19: "The nations shall come from the ends of the earth, and shall say, our fathers have inherited nought but lies;" as if Peter should say: The prophets also have proclaimed that the heathen should be redeemed from the traditions of the fathers through the precious blood of Christ. Thus will he here also point us to the Scriptures, when he says, "You are redeemed through the blood of Christ as of an innocent and spotless lamb," and explains that which is written in the prophets and in Moses. For example, that in Isaiah 53:7: As a lamb he is led to the slaughter; also, the figure in Exodus 12:3f. of the Passover or Easter Lamb. All this he explains here and says, Christ is the spotless and innocent lamb, through which, as it stands written in Exodus 12:5, it shall be without blemish, is signified that Christ's blood was shed for our sins.

v. 20. *Who was foreknown indeed before the foundation of the world, but was manifested at the end of the times.*

That is, we have not merited it, neither have we moreover at any time prayed God that the precious blood of Christ should be shed for us; therefore we cannot glory in ourselves, the praise belongs to no one, but to God alone. God promised it to us without any merit on our part, and also revealed or made known that which he knew and ordained from eternity, before the world was created. In the prophets it was truly promised, but dimly and not publicly; however, now since the resurrection of Christ and the sending forth of the Holy Ghost it is publicly preached and sounded forth in the whole world.

The end of the time, however, of which Peter here speaks, is the time of grace, when the Gospel was preached in all the world by the apostles after Christ's ascension, and will continue to be preached until the last day. The prophets, apostles and Christ himself call it the last hour, not because soon after the ascension of Christ the last day would come, but because, after this preaching of the Gospel of Christ, no other shall come, and there will be no better Gospel revealed and explained than that which is now explained and revealed. For prior to Christ's coming in the flesh one revelation prepared the way for and passed into another. Wherefore God said, Exodus 6:3, "By my name, Jehovah, I was not known to them." Although the patriarchs indeed knew God, yet they did not at that time have such public preaching of God as later went forth from Moses and the prophets. But now no preaching shall come into the world more glorious and more public than the Gospel; therefore it is the last. All the ages have now passed away, but today at last it is revealed unto us.

In the next place, according to time, it is not long to the end of the world, as Peter makes very clear in 2 Peter 3:8, where he says, "One day is with the Lord as a thousand years, and a thousand years as one day"; which leads us to the right calculation of this time and it has already an end, that which remains being as nothing before God. Salvation is now already revealed and completed, God permits the world to stand yet longer that his name may be still further honored and praised, although he is as for himself already revealed in the most perfect manner.

v. 21. *For your sake, who through him are believers in God, that raised him from the dead, and gave him glory; so that your faith and hope might be in God.*

For our sake, he says, is Christ revealed through the Gospel; for neither God nor Christ was in need of it, but it is done for our benefit, that we should believe in God, and that not through us but through Christ, who redeemed us by his precious blood and advocates our cause before God the Father, whom he gave even for that very purpose unto death, and again raised him from the dead and caused to be preached in all the world repentance and forgiveness of sins in his name; so that all who believe on him have access unto the Father through him, and without whom they could never come unto him. Thus we have faith toward God and also hope through that same faith. Faith alone saves us, but it must be a faith in God, for if God help not, then there is nothing that can help, although you had even the favor and friendship of all mankind. Hence you must have the friendship of God that you may glory in that he is your Father and you are his child, that you trust him more than your natural father and mother, that he will help you in all need, and that he will do all this alone through our only Mediator and Savior, Christ our Lord. Therefore he says that such faith does not come from human strength, but God creates it in us, for the reason that Christ merited it with his blood, to whom he therefore gave glory and placed him at his right hand, that he might work such faith in us through the power of God.

Thus far have we now heard how Peter exhorts us to gird up the loins of our mind, so as to remain pure in heart and live in faith. Then he urges, since our redemption has cost such a precious treasure, that we pass the time of our sojourning in fear, and do not depend upon the mere fact we are called Christians, sense God is a judge who asks not concerning the person, judges one like another without any respect of persons. Now he says further and closes his first Epistle:

vv. 22-25. *Purify your souls in your obedience to the truth unto unfeigned love of the brethren, love one another from the heart fervently: having been begotten again, not of corruptible seed, but of incorruptible, through the word of God, which liveth and abideth. For, all flesh is as grass, and the glory thereof as the flower of grass. The grass withereth, and the flower falleth: but the word of the Lord abideth forever. And this is the word of good tidings which was preached unto you.*

Paul, in Galatians 5:22, mentions the fruits which follow faith; and likewise Peter says here one fruit of faith is when we purify our souls in obedience to the truth through the Spirit. For where there is a righteous faith it brings the body under subjection to it and controls the lusts of the flesh; and although it does indeed not put to death the body, it brings it into obedience to the Spirit and holds it with a bridle. This is just the meaning of Paul also, when he speaks of the fruit of the spirit. A great work it is indeed that the spirit should become lord over the flesh and tame the evil lusts, which are born into us from our father and mother; for it is not possible to do this without grace, namely, to live in the married state chaste, not to say anything of the unmarried state.

But why does he say: "Make your souls chaste"? He well knows that the desires of the flesh remain in us after baptism until we are in our graves. Therefore it is not enough for one to abstain from the activities of life and continue pure and chaste outwardly and let the evil lusts stick in the heart; but one must strive to the end that his soul becomes pure and chaste through faith; also, that lust may take its departure from the heart and that the soul may become an enemy of evil lusts and desires, and continually strike them with faith until the soul is free of them.

And here he adds an excellent clause: that we purify (make chaste) our souls, "through obedience to the truth in the Spirit." There has been much preaching on chastity, and many books written on the subject, in which they said, we should fast for a certain time, we should not eat flesh, we should not drink wine, etc., that we may be free from temptation. These things may perhaps have aided some to that end, but they have not been enough. They have not subdued lust. So St. Jerome writes of himself, that he had mortified his body to such an extent that he had become like an African; still it was of no avail, and he dreamed of being in Rome at a revelry (*singetanz*, a dance accompanied with singing) among harlots. St. Bernard also subjected himself to such austerities, and so mortified his body that it became offensive, as I said above. They had severe temptations, and tried thus to subdue lust by external methods. But since they are external, they are only an outward plaster, with no inward application. So they do not suffice to subdue lust.

But here Peter has prescribed an appropriate remedy, namely, obedience to the truth in the Spirit, like the Scriptures also have done in other places; as Isaiah 11:5: "Faith shall be the girdle of his reins." This is the true plaster that girds the reins, for it must proceed from within outward, not from without inward. For it has penetrated into the flesh and the blood, the marrow and the veins; it is not outward in the dress or clothing. Therefore it is not to be expected that we should subdue lust with outward means; we may weaken the body and destroy it with fastings and labors, but the evil lusts are not in this way banished; yet faith can subdue them, and guard them, that they be compelled to give the Spirit place.

So likewise the prophet Zechariah speaks, in 9:17, of the wine Christ has, from which virgins grow, and of which he gives them to drink. Other wine usually invites to wicked lust, but this wine, the Gospel, subdues it and makes the heart chaste. This is what Peter speaks of when anyone heartily embraces the truth and is obedient to it in spirit. This is the true help and the most powerful remedy for it, aside from that you will find none that can still all evil thoughts like it. For if this enters our hearts, evil inclinations quickly leave. Let whoever will try it, he shall find it true, and whoever has tried it, knows it well. The devil lets no one attain it in an easy way, and comprehend the Word of God so as to delight in it; for he well knows how powerful it is to subdue evil lusts and thoughts.

Peter therefore would say here, if you wish to remain chaste, then you must lay hold on obedience to the truth in the Spirit, that is, you must not only read and hear the Word of God, but lay hold on it in your heart. Therefore it is not enough for a man to preach or hear the Gospel once, but he must ever persevere and advance in it. For such grace the Word possesses, that the more we taste it the sweeter it is; although there is continually one and the same doctrine of faith, yet it cannot be heard too much where hearts are not too impudent and barbarous. Now the apostle adds further:

v. 22b. *Unto unfeigned love of the brethren.*

To what end then are we to live a chaste life? In order that we may be saved thereby? No! In order that I may restrain my sin. I am to lay hold on obedience to the truth in the Spirit. But why am I to restrain it? In order to be of service to others, for I must first control my body and flesh by the Spirit, and then I can be of service later to others. It follows further:

v. 22c. *Love one another from the heart fervently.*

The apostles Peter and Paul distinguish brotherly love from love in general. Brotherhood means that Christians should all be as brethren and make no distinctions among themselves. For since we all have one Savior, one baptism, one faith, one treasure, I am no better than thou; that which thou hast, I have also, and I am just as rich as thou. The treasure is the same, except that I may have it in a better chest than thou, since I may have it lying in gold, but thou in a poor garment. Therefore as we have the grace of Christ and all spiritual blessings in common, so should we also hold body and life, property and honor, in common, that one may be of service to another in all things.

Now he speaks plainly: "Unto unfeigned love of the brethren." The apostles love to use these words, but they clearly perceived that were we called Christians and brethren universally one with another, it would be false, a feigned or imagined thing, and would be only hypocrisy. We have many brotherhoods set up in the world, but they are vain, misleading, and a defense of falsehood. The devil has devised and brought them into the world, and they are only antagonistic to the true faith and to genuine brotherly love. Christ is mine as well as St. Bernard's; thine as well as St. Francis'. If one therefore should come to you and say, I shall go to heaven if I belong to this or that brotherhood, then tell him he is deceived; for Christ cannot suffer it and will not have any other than the common brotherhood we all have one with another. Yet you come here, you fool, and will set up one of your own. This I will readily permit that they be set up, not to help the soul, but as some one's endowment, and thus serve as a fund from which they who are in need shall be helped.

Thus we all, as Christians, have acquired a brotherhood in baptism, of which no saint possesses more than you or I. For at the costly price that one was purchased, at the same price was I also purchased. God has devoted as much to me as to the greatest saint, except that he may have laid hold on the treasure better, and may have a stronger faith than I.

But love is greater than a brotherhood, for it extends even to our enemies, and especially to those who are not worthy of love. For as faith performs its work where it sees nothing, so also should love see nothing. There especially can it exercise its office where there appears nothing lovely, but only disaffection and hostility. Where there is nothing that pleases me I should the more seek to be pleased. And this spirit should go forth fervently, says Peter, from the whole heart, just as God loved us when we were not worthy of love. Now follows further:

v. 23a. *Having been begotten again.*

In the third place we should do this, because we are not

what we were before, he says, but have become new creatures. This has not come to pass through works, but is a con-
sequence of the new birth. For thou cannot make the new
man, but he must grow, or be born. Likewise a carpenter cannot make a tree, but it must grow of itself out of the earth.
And similarly we all are not made the children of Adam at the
same time, but are born so and have derived sin from our
parents. Just so here it cannot come to pass through works
that we become the children of God, but we must also be born
anew. This therefore is what the apostle would say; since ye
then have become new creatures, ye should conduct yourselves otherwise than ye did, and lead a new life. As ye before
lived in hate, ye are now to walk in love; in all respects the
reverse. But how has the new birth taken place?   Thus, as
follows:

v. 23b. *Not of corruptible seed, but of incorruptible, through the
word of God, which liveth and abideth.*

Through a seed are we born again, for nothing grows as we
see except from seed. Did the old birth spring from a seed?
Then must the new birth also spring from a seed. But what is
this seed?   Not flesh and blood!   What then?   It is not a
corruptible, but an eternal Word. It is moreover that on which
we live; our food and nourishment. But especially is it the
seed from which we are born again, as he here says.
    But how does this take place? After this manner: God lets
the word, the Gospel, be scattered abroad, and the seed falls
in the hearts of men. Now wherever it sticks in the heart, the
Holy Spirit is present and makes a new man. Then there will
indeed be another man, of other thoughts, of other words and
works. Thus you are entirely changed. All that you before
avoided you now seek, and what you before sought that you
now avoid. In respect to the birth of the body, it is a fact that
when conception takes place the seed is changed, so that it is
seed no longer. But this is a seed that cannot be changed; it
remains forever. It changes me, so that I am transformed in it,
and whatever is evil in me from my nature passes away. Therefore it is indeed a wonderful birth, and of extraordinary seed.
Now Peter says further:

vv. 24-25a. *For all flesh is as grass, and all the glory thereof as the flower of grass. The grass withereth, and the flower falleth: but the word of the Lord abideth forever.*

This passage is taken from the prophet Isaiah, 40:6-8, where the prophet speaks in this manner: "Cry! what shall I cry? Cry all flesh is grass, and all the goodliness thereof is as the flower of the field; the grass withereth and the flower falleth, but the word of the Lord abideth forever." These words Peter introduces here; for this is, as I have said, a rich epistle and well spiced with Scripture quotations.

Thus the Scripture now says that the Word of God abides forever. What is flesh and blood is corruptible like the grass, while it is yet green, hence it blooms. So whatever is rich, strong, wise, and fair, and thus is flourishing, all which belongs to the bloom, yet you observe its bloom wither. What is young and beautiful will become old and ugly. What is rich will become poor, and so on, and all must fall by the Word of God. But this seed cannot perish. Now Peter concludes:

v. 25b. *And this is the word of good tidings which was preached unto you.*

As though he would say, ye need not look far in order to meet the Word of God; ye have it before your eyes; the Word is that which we preach; with it you may subdue all evil lusts. You are not to seek it far away; you have nothing more to do than to lay hold on it when it is preached. For it is so near us that we can hear it, as Moses also says, in Deuteronomy 30:11-14: "The word that I command you is not far from thee, that thou must go far away for it; either ascend into heaven or go beyond the sea; but it is near thee, even in thy mouth and in thy heart." It is indeed soon spoken and soon heard. But if it enters the heart it cannot die or perish, and will not suffer you to perish; as long as you cleave to it, it will cleave to you. As, when I hear that Jesus Christ died to take away my sins, has purchased heaven for me, and bestows upon me all he has, then I hear the Gospel. The word is quickly gone when one preaches it, but if it falls into the heart and is apprehended by faith, it can never pass away. This truth no creature can overthrow. The gates of hell cannot prevail against it, and if I were already fast in the jaws of the devil and could yet only grasp the word, I would still have to be rescued and abide, where the word abides. Therefore he well says, you need look for no other Gospel than that which we have preached to you.

So Paul says, in Romans 1:16: "I am not ashamed of the Gospel; for it is the power of God unto salvation to every one that believeth." The word is a divine and eternal power; for although the voice or speech is soon gone, yet the substance remains; that is, the sense, the truth, which is conveyed by the voice. As when I put to my mouth a cup containing wine, I swallow the wine, although I do not thrust the cup down my throat.

So likewise is the word that the voice conveys. It falls into our hearts and lives, while the voice remains without and passes away. Therefore it is indeed a divine power; yea, it is God himself. For thus he speaks to Moses in Exodus 4:12: "I will be with thy mouth;" and Psalm 81:10: "Open thy mouth wide, proclaim glad tidings; say thou art hungry, I will satisfy thee, I will presently speak to thee comforting things."

So also, in John 14:6, Christ says, "I am the way, the truth, and the life." Whoever confides in this is born of God; so that his seed is our Lord God himself (1 John 4:7; 5:1). All this goes to teach us that we cannot be helped by works. Although the word is a small thing and seems as nothing while it proceeds out of the mouth, yet there is such an immense power in it that it makes those who confide in it the children of God (John 1:12). Thus does our salvation raise us to exalted blessedness.

This is the first chapter of our epistle, and you perceive in what a masterly manner Peter preaches and discusses faith, and here we readily see that this epistle is the true gospel. Now comes the second chapter that will instruct us how we should conduct ourselves in our good works to our neighbor.

1 Peter 2

The Works and Fruits of the Christian Life

Outline

I. In General, of all Christians, vv. 1-12.
   A. The first fruit and work of the Christian life, v. 1a.
      1. The ground and cause of these fruits and works.
      2. Their nature.
   B. The second fruit and work the Christian life, v. 1b.
   C. The third fruit and work the Christian life, v. 2a.
      1. Their nature. How a teacher or a pastor should treat the beginners in the Christian life, v. 2.
      2. The ground and cause of this fruit, vv. 2b-3.
      3. Among whom is this fruit and work to be found and among whom not, v. 4.
   D. The fourth fruit and work of the Christian life.
      1. Its nature, v. 5a.
      2. How to use this fruit and work against the papists. All Christians are holy and spiritual priests.
      3. An objection, and the answer. How there is no difference among Christians. Of the spiritual priesthood.
      4. How this fruit and work are illustrated and confirmed by quotations from the Prophets.
   E. The first prophecy, v. 6
      1. This is truly one of the chief prophecies.
      2. Its true sense and meaning.
      3. How this prophecy is to be used against free will. Who have a part with Christ and who not, vv. 7-8a. The teachers of work-righteousness are the builders who reject Christ as the cornerstone.
   F. The second prophecy, vv. 7-8.
      1. The prophecy itself.
      2. Its true sense and meaning.
   G. The third prophecy, v. 9a.
      1. How it is to be used against the papists. To what extent all believers are priests and kings.
      2. How the title, power, and praise of the Christians are set forth in this quotation.

H. The fourth prophecy, v. 9b.
  1. How the highest office of the priest is set forth in this quotation.
  2. How reason is presented in this passage as mere darkness. What is the chief office of a Christian? This is the substance of the sermons of the Prophets.
I. The fifth prophecy, v. 10.
J. The fifth fruit and work of the Christian life, vv. 11-12.
  1. How this fruit and work are connected with the foregoing. In what way can we rightly enforce the Christian teaching.
  2. The nature of this fruit and work.
  3. How to defend this fruit and work against the interpretation of the sophists. To what extent can Christians be called saints and to what extent may they be called sinners?
  4. Answer to a question that is raised by this fruit and work. Satan attacks the believers, but lets the godless go on in their security. How a Christian is to contend against evil thoughts. In what does a truly Christian life consist and in what does it not consist?
  5. The foundation and cause of this fruit and work. The witness of Pliny to the early Christians.

II. Works and Fruits of the Christian Life in Particular, vv. 13-25.
  A. As applied to the subject of civil government, vv. 13-17.
    1. The first fruit and work.
      a. How this fruit and work are to be connected with the preceding.
      b. The nature of this fruit and work.
      c. The foundation of this fruit and work.
        (1.) The nature of this foundation. To what end does the government serve. How believers are obedient even to heathen governments.
        (2.) The objection that can be raised to this foundation, and the answer. Of the Christian and the worldly government.
        (3.) Further light on this foundation, v. 16. Of Christian liberty. Of the honor one Christian owes another, v. 17a. Of the brother-love of Christians, v. 17b.
    2. The second fruit and work.
      a. Their nature.
      b. An objection that may be raised by this fruit and work, and the answer, v. 17c. How far the authority of the civil government extends.

I. Works and Fruits of the Christian Life in General, of All Christians (vv. 1-12)

vv. 1-5. Putting away therefore all wickedness, and all guile, and hypocrisies, and envies, and all evil speakings, as newborn babes, long for the spiritual milk which is without guile, that ye may grow thereby unto salvation; if ye have tasted that the Lord is gracious: unto whom coming, a living stone, rejected indeed of men, but with God elect, precious, ye also, as living stones, are built up a spiritual house, to be a holy priesthood, to offer up spiritual sacrifices, acceptable to God through Jesus Christ.

Here he begins to teach what the characteristics and fruits of a Christian life should be. For we have said often enough that a Christian life consists of two things; faith toward God and love toward our neighbor. Also, Christian faith has been given to us, yet as long as we live, many evil lusts constantly remain in the flesh—since there is no saint who is not in the flesh. But what is in the flesh cannot be entirely pure. Therefore Peter says, be ye armed, that ye may guard yourselves against the sins which still cleave to you. Watch and strive continually against them. For the worst enemies we have hide themselves in our bosoms, and in our very flesh and blood. They wake, sleep, and live with us, like a wicked spirit that we have brought home with us and we cannot get rid of. Wherefore, since Jesus Christ is entirely yours through faith, and ye have obtained salvation and all his blessings, let it be your office henceforth to put away all wickedness, all that is evil, and all guile, so that no one may act toward another deceitfully or falsely. With the world it has become a common expression to say, "the world is full of unfaithfulness," which is indeed true. But we Christians should not act with such deceit. Instead we should behave uprightly and with pure hearts toward men as toward God, acting fairly and justly, so that no one take the advantage of another in selling, in buying, or in our solemn vows, and the like.

Likewise also Paul says to the Ephesians, "Put away lying, speak ye truth each one with his neighbor" (4:25). Truth is, that yea be yea, and nay, nay. But hypocrisy comes when one represents himself by his outward manner different than he means it. Solemn is the obligation that we appear just as we are in heart. A Christian should so act as to permit all men to see and know what he thinks in his heart. Also, in all his walk and conduct, he should be anxious only to praise God and serve his neighbor and be afraid of no one and let everyone be in the depth of his heart what he is in appearance and not fight a sham battle so as to make others gape with wonder.

Furthermore, Peter says, we should put away envies and evil speakings. Here he fitly takes up the common vices among men, in their intercourse with one another. This evil speaking is exceedingly common and injurious. It is so soon done that none of us is aware of it. Therefore he says, be on your guard, if ye already have a Christian spirit, that ye may know what are the fruits of this spirit.

v. 2a. As newborn babes, long for the spiritual milk which is without guile.

Here he institutes a comparison and would say, Ye are newly born by the Word of God, therefore be ye like newborn babes who seek nothing but milk. As therefore they strive for the breasts and milk, so be ye also eager for the Word. Long for it, have a craving for it, that ye may suck in the intelligible, unadulterated milk.

These words are indeed figurative. He did not mean literal milk, or literal sucking, as he does not speak of a literal birth. But he speaks of another milk that is intelligible, which is produced by the soul, which the heart must imbibe. It must be moreover sincere, or unadulterated, not as the custom is to sell false wares. There is indeed strong obligation and great need, that to the newborn and young Christian the milk should be given pure and not adulterated. But this milk is nothing but the Gospel, which is also even the seed whereby we are conceived and born, as we have heard above (1 Pet. 1:23). Moreover it is also the food that nourishes us when we arrive at maturity; it is also the armor wherewith we equip and clothe ourselves; yea, it is all these in common. But whatever is appended to it is human doctrine, whereby the Word of God is falsified. Therefore the Holy Spirit requires that every Christian shall see to it what he sucks for milk, and shall himself learn to decide in regard to all doctrines.

But the breasts that yield this milk and that the babes suck are the teachers and preachers in the Christian church. As the bridegroom says to the bride, in Song of Solomon 4:5, "Thou hast two breasts like two young roes;" they are as though they were hung with a bundle of myrrh, as the bride says, "My beloved is unto me as a bundle of myrrh that lies continually between my breasts" (1:13). That is, we should ever preach Christ. The bridegroom must resort to the breasts; otherwise it is unjust, and the milk will be adulterated if we do not preach Christ in his purity.

Now this is accomplished if we preach that Christ died for us and rescued us from sin, death, and hell. This is delightful and sweet like milk. But later, the cross also must be preached, that we are to suffer as Christ did—this is strong drink, it is strong wine. Therefore, Christians should first be given the weakest drink, and that is milk. For we cannot preach to them anything better than to preach to them Christ alone; which is not bitter, but is mere sweet, rich grace, from which you receive no harm whatever. This is the true, intelligible, unadulterated milk.

But here Peter has well supported himself by Scripture, as he is throughout rich in passages from the Scriptures. In the Old Testament it is written, both in Exodus 23:19, and Deuter-

onomy 14:21, "Thou shalt not boil a kid in its mother's milk."
Beloved, why did God permit that to be written? Of what
concern to him was it that no suckling should be killed while
as yet it was imbibing its mother's milk? Because he would
thereby help us to understand that which Peter here teaches.
It is as if he had said, preach gently to the young and weak
Christians, let them be carefully fed, and grow fat in the knowledge of Christ. Burden them not with strong doctrine, for they
are as yet too young, but after they have become strong, let
them then be slaughtered and sacrificed on the cross.

So also we read in Deuteronomy 24:5, "When a man taketh
a new wife, he shall not go out to war the first year, lest he be
slain; but abide at home and cheer his wife." All this tends to
the point, that we should bear for a time with young Christians, and proceed tenderly with them. But when they have
grown, God brings them to the holy cross, lets them even die
like other Christians, so then the kid will be sacrificed. Now
follows further:

*vv. 2b-3. That ye may grow thereby unto salvation if ye have tasted
that the Lord is gracious.*

It is not enough to hear the Gospel once; we must ever
make use of it, that we may grow. After faith has become
strong, we must provide for and feed each individual Christian according to his growth. But to those who have not heard
the Gospel, this is not said; they know neither what is milk or
what is wine. Therefore he adds, if ye have besides tasted it, to
him it is not a thing of the heart, to him it is not sweet. But
they who have tried it, nourish themselves with this food and
with the Word constantly. To them it tastes pleasant and is
sweet.

But it is said to be tasted, when I believe with my heart that
Christ gave himself for me, and has become my own, and my
sin and misery are his, and his life also is mine. When this
reaches my heart, then it tastes. For how can I but receive joy
and gladness from it? I am heartily glad, as though some good
friend had given me a hundred florins. But he whose heart it
does not reach cannot rejoice over it. But they taste it best who

lie in the straits of death, or whom an evil conscience oppresses; for in that case hunger is a good cook, as we say, that makes the food have a good relish; for the heart and conscience can bear nothing more soothing. When they feel their misery, for this they are anxious. They smell the provision afar off and cannot be satisfied. So also Mary says in the Magnificat: "The hungry he hath filled with good things" (Luke 1:53). But that hardened class who live in their own holiness, build on their own works, and feel not their sin and misery, they taste this not. Whoever sits at the table and is hungry relishes everything heartily; but he who has previously been satisfied, relishes nothing. He can only murmur at the most excellent food. Therefore the apostle says, "If ye have tasted that the Lord is gracious." But it is as though he had said, If ye have not tasted it, then I preach to you in vain. He further says:

v. 4a. Unto whom coming [as to] a living stone.

Here he falls back again upon the Scriptures and quotes the prophet Isaiah: "Hear the word of Jehovah, ye scoffers; ye say, We have made a covenant with death, and with Sheol are we at agreement; we have made lies our refuge. Therefore thus saith the Lord Jehovah, I lay in the foundation of Zion an elect, precious cornerstone, or foundation stone" (28:14-16). This passage Paul has also quoted in Romans 9:33, and it is an important passage of Scripture, for Christ is the precious headstone which God has laid, on which we must be built.

And observe how Peter quotes the expression and shows that the stone signifies Christ. Hence as Isaiah says, "Trust in him" is the same as Peter says, "Build upon him." That is called explaining the Scriptures rightly.

Christ is this precious foundation or cornerstone upon which both the Jews and the Gentiles must be built through faith, if they are not to be terrified, that is, if they are not to doubt in their abyss of sin and thus be ruined and die.

As builders lay the cornerstone where it will rest secure and firm so as to bear up the entire building; just so God laid Christ as a cornerstone and he will indeed remain such. All who build upon him, that is, all who are called through the

Gospel and accept and believe it, may become righteous and be saved. They shall indeed be secure and unmovable in the face of all misfortune, be it caused by sin, death, or Satan. On the other hand, those who are not built upon him must be lost and condemned, there is, in short, no help or counsel for them.

He is moreover a test-stone, who has indeed been kept and in every way tempted through suffering and the cross, so that he can truly sympathize with and help those who are tempted, since all who are built upon him meet such experiences, for they must be made in his image (Rom. 8:17). He is also a precious cornerstone. Precious is he in the hearts of the believers in Christ and in the presence of God; but in the eye of the world he is despised and rejected by the builders, namely, the best people of the world who teach and govern differently. But the prophet designates him as the cornerstone, for he has united the two walls, the two peoples, the Jews and the Gentiles and made them one people and one church. Thus Christ, the living stone, bears up the whole building and joins all parts harmoniously so that it grows into a living temple in the Lord, against which all the gates of hell cannot prevail. For whoever is built upon this foundation-stone, that is, whoever believes, shall not, as the prophet clearly shows, be put to shame. Of this more will be said later.

v. 4b. Rejected indeed of men, but with God elect, precious.

Here he cites a passage in Psalm 118:22, 23: "The stone which the builders rejected is become the head of the corner. This is Jehovah's doing; it is marvelous in our eyes." Christ also quotes the same passage in Matthew 21:42; as does Peter in Acts 4:11, where he says, "He is the stone which was set at nought of you the builders, which was made the head of the corner;" as if Peter should say: You are the builders, God has charged you with the building of his house, that is, his people, making them better and teaching them the way of salvation; he instituted your priesthood, Aaron, whose successors you are, he himself consecrated and committed unto you the Law, the Scriptures, and the office of preaching. And thus he has made you builders, so that you should esteem the stone which he himself laid, and build yourselves and your people upon him. That is, you should accept him and point your people to him as the true Lord and Savior, so that whoever believes on him shall not be put to shame. But what do you do? You have not only not accepted him, but in the most shameless and ignominious manner you have rejected him, yea, condemned and put him to death on the cross as a blasphemer of God, as a seducer and as a rebel. This you have done so that he who was truly despised and rejected by you builders and your disciples, is chosen by God and is precious in his sight; he made him the foundation and cornerstone so that he might carry the entire building and join together the two walls, to the end that all who are built upon him by faith may never be put to shame. Therefore since you rejected him, God has in turn rejected you and accepted the heathen as his people.

In like manner Christ himself makes use of this analogy in Matthew 21:42. So Peter does in Acts 4:11, where he says, "He is the stone which was set at nought of you the builders." Ye are builders, he says: for they taught the people, went about with great speeches, laid down many laws, but built up mere work-saints and hypocrites. Then Christ comes and tells them, ye are hypocrites and broods and vipers in Matthew 23:33. He pronounces upon them many terrible judgments; he considers them as sinners and not as great saints. And as they could not endure this, they even reject him, and say to him, "You are a heretic; and do you caution we should not do good works? Ay! you must die." Therefore Peter says, here, this is the corner that was indeed rejected of men, upon which ye must be built by faith. This is now marvelous in our eyes, as the prophet says in Psalm 118:23. It seems strange to us, and where the Spirit does not teach, it is utterly incomprehensible. Therefore he says, in God's eyes the stone is elect, and an extremely precious stone; it is of great importance also that it takes away death, satisfies for sin, and rescues from hell—besides it freely gives us heaven.

v. 5a. Ye also, as living stones, are built up a spiritual house.

How can we build ourselves up? With the Gospel and that

which is preached. The builders are the preachers; the Christians who hear the Gospel are they who are built and are the stones which are to be fitted on this corner-stone. We are to repose our confidence on him and let our hearts stand and rest upon him. I must therefore take heed to myself that I have the form which this stone has, for if I am laid upon him by faith, then I must also bear such marks and polish as he had, and everyone else with me. It grows out of faith and is a work of love, that we all be fitted one to another, and all thus become one building. To the same end also Paul speaks on this subject, although in a different manner in 1 Corinthians 3:16: "Ye are the temple of God." The house of stone or wood is not his house; he will have a spiritual house, that is, the Christian congregation, where we are all alike in one faith, one resembling the other, and all laid and fitted one to the other, and locked into one another by love, without any wickedness, deceit, hypocrisy, hatred, and slander, as he has said.

v. 5b. To be a holy priesthood.

Here he casts down the outward and temporal priesthood, which had existed before under the old dispensation, as also the outward church, which he takes entirely away; as though to say: That outward institution of the priesthood has all ceased, wherefore another priesthood now begins, and another sacrifice is offered, even one that is entirely spiritual. We have had much discussion on this point, maintaining that those who are now called the clergy are not priests in the sight of God; and it is founded upon this passage of Peter. Therefore apprehend it well, and if one should meet you with the objection and attempt to show, as some have done, that he speaks of a twofold priesthood—of outward and spiritual priests— then bid him lay aside his spectacles that he may see clearly and take *nieswort*, or aromatic snuff (Bucer in his Latin translation, *Nasturtium*), that he may clear his brains. Peter says also, "Ye are to build yourselves up into a spiritual or holy priesthood." Ask now those priests whether they are holy: Their life clearly shows, as we see, that this wretched set of men is plunged into avarice, fornication, and all manner of vice. Whoever fills the office of this priesthood must certainly be holy. Whoever is not holy does not possess it. Therefore Peter speaks here only of one kind of priesthood.

We ask further whether he makes a distinction between spiritual and worldly or secular person, since the clergy are now called spiritual and other Christians worldly? Then they must confess, and no thanks to them for it, that Peter here speaks to all who are Christians, even to those who lay aside all wickedness, deceit, hypocrisy, and malice, and are like newborn children, who drink the pure milk. Their lie must bite itself in their mouth. Because it stands forth not to be gainsaid, that Peter speaks to all Christians, whence it is clear that they lie, and that Peter says nothing of their priesthood, which they have fancied and arrogate to themselves alone. Therefore our bishops are nothing but Nicholas-bishops [which Bucer renders in his Latin translation, *idols* or *vain persons*, boys set up as their bishops on the festival of D. Nicholas, See *St. Louis Walch*, vol. 19:675, 1358; translator's note]. And as is their priesthood, so are also their laws, sacrifices, and works. It might be an excellent play to act out on Shrove-Tuesday, the carnival period of the year, except that under the mask the divine name is reviled.

Therefore those alone are the holy and spiritual priesthood, who are true Christians and are built upon this stone. For since Christ is the bridegroom, and we all are the bride, the bride has all that the bridegroom has, even his own body. For if he gives himself to the bride, he gives himself to him. Now Christ has been anointed the high and most exalted priest of God himself; he also sacrificed his own body for us, which is the office of the high priest. Besides, he prayed on the cross for us. And in the third place, he also preached the Gospel and taught all men to know God and himself. These three offices he has also given to all of us. Therefore, since he is a priest and we are his brethren, so all Christians have it in their power and charge, and the obligation rests upon them, to preach and to come before God, and one to pray for another, and offer himself up to God. And in spite of the fact that one does not raise his voice to preach or to speak he is nevertheless a priest.

v. 5c. To offer up spiritual sacrifices.

Thus the bodily or temporal sacrifices of the same priesthood are at an end, so that both the priesthood and the sacrifice have not been annulled, and all at present is new and spiritual. For the true, eternal high priest, Christ, is at hand, as Revelation 1:5, 6 says, Him that loved us, and washed us from our sins by his blood; and he made us to be a kingdom, to be priests unto his God and Father. And just as he has sacrificed his body, so we should sacrifice also ours (Rom. 12:1). Here is now fulfilled all that is signified by the outward sacrifice of the Old Testament, as they all were held and meant in short to preach the Gospel; for whoever preaches the Gospel observes and fulfills all, he sticks the calf dead, namely, kills the carnal mind and slays the old Adam. For this stubborn nature in the flesh and blood we should sacrifice and destroy there on the cross. There the true office of the priest is administered when we sacrifice to God the wicked rogue, the corrupt old stupid fellow, namely, the carnal man. For at last all must be laid aside that we have inherited from the old Adam, as we have heard before in the first chapter. This is the only sacrifice that is pleasing and acceptable to God. From this you can see where our fools and blind leaders have led us with their trickery, who have not understood what the true priesthood is nor what kind of sacrifices we should offer unto God.

Now you may say: If it be true that we all are priests and should preach, what state of things would there then be? Shall there be no difference among the people, and shall the women also be priests? Answer: Under the New Testament no priest should by right wear the tonsure; not that it is wrong in itself that one should even permit his head to be shaved; but because one should not make a difference between those who until the present time are called priests and the ordinary Christian man, which faith cannot allow. It ought to be so arranged that those who are now called priests should all become plain laymen like other people, and only some of them who are competent should be chosen out of the congregation to the preaching office. Thus there is only an outward distinction for the sake of the office, in that one is called out of the congregation. But before God there is no distinction. Certain ones are selected from the large company of the congregation so that, as representatives of the congregation, they may bear and fill the office which they all have. Hence, as we have said, all Christians shall sacrifice, pray, and preach and confess the grace of God in Christ. Therefore shall no one self-chosen stand up and preach in the congregation; but they ought to be selected out of the company of believers and appointed thereto, who may be removed in case they are found unfaithful. For Paul teaches in 1 Timothy 3:2 and Titus 1:6: such persons shall be blameless, without reproach.

Therefore the pope, contrary to the Word of God, has devised his own priesthood, and in doing so has shamefully and in an unchristianlike manner misrepresented the truth by teaching that they are holy and spiritual who live in the state of the priests. Beloved, outward anointing and shaving the tonsure make no one holy and spiritual. If they did, God would have indeed permitted the Levitical priesthood to continue, which he himself instituted. But Christ, the eternal Priest himself, had to intercede in our behalf, die on the cross, and shed his blood and with it cleanse us from our sins. Such doctrines and confession however the troublesome pope has rooted out with his priesthood, and he has brought it to pass that among us Christians there is indeed a greater difference than between us and the Turks. If you wish to see Christians, then you dare not make a distinction among them and say: That is a man or woman, a servant or a master, old or young; but as Paul says in Galatians 3:28: "Ye all are one man in Christ Jesus." Hence they all are even priests and all proclaim the wonderful works of God, each one in his own home; those to whom it is appointed, in the Church; all pray and offer praise to God. For, as I said, in the congregation no one shall teach publicly unless he is called to do so.

This is now the true priesthood, which consists of three parts: that we offer spiritual sacrifices, that we pray for all present needs, and that we preach the Word. Whoever now believes on Christ, so that he is cleansed from all sins through his blood is a priest, and is under obligation to proclaim such inexpressible grace and love shown us in Christ. Likewise he prays and bears the holy cross, by which the old Adam is put to death and thanks are offered to God. Hence we should not be misled by the monkey play of the papists, who wish to be the only priests and to be spiritual. They have no other office than what they wear the tonsure and are anointed. By such jugglery, as I said, we are not consecrated to be priests; it must be by another consecrating bishop, of whom it is written in Psalm 110:4 "Jehovah hath sworn, and will not repent: thou art a priest forever...."

v. 5d. Acceptable to God through Jesus Christ.

Since Christ is the cornerstone upon which we are anchored, it follows that whatever we wish to undertake relative to God must be realized only through him, of which we have heard sufficient. For God has no regard for my good works and my cross though I afflict myself to death. But he has regard for Christ through whom my works avail before God, which without Christ are not worth a straw. Hence the Scriptures rightly call Christ a precious cornerstone, which communicates his virtue to all who build upon him by faith. Thus Peter teaches us in this passage how Christ is the living stone and what Christ is. It is a beautiful figure, from which we easily understand how we are to believe on Christ. Hence it now follows further:

vv. 6-10. Because it is contained in scripture, Behold, I lay in Zion a chief corner stone, elect, precious: and he that believeth on him shall not be put to shame. For you therefore that believe is the preciousness: but for such as disbelieve, the stone which the builders rejected, the same was made the head of the corner; and, a stone of stumbling, and a rock of offense; for they stumble at the word, being disobedient: whereunto also they were appointed. But ye are an elect race, a royal priesthood, a holy nation, a people for God's own possession, that ye may show forth the excellencies of him who called you out of darkness into his marvelous light: who in time past were no people, but now are the people of God: who had not obtained mercy, but now have obtained mercy.

I have before said that Peter has enriched and fortified his epistle well with Scripture, just as all preachers should do, in order that their foundation may rest entirely on the Word of God. Here also he introduces four or five texts, one after another. The first he has taken from Isaiah 28:16, word for word, that Christ is a precious cornerstone or foundation. It is the very passage we have just treated and in part explained. It is truly an eminent proof text of the doctrine of faith, which is to be laid down as a foundation when we preach in a place where Christ has not been preached before. For it must be confessed that Christ is the stone on which faith should be built and should stand.

But that the prophet does not here speak of a material stone is evident as it follows, "Whoever believes on him shall not be put to shame." If I am to believe on him, it must be a stone in a spiritual sense. For how am I to believe on stone and wood? Besides he must be truly God, since in the first commandment God has forbidden us to believe on anything else, but on himself only. Since then this stone is laid as a foundation in which we are to trust, God alone, but must also in addition be man, because he must be a part of the building, and not merely a part, but the head. If a man then erects a building, one stone must be like the other, that each have the complexion, nature, and form of the other. Therefore, since we are built on Christ, he also must be like us, and of the same nature with the other stones, that rest upon him, even a real human person as we all are. Thus do the Scriptures, in simple and few words, express so great a theme, even the entire summary of our faith, and in such brief words comprises more than any man can express.

Now what the building is, I have already said; namely, faith, whereby we are laid on Christ and repose our trust upon this stone, and thus become like him. It also must follow, that the building must be fitted one part to the other. For the other stones must all be laid and placed upon this stone. That is, of course, love—a fruit of faith.

But why does the prophet call him a foundation stone? Because no man can build a house except he lay one stone first as a foundation; for the other stones in the building cannot stand except on the foundation stone.

So all of us must rest on Christ and confess him as our foundation stone. Therefore we are not to pride ourselves that the stone must receive something from us, but we must receive blessing from it alone; for we do not bear it up, but it bears us up, and upon him lies sin, death, hell, and all we have to bear. So that all this, and whatever jars against us, cannot injure us if we have been placed on this foundation. For if we remain resting on him and rely upon him, we must then remain where he is—just as natural stones must be left on their foundation stone.

Besides, the prophet calls him a "corner-stone." The Holy Spirit has a way of his own to say much in few words. Christ is a cornerstone because he has brought Gentiles and Jews together who were at dead enmity one with the other, and thus the Christian church has been gathered from both classes, of which the apostle Paul writes extensively in Ephesians 2:14-22. The Jews gloried in the law of God, and that they were God's people. Thus they despised the heathen. But now Christ has come, has taken away boasting from the Jews, and called us who were Gentiles. Thus he has made us both one, by one faith, and he has so dealt with us that we both must confess we have nothing of ourselves, but are all sinners. Therefore we must expect righteousness and heaven only from him, and we Gentiles may as justly claim Christ has come to help us, as he did to help the Jews. Therefore he is the cornerstone that joins together in one, both walls, the Jews and the Gentiles, so that it becomes one building and one house. Of this Paul writes in Ephesians 2:20f.

Now the prophet closes thus: "Whoever believes on him shall not be put to shame." When the Holy Spirit says, they shall not be put to shame who believe on Christ, he gives us to understand what he has in view: He has already published and confirmed the sentence, that the whole world must be confounded and put to shame. Yet he would rescue some out of the multitude, so that no one may escape the shame except he who believes on Christ. So Christ explains himself in the last of Mark 16:16: "He that believeth and is baptized shall be saved; but he that disbelieveth shall be condemned." In which words he also refers to the prophets. Therefore Peter well said in 1 Peter 1:10, the prophets sought out the time and diligently inquired after the salvation and concerning the future grace that was previously promised. So now we are to preach Christ, that he it is who has rescued us from this shame into which we all were plunged.

Now let anyone come forward who so desires, to exalt free will and to defend human ability. If you should wish to overthrow with one stroke all human works and doctrines, and whatever springs from man, you have enough in this single passage to do it, so that all must fall like dry leaves from the tree. For it is ordained that whoever does not rest upon this stone is already lost. God does not suffer you to accomplish anything by works. Of such simplicity the Spirit and the Divine Majesty speak, that no one esteems it, yet of such power that it overthrows all things. Who then will set himself against it, or who will not be terrified by it? Therefore God would have us entirely despair as regards ourselves. He would have us appropriate to ourselves only the blessings he has, and build on the foundation which no creature can overthrow. That way no one should trust in his own righteousness, but in Christ's righteousness, and in all that Christ has. But what is it to rest upon his righteousness? Nothing else but to despair in regard to myself, and to think, my righteousness and my truth must go to pieces; and build upon this, namely, that his righteousness, his truth, his life, and all the blessings he has, are eternal. There lies the foundation on which I stand; whatever rests not on this foundation will all necessarily fall. But whoever falls back on this foundation, he alone shall not be put to shame and shall rest—safely, so that no violence shall ever injure him in the least. Therefore Christ shall not only be a stone, but God will lay also him as a foundation on which we should confide. God has said this, he cannot lie.

Now this stone does not serve itself, but it suffers to be trodden on and buried in the earth so that it cannot be seen, and the other stones lie upon it and are seen. Wherefore, it is given to us to partake of him and rest upon him and believe what he has shall all be ours, since he has procured it for our benefit; so that I may say, this is my own property and treasure, over which my conscience can exult. But Peter says further:

vv. 7-8a. For you therefore that believe is [he precious] the preciousness [honor]: but for such as disbelieve, the stone which the

builders rejected, the same was made the head of the corner; and, a
stone of stumbling, and a rock of offense.

This good, precious stone, says Peter, is indeed to some
precious and honorable. But on the other hand, to many it is
not precious, but despised, and a stone of stumbling (Isa. 8:14).
How is this? The Scriptures ascribe to it a twofold aspect,
inasmuch as there are some who believe in it, and on the other
hand there are many who do not thus believe. To them who
believe is he precious, so that my heart must be glad if I repose my confidence and trust in him. Therefore he says, "To
you that believe he is precious"; that is, ye are greatly depend-
ent on him. For although he in himself is precious and excellent, yet this may be of no service or help to me. Therefore he
must be precious to us because he gives us so many precious
blessings; as an exceedingly precious stone, which does not
retain its virtue in itself, but breaks forth and imparts all its
powers, so that I have all that he is and has.

Unbelievers however do not esteem him as such a precious
stone, but reject him and stumble upon him—therefore he is
not pleasing to them, but obnoxious and hateful; although he
is delightful in himself. These are not only the great, public
avowed sinners, but much more those great saints who rest
on their freewill, on their own works and righteousness, who
must stumble at this stone and be dashed upon it. Now God
pronounces the sentence, that they who rest thereon without
works, are justified through faith alone; but others do not attain to justification because they wish to be justified by their
own righteousness, as Paul says in Romans 9:31 and 10:3.

Therefore this has become the stone, says Peter, which the
builders rejected. And here he dovetails the Scriptures into
one another, but explains the passage he quoted above from
Psalm 118:22, "The stone which the builders rejected is become the head of the corner." Who the builders are, I have
sufficiently shown (v. 5); even those who taught and preached
the law, and would justify men by their works; who agree
with Christ, as summer and winter with each other. Therefore, ministers who preach work righteousness reject this stone.

Besides this, he quotes another passage from the prophet
Isaiah. In Isaiah 8:13, 14, the prophet has there described that

which was to take place, as Peter here does, and speaks thus: "Jehovah shall be your dread, who shall be to you for a sanctuary (holiness), but for a stone of stumbling and a rock of offense shall he be to both the houses of Israel." The sense of the prophet is this: Jehovah shall be to you for holiness; that is, he shall be hallowed in your hearts; ye are to have no other sanctification, neither this nor that, except as ye believe. To the others, he shall be a stone on which they shall stumble and be offended.

But what now is this offense and this running or stumbling? It is this: When we preach Christ, and say, See why this stone is laid for a foundation, namely, that you wholly desponding and despairing in yourself might hold your works and your own righteousness as condemned, and might place your confidence in him alone, and believe that Christ's righteousness becomes your righteousness. When men hear this, they revolt at it, stumble and are offended, and say, How? Do you mean to say that virginity, and masses, and the like good works, amount to nothing? It is the devil that bids you say that! For they cannot reconcile themselves to the thought that their claims are no good. They think they have done well in the sight of God. They quote passages to prove it from the Scriptures and say, "God has commanded that we should perform good works. If we dispute this, they cry out, "Heretic! Heretic!" "Fire! Fire!" So they cannot endure this stone, and they stumble against it. They then bounce against one another, so that they cannot help being rushed by this stone, as Christ said in Matthew 21:42, "Have ye never read in the Scriptures, the stone which the builders rejected, the same is become the head of the corner?" And it follows, "And he that falleth on this stone shall be broken to pieces; but on whomsoever it shall fall, it will scatter him as dust" (Matt. 21:44). Therefore, do as ye will, ye cannot dishonor the stone; it is laid, and it will continue to lay where it was placed. Whoever then will rush upon it and dash himself on it, must necessarily be scattered as dust.

This is the stumbling and the offense of which Scripture speaks so much. Thus the Jews stumble to this day against this stone, and this stumbling will not cease until the last day shall come. Then shall this stone fall upon all the unbelieving and grind them to powder. Therefore, although Christ is such an elect, precious stone, he must yet be called a stone of offense and stumbling, by no fault of his. And just as the Jews did, we continue to do at the present day; for as they gloried in the name of God, that they were God's people, so it is the case now, men under the name of Christ and the Christian church, deny Christ and reject the precious stone. (The reason is, they are required to renounce their own wisdom, righteousness, holiness, and that they will not and cannot do. They rather reject this chosen, precious stone. Nevertheless he remains indeed unrejected but they must on its account go to the bottom and descend to the devil, and nothing can prevent it. Ed. 1539.) He has come that they might reject their own works; but this is a thing they cannot suffer, and they reject him. Therefore it follows:

v. 8b. For they stumble at the word, being disobedient: whereunto also they were appointed.

Here you hear what the cause is: The word and the preaching of Christ, that we must either be built upon him or be lost, find no entrance or welcome in their hearts. Hence when they hear that no one can be justified before God through the works of the law, or that to praise and practice chastity, poverty and obedience appeases not the wrath of God, but faith in Christ does, they do not believe such preaching of grace. Yea, they moreover take offense and stumble. Consequently Paul calls the Gospel the offensive Word of the Cross, which those who are lost consider pure foolishness. He says: "We preach Christ crucified, unto the Jews a stumbling block, and unto the Gentiles foolishness; but unto them that are called both Jews and Greeks, Christ the power of God, and the wisdom of God" (1 Cor. 1:23, 24).

If they are told their works are not good and are of no avail before God, they cannot and will not hear it. Now God has laid Christ as a foundation, whereon they should have been placed, and through him have obtained complete salvation; and he has caused him to be preached throughout the whole world, that they through the proclamation of the Gospel might be grounded on him. Yet they would not accept him, and they remained in their own nature and works. For if they suffered themselves to rest upon him, then would their own honor, riches, and power fall, so that they could never be raised again. Peter says further:

v. 9a. But ye are an elect race [a chosen generation] a royal priesthood, a holy nation, a people for God's own possession.

There he gives Christians a true title, and has quoted this passage from Moses. Who said to the Jews, "For thou art a holy people unto Jehovah thy God; Jehovah thy God hath chosen thee to be a people for his own possession, above all peoples that are upon the face of the earth" (Deut. 7:6). Thus in Exodus 19:5,6, he says: "Ye shall be mine own possession from among all peoples, and shall be unto me a kingdom of priests, and a holy nation." There you see where Peter's words are from. As I have said before (v. 5), so I say again, that it should be understood how Scripture is wont to speak of priests. Let no one be troubled as to those whom the people call priests; let everyone call them as he pleases, but abide thou by the pure Word of God, and whom this calls priests call thou priests also. We can well endure that they call themselves priests whom the bishops and the pope consecrate. Let them call themselves as they will, only see to it that they do not call themselves "priests of God," for they cannot quote a word from Scripture in support of their claim.

But should they claim that in this passage he speaks of them, answer them as I have instructed you under verse 5, and ask them to whom Peter is here speaking, and then of necessity they shall be made ashamed. For it is certainly clear and plain enough that he speaks to the whole congregation, to all Christians, in that he says, "Ye are a chosen generation" and "a holy people," since he has hitherto spoken of none but of those who are built upon this stone and believe. Therefore it must follow that whoever does not believe is no priest. If they say, then: Ah! we must explain the passage just as the holy fathers have interpreted it; then reply: Let the fathers and teachers, whoever they may be, explain as they will, yet

Peter, who has received greater testimony from God than they,
besides being more ancient, tells me so and so, therefore I will
hold with him. The passage moreover needs no comment, for
he speaks in express words of those that believe. Now they
are not the only believers who are anointed and wear the
tonsure. Therefore we will readily allow that they call themselves by this name, for the question is not what they permit
themselves to do. The dispute is whether they are styled priests
in the Scriptures, and whether God calls them by this name.
There may be some selected out of the congregation as its
officers and ministers, and appointed to preach in the Church
and administer the sacraments, but we all are priests before
God if we are Christians. For since we are built upon this
stone, which is our high priest before God, we must also possess all that he has.

Therefore I would be glad to find this word *priests* becoming as common as it is for us to be called Christians. For it is
all one thing—priest, baptized, Christian. As little as I would
suffer that those who are anointed and shorn should be called
Christians and the baptized, so little would I endure that they
only should be regarded as priests. Yet they have arrogated
the name entirely to themselves. So too they have named the
church which the pope and his cardinals rule. But Scripture
refutes this. Therefore mark well, that you may know how to
establish the distinction as to how God names us priests, and
how men call themselves such. For we must yet again state
this word *priest* should become as common as the word *Christian*. For to be a priest belongs not to an office that is external,
it is only such an office that is administered before God.

So we conclude that we are all kings. *Priests* and *kings* are
all spiritual names, as *Christians, saints,* and *Church.* And just
as you are not called a Christian because you have much gold
or wealth, but because you are built upon this stone and believe on Christ, so you are not called a priest because you
wear a tonsure or long robe, but because you dare come into
God's presence. Likewise you are not a king because you wear
a gold crown and have many lands and people subject to you,
but because you are lord over all things, death, sin and hell.
For you are as really a king as Christ is a king, if you believe

on him. Still he is not a king as the kings of this world are. He wears no crown of gold, rides forth with no great pomp and large equipage. But he is a king over all kings, one who has authority over all things and at whose feet all must bow. As he is a lord, so also am I a lord; for what he possesses that have I also. For through him are we children and heirs of God, his brethren and joint heirs (Rom. 8:17).

Therefore mark well that you know how to distinguish those who are priests before God—namely, those who show forth and preach to us the glory and goodness of God in Christ, pray, do good, suffer evil—from those who are called priests because of the consecration, tonsures, and long robes. They are priests like Baal's priests were prophets.

Now, just as Christ is not a worldly king—for he had not any where to lay his head; but a spiritual, eternal King, to whom God committed all things so that he could rescue his own in every time of need, justify, and save them—so are they who believe in him spiritual kings and partakers of the heavenly possessions, of which neither death nor Satan can rob them. I have spoken these words that you may learn rightly to consider and understand the words *priest*, and *king*, as they are used in the Scriptures. Do not use them as the world does, that knows nothing to say of other kings than those who wear golden crowns, have countries and peoples subject to them, who can indeed be also wicked, godless persons, as they generally are. These in the eye of the world are lordly, powerful, rich, and proud. But when death comes, their power and glory have an end. But with the kings of whom Peter here speaks it is just the opposite. Upon earth they are generally poor, miserable, oppressed, and despised people, but before God they are the richest and the most glorious. They have little or nothing and yet they have all. They are poor, and yet they make many rich. Whoever does not acknowledge and know Christ and what God has given to us through him, understands nothing of this.

But perhaps someone may reply. Peter says here that Christians are also kings, while we have before our eyes the fact that we are not all kings, so that this passage is not to be understood as though he spoke of all in general. For whoever is a Christian is certainly not a king in France or a priest at Rome. But when I ask whether the King of France is also a king in the sight of God, this he passes over, for God will not judge by the crown. On earth and before the world he is indeed a king, but when death comes, then his kingdom is at an end; for then he must lie at the feet of those that believe. We are speaking of an eternal kingdom and priesthood, inasmuch as everyone who believes is in truth a king before God; but who does not know that we are not all shorn and anointed priests? Because some men have been anointed, they are not therefore priests in the sight of God; just as they are not kings before God because they have been crowned. Crowned kings and anointed priests are of the world, and are made by men. The pope may make as many such priests as he chooses, but far be it that he should make one a priest before God, for these God himself will make.

Therefore, when Peter says here, "Ye are a royal priesthood," it is as much as if he had said, "Ye are Christians." Would you now know what sort of a title and authority and glory Christians have; you learn it here that they are kings and priests, and a chosen people. (Why they are consecrated to be priests and how they are to fill their office, follows. Ed. 1539.) What the priest's office is, follows:

v. 9b. That ye may show forth the excellencies [German: tugend, virtue] of him who called you out of darkness into his marvelous light.

It belongs to the office of a priest to be a messenger of God and receive from God himself the command to preach his word. The excellencies or praises, says Peter, that is, the wonderful work that God has performed in you, in bringing you out of darkness into light, you are to proclaim. This is the highest office of a priest. And the way you are to preach is by one brother proclaiming to another the powerful work of God; how ye have been called to eternal life. Thus shall you also instruct others how to come to the same light. For your whole duty is discharged in this, that you confess what God has done for you; and then let it be your chief aim to make this known publicly and to call everyone to the light, to which ye have been called. Where you see people who are ignorant, you are to direct and teach them as you have been taught, namely, how a man may be saved through the virtue and power of God, and pass from darkness to light.

And here you observe Peter plainly saying that there is only one single light, and he concludes that all our reason, however sharp-sighted it is, is mere darkness. For although reason may count one, two, three, and also discern what is black or white, great or small, and judge outwardly of other matters, still it cannot understand what faith is. Here it is stark blind, and if all men should put their wits together, they could not understand a letter of this divine wisdom. Therefore Peter speaks here of another light and that is truly wonderful; and he tells us earnestly that we are all alike in darkness and blindness if God hath not called us to his true light.

Experience teaches us this also. For when we preach that we cannot come before God by our works, but must have a mediator who may come into God's presence and reconcile us to him, reason must confess that she never could have known such a thing. So if she would understand it, she must have another light and knowledge. Therefore all that is not of God's Word and faith is darkness. For here reason gropes like a blind man. It is ever-changing from this to that, and it knows not what it does. But if we speak in this manner to the worldly, learned, or wise, they begin to cry out and rage against it. Therefore Peter is a bold apostle indeed, in that he dares to make darkness what all the world calls light.

So we see that the first and most eminent office we as Christians are to discharge is that we make known the praise of God. What then are the praiseworthy things and the noble deeds God has wrought? They are, as we have often said (1 Peter 1:3, 13), that Christ, through the power of God has wounded death, chained hell, subdued sin, and brought us to eternal life. These are excellencies or virtues so great that it is impossible for any man to comprehend them, and as to doing them, that is out of the question. Therefore it is of no avail that human doctrines be preached to us Christians. For we are taught of a power that subdues the devil, sin, and death.

And here Peter has once more brought together many proof-texts, and it is throughout common with him thus to heap passage upon passage. For all the prophets declare that God's name and honor, and his arm or power should be honored and extolled, and that he would perform a work of which the whole world would sing and speak. Of this the prophets in all places are full; to all these Peter here refers. Beside, they have spoken much of light and darkness, that we must be enlightened with God's light, thereby showing that all human reason is darkness. Peter says further:

v. 10. Who in time past were no people, but now are the people of God; who had not obtained mercy, but now have obtained mercy.

This passage is written by the prophet in the book of the prophet Hosea 2:23, and Paul has also quoted it in Romans 9:25: "I will call that my people, which was not my people." The import of all is this: Almighty God chose his people Israel as a peculiar people, manifested his great power in their behalf, gave them many prophets, and performed many wonderful works among them so that he might from that people permit Christ to become man. For the children's sake it has all taken place. Therefore they are called in Scripture the people of God. But the prophets extended this further by saying that this election should be more comprehensive and should even include the Gentiles.

Therefore Peter says here: Ye are now the people of God, who once were not the people of God. Hence it is evident that he wrote the epistle to the Gentiles and not to the Jews. By this he shows that the passage out of the prophet has been now fulfilled; that they are now a holy people; that they have the property, priesthood, kingdom, and all that Christ has, if they believe. It follows now further:

vv. 11, 12. Beloved, I beseech you as sojourners and pilgrims, to abstain from fleshly lusts, which war against the soul; having your behavior seemly among the Gentiles; that, wherein they speak against you as evil-doers, they may by your good works, which they behold, glorify God in the day of visitation.

Peter here uses a different mode of speech from that of Paul, who would not speak in this manner, as we shall hear; for every apostle has his own characteristic way of speaking, just as each prophet has. He has hitherto been firmly laying the foundation of the Christian faith, which may serve as his text. Now he proceeds and teaches how we should conduct ourselves toward all men. This is the true method of preaching, first to set forth faith, what it does, and what its power and nature are, even that it gives to us enough of everything that is necessary to holiness and salvation; that we can do nothing except by faith, and through this we have all that God possesses. God has thus proceeded with us and given us all that is his, and has himself become our own, so that we have through faith all things that are good and needful for us. What then are we to do? Are we to live in indolence? Then it would be the best that we should die, so that we might have it all. But while we live here we should act in our neighbor's behalf and give ourselves to his welfare, as God hath given himself to us. Thus faith saves us, but love leads us to give to our neighbor whenever we have enough to give. That is, faith receives from God; love gives to our neighbor. This theme is mentioned in few words, yet much may easily be preached on it, and it may be extended further than has been done by Peter.

This is now the sense of the apostle, when he says, "Dear brethren, I admonish, beseech, you as sojourners and as pilgrims." Since you are one with Christ, form one household, and his goods are yours, your injury is his injury, and he takes as his own all that you possess. Therefore you are to follow him and conduct yourselves as those who are no longer citizens of the world. Your possessions lie not upon the earth, but in heaven. And though you have already lost all temporal good, you still have Christ who is more than all else. The devil is the prince of this world and rules it; his citizens are the people of this world; therefore, since you are not of the world, act as a stranger in an inn—one who has not his possessions with him but procures food and gives his gold for it. For here it is only a sojourning, where we cannot tarry, but must travel farther. Therefore we should use worldly blessings no more than is needful for health and appetite, and then leave them and go to another land. We are citizens of heaven; on earth we are pilgrims and guests (Heb. 13:14).

v. 11b. Abstain from fleshly lusts, which war against the soul.

I will not determine here whether Peter speaks of outward impurity, or like Paul does, of all that is called carnal—that is, whatever man does without faith, while he is in the body and in a carnal life. I hold however that Peter had a different mode of expression, yet I do not think he uses the word *soul*, as Paul does, for spirit; but Peter has held more to the common Greek word than Paul. Yet much stress is not to be laid upon this; let it be understood of all kinds of lust, or all kinds of carnal desire or impurity. But this at least he would teach us, that no saint on earth can be fully perfect and pure. The high schools have even trodden this passage under their feet, and they do not understand it; they think it is said only of sinners, as though the saints had no wicked lust remaining in them. But whoever will study carefully the Scriptures must note a distinction. The prophets sometimes speak of the saints in a manner, as though they were indeed perfectly holy in every respect; while on the other hand they speak also of them as having evil lusts and being troubled with sins. In regard to these two distinctions those persons cannot judge. Therefore understand it thus: That Christians are divided into two parts; into an inward nature which is faith, and an outward nature which is the flesh. If we look upon a Christian as respects faith, then he is pure and entirely holy; for the Word of God has nothing impure in it, and wherever it enters the heart that depends upon it, it will make that also pure; because, in respect to faith all things are perfect. According to that, we are kings and priests and the people of God, as was said above in 1 Peter 2:9. But since faith exists in the flesh, and we still live on the earth, we feel at times evil dispositions, such as impatience and fear of death. These are all the fault of the old man, for faith is not yet mature and has not attained full control over the flesh.

This you can understand from the parable in Luke 10:30 of the man who went down from Jerusalem to Jericho and fell among thieves. They beat him and left him lying half dead.

But the Samaritan afterward took him up, and bound his wounds, and cared for him, and saw to it that he should be nursed. There you perceive that this man, since he is to be nursed, is not sick unto death, his life is safe. All that is wanting is that he should be restored to health. Life is there, but he is not completely restored, for he lies yet in the hands of the physicians and must yet give himself up to be healed. So we have also the Lord Jesus Christ in his completeness; we are assured of eternal life, yet we have not perfect health; some of the old Adam still remains in the flesh.

Similar also is the parable in Matthew 13:33, where Christ says: "The kingdom of heaven is like unto leaven which a woman takes and mingles in the meal until it is leavened throughout." When meal is made into dough, the leaven is all in it. But it has not penetrated and worked through it, but the meal lies working until it is leavened throughout, and no more leaven need be added. Thus through faith you have all that you need to apprehend the Word of God, yet it has not penetrated throughout, wherefore it must continue to work till you are entirely renewed. In this way you are to discriminate in regard to the Scriptures, and not martyr them as the papists do.

Therefore I say, when you read in the Scriptures of the saints, that they were perfect, understand that as to faith they were entirely pure and without sin, but the flesh still remained and that could not have been entirely holy. Therefore Christians desire and pray that the body or the flesh be mortified, that they may be entirely pure. Those who teach otherwise have neither experienced nor relished this, which leads them to speak just as they imagine and conceive with their reason; wherefore they must err. In regard to this, those great saints who have written and taught much, have greatly stumbled. Origen has not a word of it in his books. Jerome never understood it. Augustine, had he not been driven to contend with the Pelagians, would have understood it no better. When they speak of the saints, they extol them so highly as if they were something different from, and better than, other Christians; just as though they had not felt the power of the flesh and complained of it as well as we do.

Therefore Peter says here, as ye would be pure and have complete sanctification, continue to contend with your evil lusts. So also Christ says in the gospel of John 13:10: "Whoever is washed, must also wash his feet." It is not enough that his head and hands be clean; therefore, he would yet have them wash their feet.

But what does Peter mean in that he says, abstain from the lusts that war against the soul? This is what he would say: You are not to imagine that you can succeed by sports and sleep. Sin is indeed taken away by faith, but you have still the flesh which is impulsive and inconsiderate; therefore take good care, that ye overcome it. By strong effort it must be done; you are to restrain and subdue lust, and the greater your faith is, the greater will the conflict be. Therefore you should be prepared and armed, and you should contend with it incessantly. For they will assault you in multitudes and would take you captive.

Hence Paul also says: "I delight in the law of God after the inward man; but I see a different law in my members, warring against the law of my mind, and bringing me into captivity" (Rom. 7:22, 23), so that I do what I would not. As though he had said, I fight indeed against it, but it will not finally yield. Therefore I would gladly be free, but in spite of my good will it cannot come to pass. What then am I to do? "Wretched man that I am! who shall deliver me out of the body of this death" (Rom. 7:24). In this same manner all the saints cry out. But people without faith the devil leads in such a way that he permits them only to enter on a sinful course, and he follows them, but does not destroy them entirely by sin. But as to the others, he thinks, I have already taken them captive by unbelief. I will permit them to go so far only, as to do no great sin and have no great assault, and be kept from swearing and knavery. But believers have always opposition enough; they must ever stand in the attitude of struggle. Those who are without faith and have not the Spirit, do not feel this nor do they have such an experience. They break away and follow their wicked lusts. But as soon as the Spirit and faith enter our hearts, we become so weak that we think we cannot beat down the least imaginations and sparks of temptation, and we see nothing but sin in ourselves from the crown of the head even to the foot. For before we believed, we walked according to our own lusts, but now the Spirit has come and would purify us, and a conflict arises when the devil, the flesh, and the world oppose faith. Of this all the prophets complain here and there in the Scriptures.

Therefore Peter now means that the strife does not take place in sinners, but in believers, and he gives us the consolation that we may check evil lusts thus, namely, by barking against them. If thou then hast wicked thoughts, thou shouldst not on this account despair; only be on thy guard, that thou be not taken prisoner by them. Our teachers have proposed to relieve the matter by directing men to torture themselves until they had no more evil thoughts, that they at last became frantic and insane. But learn, if you are a Christian, that you must experience all kinds of opposition and wicked dispositions in the flesh. For wherever faith exists, there come a hundred evil thoughts, a hundred struggles more than before. Only see to it that you act the man and not suffer yourself to be taken captive. Continue to resist and say, I will not, I will not. (Lord Christ then hast said: "Ask and ye shall receive." Help, dear Lord, against all temptations. Ed. 1539.) For we must here confess that the case is much like an ill-matched couple who are continually complaining of one another, and what one will do the other will not.

That may still be called a truly Christian life which is never at perfect rest nor and has not advanced so far that we feel no sin, but that we indeed feel sin, only we do not allow it admittance. Thus we are to fast, pray, and labor to weaken and suppress lust. So you are not to imagine you are to become a saint like these fools speak of. Since flesh and blood continue as long as sin remains; therefore we are to constantly war against it. Whoever has not learned this by his own experience must not boast that he is a Christian.

Before, we have been taught that when we made confession or joined some spiritual institution, we were at once pure and needed no longer to contend with sin. They have said, moreover, that baptism purifies and makes holy, so that nothing evil remains in the person. Hence they thought, now I will have a pleasing rest; then the devil came and assaulted them worse than before. Therefore, understand this well: Though you confess and receive absolution, you must do even as the soldier who in battle runs upon the points of the javelins, when the critical moment approaches and the conflict rages, compelling him to strike for the right, as if to repel outrage. Then he must draw out his sword and strike right and left. But now while the strife threatens only, there must be untiring vigilance. So, if you have been baptized, be on your guard, inasmuch as you are not safe for an hour from the devil and from sin, even though you think you will have no more attacks. Therefore a Christian life is nothing else than a conflict and encampment, as the Scriptures say (Job 7:1f); and therefore the Lord our God is called the Lord of Sabaoth, "*Dominus Sabaoth*" (Ps. 24:10), that is Lord over hosts. So also, "*Dominus potens in praelio*," the Lord is mighty in battle (Ps. 24:8). By these words, God shows that he is almighty for he triumphs in a wonderful way through us against the prince and God of this world, the devil and the gates of hell. Yet we are very weak, hardly to be counted a feeble fly compared to Satan. Hence Paul says in 2 Corinthians 4:7, "But we have this treasure in earthen vessels, that the exceeding greatness of the power may be of God" and not from ourselves.

And thus he shows how powerful he is, that he permits his people to be exposed in the conflict and rush upon the points of the javelins; yet while the trumpets are ever-sounding, he is ever-observant, saying, beware here, beware there; thrust here, strike there. Besides, it is a lasting conflict, in which you are to do all you can to strike down the devil by the Word of God. We must therefore ever offer resistance, and call on God for help, and despond of all human powers. Now follows further:

v. 12. Having your behavior seemly [an honest life] among the Gentiles; that, wherein they speak against you as evil-doers, they may by your good works, which they behold, glorify God in the day of visitation.

Note here what excellent order Peter observes. He has already taught us what we should do in order to subdue the flesh with all its lusts. Now he teaches us again why this should be. Why I should subdue my flesh? That I may be saved? No, but that I may lead an honest life before the world. For this honest life does not justify us, but we must first be justified and believe before we attempt to lead an honest or pious life. But as to outward conduct, this I am not to direct to my own profit, but that the unbelieving may thereby be reformed and attracted, that they may through us come to Christ; which is a true mark of love. They slander and abuse us, and hold us to be the worst wretches; therefore we should exhibit such an excellent course of behavior, that men shall be compelled to say, "Ah! We cannot find them guilty of any wrong."

We read when the emperors reigned and persecuted the Christians, no fault could be found with the believers, except that they called on Christ and considered him as God. So Pliny writes in his letter to Trajan, the Emperor, that he knew of no wrong that the Christians did, except that they came together every morning, early, and sang songs of praise in order to honor their Christ and receive the sacrament; besides this, none could bring any charge against them. Therefore Peter says: Ye must endure to have men reproach and abuse you as evil-doers, and for this reason you are to lead such a life that you shall do no one any injury, and in this manner you shall bring about their reformation. "Till that day arrive;" that is, ye must endure it as long as men reproach you, till once all shall break forth and be revealed, so that it shall be seen how unjust they have been toward you, and that they be compelled to glorify God on your account. Thus Peter now continues:

II. Works and Fruits of the Christian Life in Particular (vv. 13-25)

A. As Applied to Subjects of Civil Government (vv. 13-17)

vv. 13-17. Be subject to every ordinance of man for the Lord's sake: whether to the king, as supreme; or unto governors, as sent by him for vengeance on evil-doers and for praise to them that do well. For so is the will of God, that by well-doing ye should put to silence the ignorance of foolish men: as free, and not using your freedom for a cloak of wickedness, but as bond-servants of God. Honor all men. Love the brotherhood; fear God; honor the king.

In this beautiful order Peter proceeds and teaches us how we should conduct ourselves in all things. Hitherto he has spoken in a general manner of the conduct that becomes every condition in life. Now he begins to teach us our duties to the civil government. For since he had said enough on the first theme, our duty to God and ourselves, he now adds how we are to behave toward all men. And he would say in the first place and before all else, since ye have done all that was necessary to attain to true faith and you hold your body in subjection, let this now be your first business, to obey the civil authorities.

This, which I have here rendered in the German, every *ordinance (ordnung)* of man, is the Greek *ktisis,* and in Latin *creatura.* This has not been understood by our learned men. The German language well expresses what the word means, where it is said, "we are to obey what the world ruler enacts or creates." So he uses the word here as though he said, "yield obedience to what the public government enacts or creates." For to enact is to lay down a command and ordinance, and it is a human creation. But they have hence inferred that *creatura* means a creature, an ox or an ass, as the pope also speaks of it. If this were Peter's meaning, then we should need to become subject even to a slave. But he here means a human ordinance, law or command, and what they enact we are to do. What God makes, authorizes, and requires as his ordinance we should believe. So also, that is a human and secular creation which is constituted by commands, as external government must be. To this we are to be subject. Therefore understand the expression, "creatura humana," as meaning *"quod creat et condit homo,"* what man makes and constructs.

v. 13b. For the Lord's sake.

We are not bound to obey the sovereign power for its own sake, he says, but for God's sake, whose children we are. We should be moved to obey, but not that we may thereby acquire merit. For what I do for God's sake, I must freely do as an act of service; moreover, I should do from pure cheerfulness whatever his heart desires. But why should we be obedient to the civil powers for God's sake? Because it is God's will that evil-doers should be punished and that those who do well should be protected, so there can be concord in the world. Therefore we should demand that there be public peace, which God requires. For since we are not all believers, but the majority unbelievers, he has enacted and ordained so as to save the world from anarchy that the civil power should bear the sword and restrain the wicked, in case they are not disposed to observe the peace, they may be compelled to do so. This he executes through the civil powers, so that the world may be ruled for the good of all. Whence you see if none were wicked, there would be no need of civil government; wherefore he says, "for vengeance on evil-doers, and for praise to them that do well" (v. 14). The just should have honor when they do right, since they exalt and crown the worldly authorities, insomuch that others may take example from them, not however that anyone may thereby merit anything before God. Such is Paul's language also, in Romans 13:3: "For rulers are not a terror to the good work, but to the evil. And wouldst thou have no fear of the power? do that which is good."

v. 15. For so is the will of God, that by well-doing ye should put to silence the ignorance of foolish men.

With these words Peter silences vain babblers who glory in their Christian name and rank. He prevents them from alleging and saying, "Since faith is sufficient for a Christian, and works do not justify, what is then the need of being subject to the civil power, and paying tribute and taxes?" He tells them thus, although we have no benefit from it, we ought readily to do it to please God, so that the mouth of those enemies of God who revile us may be stopped, and that they be not able to bring anything against us, but be compelled to say we are honest, obedient people. So we read of many saints, that they were summoned to war under heathen rulers and slew the enemy, yet were as subject and obedient to those that summoned them as we Christians are bound to be to the civil rulers, although at present it is maintained we could not be Christians if we lived among the Turks.

Now you may perhaps say, But still Christ has commanded that we should not resist evil, but if anyone strike us on one cheek we are to turn the other also (Matt. 5:39). How then can we strike and execute others? Answer: The heathen formerly objected in like manner to the Christians, and said, if such and such should come to pass, your government must be suppressed. But we reply: It is true that Christians for themselves should not resist evil, neither should they revenge themselves when injured, but endure injustice and violence. Therefore they cannot be severe even toward those who do not believe. But the civil power of the sword is not thereby forbidden. For although pious Christians have no need of the sword and the law since they live so that none can complain of them and since they do no man any wrong, but treat everyone kindly and cheerfully endure all that is done to them; yet the sword must be borne on account of the unchristian people, that they— when they injure others—may be punished. This will preserve the general peace and protect the godly. Thus God has provided another government, that they who would not of themselves be restrained from evil might be compelled by the civil power to do no one any injury.

Therefore God has established the civil authorities for the sake of the unbelieving, so that even Christian men might exercise the power of the sword and come under obligation thereby to serve their neighbor and restrain the wicked so that the good people might remain in peace among them. And still the command of Christ abides in force that we are not to resist evil; also, that a Christian, although he bears the sword, does not use it for his own sake nor to revenge himself, but only for others. And moreover this is a work of Christian love, that with the sword we support and defend the whole community and not suffer it to be injured. Christ teaches only those who, since they believe and love, are also obedient. But the greater multitude in the world, as it does not believe, obeys not the command. Therefore they must be ruled as unchristian people, and their caprice be put under restraint; for if their power were allowed to obtain the upper hand, no one could stand before them.

Thus there are two kinds of government in the world, as there are also two kinds of people, namely, believers and unbelievers. Christians yield themselves to the control of God's Word; they have no need of civil government for their own sake; but the unchristian portion require another government, even the civil sword, since they will not be controlled by the Word of God. Yet if all were Christians and followed the Gospel, there would be no more need or use of the civil sword and the exercising of authority; for if there were no evil-doers, there certainly could be no punishment. But since it is impossible for us all to be righteous, Christ has ordained the civil government for the wicked, that they may rule as they must be ruled. But the righteous he keeps for himself, and rules them by his mere word.

Therefore Christian government is not opposed to the civil, nor is civil government opposed to Christ. Civil government does not in any way belong to Christ's ministry; but it is an outward thing, like all other offices and institutions. And as these exist distinct from Christ's office, unbelievers may fill them just as well as Christians. So it is also with the office of the civil sword, since it neither makes men Christian nor unchristian. But of this I have spoken often enough elsewhere (especially in *The Civil Authority: To What Extent We Are Obliged to Obey It*).

Hence God has established the civil authorities to punish the wicked and to protect the pious. That is indeed a precious good work, which Peter says here is the will of God. Hence God calls the civil power a minister of God, for good to him who does good, but to him who does evil our avenger of wrath, for the government beareth the sword not in vain (Rom. 13:4). Therefore believers in Christ may bear the sword and know also that they do God a service when they bring the wicked into subjection and punish them, in order that the godly may be able to dwell in peace. And yet at the same time the saying of Christ must stand that we are not to resist evil, also that a Christian, if he bears the sword, does not use it for his own interest nor to avenge himself, but only for the sake of others; and thus it is also for the sake of the work of Christian love that we support and defend the whole church with the sword and not suffer it to be injured. The great mass of the world will not allow themselves to be ruled with goodness. Therefore their wantonness must be restrained, otherwise we could not live in the same community with them in safety.

v. 16. As free, and not using your freedom for a cloak of wickedness, but as bond-servants of God.

This is said especially to us who have heard of Christian liberty, that we may not go on and abuse this freedom. That is to say, under the name and show of Christian freedom we should not do all we lust after so that from this liberty shall spring a shamelessness and carnal recklessness; as we see even now takes place. It had begun even in the apostles' times, as is evident from the epistles of Peter and Paul, when men did what the great multitude do at present. We have now again, through the grace of God, come to the knowledge of the truth, and we know to be mere deception that which popes, bishops, priests, and monks have hitherto taught, enacted, and enforced. Our conscience is enlightened and has become free from human ordinances and from all control which they had over us, so that we are no longer obliged to do what they have commanded under peril of our salvation. To this freedom we must now hold fast and never allow ourselves to be robbed of it. But at the same time we should be carefully on our guard not to make this freedom a cloak of our shame.

The pope has here proceeded unrighteously in aiming to force and oppress men by his laws. For among a Christian people there should and can be no compulsion, and if the attempt is made to bind the conscience by outward laws, faith and the Christian life are soon suppressed. For Christ's followers are to be led and ruled only in the spirit, since they know that they through faith already have everything necessary to be saved, and stand in need of nothing more to this end. Henceforth they are under obligation to do nothing but good to their neighbor, helping him with all they have, as Christ has helped them. Moreover, all the works they do should be done freely and without constraint, and flow forth from willing and happy hearts, which thank, honor, and praise God for the blessings received from him. So Paul writes: That for the righteous no law is made, for they do freely of themselves and unsummoned, all that God requires (1 Tim. 1:9).

Now such enforcement of human doctrines is abolished and Christian liberty is preached. The reckless spirits that are without faith coincide with it, and thereby would become good Christians, inasmuch as they keep not the law of the pope, claiming this freedom which relieves them from obligation to it. Yet they observe not that which true Christian freedom requires, namely, to do good to their neighbor with cheerfulness and irrespective of its being commended, as real Christians do. Thus they make Christian freedom a mere cloak, under which to work only their shame, and disgrace the noble name and title of that freedom which Christians have.

This Peter here forbids, for what he would say is: Although ye are free in all external matters, if ye are Christians, and should not be forced by laws to subject yourselves to the control of worldly rule, since for the righteous no law is given, as we have said (I Tim. 1:9). Yet ye should do it of yourselves, voluntarily and without compulsion, not that ye must be held in obedience by necessity, but in order to please God, and for the advantage of your neighbor. This also Christ did himself, as we read in Matthew 17:24f, in that he paid tribute when he did not need to do it, but was free, and Lord over all things. So likewise he subjected himself to Pilate and permitted himself to be judged, while as yet he said to him, "Thou wouldst have no power against me, except it were given thee from above" (John 19:11), in which words he gave confirmation to the authority to which he meanwhile subjected himself, that he might please his Father.

From this you see that the multitude has no claim to Christian freedom who will do nothing, neither what the world nor what God requires, but abide in their old insubordinate disposition, although they make their boast of the Gospel. Though we be free from all laws, we must yet have respect to weak and ignorant Christians, since this is a work of love. Hence Paul says in Romans 13:8: "Owe no man anything, save to love one another." Therefore let him who would glory in his freedom do first what a Christian should do: let him first do good to his neighbor, and after that thus make use of his freedom. When the pope or any other person imposes his authority upon him and would force him to obey it, let him say, "My good fellow, Mr. Pope, I will not do it for this reason, because you choose to make a command of it and invade my liberty." We are to live in freedom as the servants of God, like Peter here says, not as bond-servants of man. Yet in case anyone desires anything of me in which I could be of service to him, I will cheerfully do it out of good will, not being scrupulous whether it has been commanded or not, but for the sake of brotherly love, and because God also requires that I should do good to my neighbor. Thus I will not be forced to become subject to worldly princes and lords, but what I do I will do of my own free will; not because they command me, but in order to do a service to my neighbor. Thus should all our works be, springing from affection and love, and all having respect to our neighbor, since we have no need on our own account to do good works. It further follows:

v. 17a. Honor all men.

This is not a command, but a faithful admonition. We are assuredly under obligation to honor everybody, although we are free; for this freedom does not extend to evil-doing, but merely to well-doing. Now we have repeatedly said that every Christian through faith attains to all that Christ has himself, and is moreover his brother. Therefore as I give all honor to the Lord Christ, so also should I do toward my neighbor. This consists not merely in outward behavior—that I should bow to him and the like—but much more: That inwardly in my heart I should highly regard him, as I also highly regard Christ. We are the temple of God, as Paul says in 1 Corinthians 3:16; for the Spirit of God dwelleth in us. If now we bend the knee before a temple of worship or a picture of the holy cross, should we not do it far more before a living temple of God? Thus Paul teaches us also in Romans 12:10, in honor to prefer one another, so that each may place himself below the other, and raise the other above himself. The gifts of God are manifold and various, so that one is in a more exalted position than another; but no one knows who is most exalted in the sight of God, for he may easily raise to the highest place a person who now occupies the meanest position. Therefore should everyone, however high he be exalted, humble himself and honor his neighbor.

v. 17b. Love the brotherhood.

I spoke under 1 Peter 1:22 of the distinction the apostles

make between love in general and brotherly love. We are required even to love our enemies; this is common Christian love. But brotherly love is that we Christians love one another as brethren and communicate one to another, since we all alike have our blessings from God. This is the love Peter here particularly requires.

v. 17c. Fear God. Honor the King.

He says not that we are to have great regard for lords and kings, but that we are to honor them, although they are heathen, as Christ also did, and those prophets who fell at the feet of the King of Babylon. But here perhaps you will say: Hence, you perceive, that we are to be obedient to the pope and are to fall at his feet. Answer: Certainly if the pope attains to temporal power and conducts himself like another sovereign, we are to be obedient even to him, as when he speaks after this manner: I forbid you wearing the cowl or tonsure; besides, on this day you are to fast, not that it is of any avail before God or necessary of salvation, but because I, as a temporal ruler, require it. But in case he goes further and says, This I, in the place of God, forbid you doing, this you are also to receive as though it came from God himself, and to observe it under pain of being excommunicated and of committing a deadly sin, then you are to say, Pardon, my master, I will not do it.

To every ordinance of man we are to be subject, and we are to do what it requires—so long as it does not bind the conscience and only forbids in respect to outward things, even if it should proceed tyrannically toward us. For Scripture says, "If any man would take away thy coat, let him have thy cloak also" (Matt. 5:40). But if it invade the spiritual domain and constrain the conscience, over which God only must preside and rule, we certainly should not obey it, but rather slip our neck from under it. Temporal authority and government extend no further than to matters external and temporal; but the pope not only arrogates this to himself, but would seize upon the spiritual authority also. Yet he has none of it, for his commands have respect to nothing but clothing, food, canonries, and prebends; matters that belong neither to civil nor spiritual control. For how is the world benefited by these things? Besides, it is contrary to God's will to make sin and good works to consist in such matters, where they do not; hence Christ cannot suffer it. But he can well tolerate civil government, since it does not encumber itself with the matters of sin and good works, and spiritual affairs. Instead it has to do with other things, such as protecting and fortifying cities, building bridges, imposing taxes, gathering tribute, extending protection, guarding the land and the people, and punishing the evil-doers. Therefore to such a prince, while he imposes no ordinance upon the conscience, a Christian may readily render obedience, and he does it unconstrainedly [for conscience sake, Rom. 13:5; Edition of 1539], since he is free in all things.

Therefore when an emperor or prince asks me what my faith is, I shall tell him, not because he commands it, but because I am under obligation to confess my faith publicly before every man. But in case he should go further, and command me to believe thus or so, then I shall tell him: My good sir, attend to your civil government; you have no authority to intrude on God's domain, wherefore I certainly shall not obey you. You cannot yourself tolerate invasion into your sovereignty: if anyone against your will passes the limits, you shoot him down with rifles. Do you imagine then that God will tolerate that you should thrust him from his throne and seat yourself in his place? Peter calls the civil power to step into God's ordinances and to make laws against faith (v. 13). But of this we have said enough. It follows now further in the Epistle:

B. As Applied to Servants (vv. 18-25)

vv. 18-20. Servants, be in subjection to your masters with all fear; not only to the good and gentle, but to the froward. For this is acceptable [thankworthy], if for conscience toward God, a man endureth griefs, suffering wrongfully. For what glory is it, if, when ye sin, and are buffeted for it, ye shall take it patiently? but if, when ye do well, and suffer for it, ye shall take it patiently. This is acceptable with God.

Peter has thus far taught us how we should be subject to

the civil power and give it honor. Wherefore, we have stated how far its authority extends, that it may not arrogate to itself matters which pertain to faith. This is said of the civil ordinances in general, and it is a doctrine for everyone to receive. But now he proceeds and speaks of such power as does not extend over a community, but only over individuals. Here he first teaches how domestics should conduct themselves toward their masters. The meaning of it is as follows:

Household servants and day laborers are just as really Christians as any other class, if like others they have the word, faith, baptism, and all such blessings. Therefore, before God they are just as great and high as others. But as to their outward state and before the world, there is a difference, since they occupy a lower station and must serve others. Wherefore, since they are called into this state by God, they should make it their business to be subject to their masters, and have respect and esteem for them. Of this the prophet David gives a fine illustration, and shows how they are to serve: "As the eyes of servants look unto the hand of their master, as the eyes of a maid unto the hand of her mistress, so our eyes look unto Jehovah our God" (Ps. 123:2). That is, servants and maidens should perform with humility and care what the master or the mistress requires. This is the will of God, and therefore it should cheerfully be done. Of this you may be certain and assured, that it pleases God and is acceptable to him, when you do this in faith. Wherefore, since these are the best works you can do, you are not to run far after others. What your master or mistress commands you, that God himself has commanded you. This is not a human command, although it is made by man. Therefore you are not to scruple as to the master you have, be he good or bad, kind or irritable and froward, but think thus; let the master be as he may, I will serve him, and do it to honor God, since he requires it of me, and since my master, Christ, became a servant for my sake.

This is the true doctrine that is always to be advocated, which now, alas! is buried in silence and is lost. But no one regards it except those who are Christians, for the Gospel appeals only to those who receive it. Therefore, if you will be a child of God, purpose in your heart to render such service as

Christ himself bids you. As also Paul teaches, in Ephesians 6:5, 6: "Servants, be obedient unto them that according to the flesh are your masters as unto the Lord Christ; not with eye-service only, as men-pleasers, but as servants of Christ, that ye obey from the heart, for God's sake, with cheerfulness." Consider that ye serve the Lord, and not man. So also, he says in Colossians 3:24: "Ye serve the Lord Christ."

Ah! if the popes, monks, and nuns were now in such a state as this, how they would thank God and rejoice! For none of them can say, God has commanded me to celebrate mass, sing matins, pray the seven times, and the like; for Scripture does not contain a word on these subjects. Therefore if they are asked whether they are confident and assured that their state pleases God, they say, No! But if you ask a little maid-servant why she scours the key or milks the cow, she can say, I know that the thing I do pleases God, for I have God's Word and commandment. This is a great blessing and a precious treasure of which no one is worthy. A prince should thank God, if he might do the same. It is true, he can do in his state what God requires, namely, punish the wicked. But when and how rarely does it happen that he can discharge such a duty aright? But in this sphere all is so ordered, that you may know when you do what you are bidden that it pleases God. God does not look to the smallness of the work, but to the heart that serves him in such little things.

However, in this it is as in other matters; what God has commanded, no one performs; what men enact and God does not ordain, everyone runs after. But, you say, Ah! how is this? What if I have such a strange and irritable master whom no one can thankfully serve, for many such may be found? To this Peter answers: Are you a Christian and desirous to please God, you are not to inquire as to that matter how strange and froward your master is, but ever direct your eyes to observe what God bids you. There you are to reason thus: I will in this way serve my master, Christ, who requires of me that I be subject to this froward master. If God should command you to wash the devil's feet, or those of the worst wretch, you are to do it; and this work would be just as much a good work as the highest of all, when God calls you to it. Therefore you are to have no regard to the person, but only to what God requires; and in this case the humblest work is more to be preferred in God's sight, when rightly performed, than all the popes' and monks' works gathered together on one heap. But whomsoever this does not incite, that it is God's will and acceptable to him, then nothing will avail to incite him. Anything better than this you cannot do, anything that is worse you cannot omit to do. And therefore this is to be done "with all fear," as Peter says, that it may be rightly pursued, since it is not the command of men, but of God. Certainly then where you hesitate you act not only against your earthly lord, but you sin against God and load yourself with the wrath of God, which is unbearable. Therefore he says, "with all fear." Again if you do what God has commanded you, then you render him an acceptable service and sacrifice. Here then the humblest work of a man servant or a maid servant before God is better, when according to his command, than the works of all the priests and monks put together.

For he is worthy of praise, he says, who has obtained a good cheerful conscience before God through faith in Christ, and thinks thus: If my lord were twice as odd and cross, I would even then not allow myself to be moved by impatience and disobedience, and much less return evil for evil, but with a strong will endure the evil and suffer the wrong. For if I should experience at the same time great injustice and suffering, what is that compared to the fact that Christ, my Lord and Redeemer, who never committed any sin, did the greatest, yea, the inexpressible benefactions of the world, and was so scandalously rewarded for it, that he had to die on the Cross between two malefactors as a blasphemer of God and as a rebel? He suffered for the sake of his good deeds, and the severest pain, the like of which no human being on the earth ever experienced and endured; him will I imitate. For the yoke and the burden he places upon me are easy and light. But whoever suffers now for their wicked deeds, as the godless, disobedient servants do, cannot have this glory.

And here Peter speaks particularly of servants according to the circumstances of those times, when they were held as property. This situation is still to be found in some places. Servants are bought and sold like cattle, are ill-treated and beaten by their masters. The masters had such license that they were not punished although they beat their servants to death. Therefore it became necessary that the apostles should carefully admonish and comfort such servants, that they might serve their hard masters, and endure the service, though suffering and injustice were imposed upon them.

Whoever is a Christian must also bear the cross; and the more you suffer wrongfully, the better it is for you; wherefore you should receive your cross from God cheerfully and thank him for it. This is the right kind of suffering that is well-pleasing to God. For what would it be if you should be cruelly beaten and had well deserved it, yet would glory in your cross? Therefore Peter says, "When ye do well, and suffer for it, ye shall take it patiently, this is acceptable with God;" that is to say, a pleasing and a great thank offering before God and real divine worship. Observe here those truly precious good works are described, which we are to do. We like fools have trodden this doctrine under foot and have invented and set up other works. Hence we should lift up our hands, thank God, and rejoice that we at length have such knowledge. Now it follows further:

vv. 21-25. For hereunto were ye called: because Christ also suffered for you leaving you an example that ye should follow his steps: who did no sin, neither was guile found in his mouth, who, when he was reviled, reviled not again; when he suffered, threatened not; but committed himself to him that judgeth righteously: who his own self bare our sins in his body upon the tree, that we, having died unto sins, might live unto righteousness; by whose stripes ye were healed. For ye were going astray like sheep; but are now returned unto the Shepherd and Bishop of your souls.

Thus we have said that the servant should resolve in his heart and be induced cheerfully to do and suffer what is required of him, since his master, Christ, has done so much for him. That they reason thus: inasmuch as my dear Master has become my servant, a thing which he was not obliged to do, and has given his body and life for me, why should not I serve him in return? He was perfectly holy and without sin, yet he so greatly humbled himself, shed his blood for me, and died to take away my sin. Ah! shall not I also suffer some if it please him? Whoever reflects on this must be a stone if it does not move him; for when the master goes forward and steps in the mire, the servant should cheerfully follow him.

The servants should picture in their hearts and stir themselves to be gladly subject to their irritable masters and to suffer wrongfully for their faithfulness and good deed. Since here they hear that the same met even Christ, their Lord and Savior, in comparison with whom they are nothing; therefore they should also keep in mind that Christ, the innocent and spotless Lamb of God, the elect, precious cornerstone, who never did any sin and in whose mouth was found no guile, sacrificed our sins in his own body on the Cross, not for his own benefit, but for the benefit of us poor miserable human beings that we might be healed by his wounds. Yet he merited by it no thanks from the wicked world. What wonder is it then that we who are by nature the children of wrath should receive evil reward for our faithful service and labor from our worldly lords?

Therefore Peter says, "for hereunto were ye called." Whereunto? That ye should suffer wrongfully like Christ. As though he would say, If you would follow Christ you must not dispute and complain much, although you are unjustly treated, but endure the same and count it for the best, since Christ has suffered all without any guilt on his part. He did not even defend his integrity when he stood before the judges. So you are to tread this right under foot, and only say, "*Deo gratias*, thanks to God"; to this end am I called that I should suffer injustice; for why should I complain when my Master did not?

So Peter wishes to say now: You servants have two reasons which should move you gladly and willingly to be subject to your irritable masters. First, your calling implies that you shall be willing to suffer for well-doing, and not only endure the evil, but even reward it with good. Secondly, the example of Christ requires it; for aside from that he has suffered for us, has delivered us from the power of Satan by his death and resurrection, and justified and saved us, he has also left us an example, that we should walk in his steps. We all, each in his calling, should show all faithfulness and kindness to their masters and to everyone, and expect as a reward for it ingratitude, hatred, envy, persecution, and all misfortune; to this Peter says, we are called. Christ also teaches us the same by his own example, who with the highest temporal and spiritual blessing, has served not only his own people to whom he was promised, healed the sick, cleansed the lepers, raised the dead, preached the Gospel to the poor; but he also became a curse in order that through him the whole world might be blessed. And for all that he received the reward that he not only had to hear—he was a Samaritan, possessed with the devil, a glutton, a winebibber, a publican and a friend of sinners. Not only that but he was finally mocked, reviled, spit upon, pierced, nailed to the cross, and there blasphemed in the most bitter and virulent manner. Hanging between two malefactors as an arch-evildoer, who had both blasphemed God and raised a sedition against the government, he died. And all this he willingly and patiently suffered, never took vengeance on his enemies, never reviled them again nor threatened; but committed his cause to him who judgeth righteously. Yea, he even prayed for them while on the cross and said: "Father, forgive them, for they know not what they do." Therefore if thou wilt be a Christian, thou shalt then imitate thy Lord, and have compassion on those who cause the suffering, and even pray for them that God might not punish them. For they do far more harm to their own souls than to your body. If you take this to heart, you shall easily forget your suffering, and suffer cheerfully. For we are to consider that we were once in such a Christless state as they, but have now through Christ been converted.

But whoever is not moved by this exhortation of Peter to bear all kinds of evil and to suffer misfortune, can by no means glory in that he is a Christian; for if the Lord himself goes ahead and steps into the mire, then the servant should follow him thither, yea, and he is right in doing so. Since Christ empties himself of his divine essence and becomes a servant of us all, much more should we, who are conceived and born in sin, most deeply humiliate ourselves, descend to the lowest depth, and become servants of others. But even if this had already been done, what were our humility, obedience, well-doing, and suffering compared to the humiliation, obedience, well-doing, and suffering of this exalted person of whom Peter bears witness. He was sinless, and this title belongs to him alone. For no saint, be he an apostle, prophet, or patriarch, can boast that he never committed any sin. But they rightly bear the title as is written in Psalm 14:3: "They are all gone aside; they are together become filthy; there is none that doeth good, no, not one." Therefore have all without exception in universal Christendom prayed: Forgive us our transgressions (Ps. 32:5), and comforted themselves so sweetly with the article of faith on the forgiveness of sins through Christ, just as we do now. This is yet a powerful sermon, and domestics are strongly exhorted to obedience with many beautiful words. But it is a doctrine and admonition for the divinely saved who follow Christ, for so readily will they not accompany him. He does it far in advance of us as an example to all. The great mass of servants, however, continue as they are. Yea, they grow worse, as now the common cry is heard everywhere that domestics are disobedient and unfaithful. They will indeed be found by God in his own time, be punished here on the earth and yonder in eternity.

In this connection Peter introduces several passages from the prophet Isaiah: "Who had done no violence, neither was any deceit in his mouth" (Isa. 53:9); "With whose stripes we are healed" (Isa. 53:5). All that Christ did and spoke in preaching, in giving counsel, and in chastising has been good, useful, comforting, and blessed. Therefore, he indeed merited that everyone should fall at his feet and bear him in their hands. He had also indeed the power and right to take vengeance on his adversaries; yet he allowed them to revile, mock, and blaspheme him and finally put him to death. It is this example that you should follow. If you consider it rightly, and earnestly aspire to imitate it, then you will sing praise and thanksgiving to God, that you were worthy to be like Christ, and not murmur nor be impatient when men cause you to suffer, since your Lord did not revile again, neither threatened, but instead prayed for his enemies, as has been said.

Here you may reply: How? Shall I then say they are right who treat me unjustly, and say of them, they have done well? Answer: No! But this is what you should say: Though I have

not deserved it, and you have wronged me, yet I will cheerfully from my heart suffer it, for the sake of my Lord and
Savior, who for his divine and inexpressible good deeds suffered all kinds of evil and finally died the ignominious death
of the Cross. "He bore our sins in his body," as Peter says,
which means he did not suffer for himself, but for the entire
human race, by which he atoned for the horrible fall of Adam
and restored again what Satan had destroyed. Whoever does
not acknowledge such fathomless love, nor is thankful to him,
will not escape the wrath and punishment of him who judges
righteously. The Jews, Greeks, Romans, had to bear the brunt;
and he will in his own time visit those who at present blaspheme and persecute the Gospel of Christ.

*v. 25. For ye were going astray like sheep; but are now returned
unto the Shepherd and Bishop of your souls.*

This however is a passage from the prophet Isaiah, who
speaks in this manner: "All we like sheep have gone astray;
we have turned every one to his own way" (Isa. 53:6). But
now have we obtained a Shepherd, says Peter. The Son of God
has come for our sake, that he might be our Shepherd and
Bishop. He gives us his spirit, feeds us, and leads us by his
word, so that we now know how we are helped. Therefore,
when you confess that through him your sins have been taken
away, then you become his sheep, and he becomes your herds-
man. Just as he is thy bishop, so art thou his soul. This is then
the comfort which all Christians have.

Thus we have considered two chapters in this epistle, in
which Peter has in the first place taught the true faith, then the
true works of love, and has spoken of two kinds of works.
First, how we all in common should act toward the civil
government, then how domestics should conduct themselves
toward their masters. And what Peter says here of servants
extends also to other persons; namely, mechanics, day-laborers,
and all kinds of hired help. Now he goes on to teach us further,
how husband and wife should conduct themselves toward
one another in a Christian manner.

1 Peter 3

The Duties of Christians in the Married State and the Duties of all Christians; Also Concerning Christ.

Outline

I. The Duties of Christian Wives and Husbands, vv. 1-7.
    A. The duties of Christian wives, vv. 1-6.
        1. The first duty, vv. 1-2.
            a. The duty itself, v. 1a.
            b. The foundation and cause of this duty, vv. 1b-2. It is a precious treasure to know what works are well-pleasing to God. That which God requires, no one will do cheerfully.
        2. The second duty, vv. 3-6.
            a. Whether this duty pertains to women only, vv. 3–4.
            b. An objection that may be raised by this duty, and the answer.
            c. The nature of this duty. Of the costly ornaments of the soul.
            d. The foundation of this duty, vv. 5-6.
    B. The duties of Christian husbands, v. 7.
        1. The duty itself, v. 7a.
        2. The reason and cause of this duty.
        a. The first reason, v. 7b.
        b. The second reason, v. 7c.

II. The Duties of All Christians, vv. 8-17.
    A. The first duty.
        1. The nature of this duty, v. 8f.
        2. How and by what this duty is hindered.
        3. How and by what this duty is furthered. The foundation and cause of this duty.
    B. The second duty, v. 8b.
    C. The third duty, v. 8c.
    D. The fourth duty, v. 8d.
    E. The fifth duty, v. 8e.
        1. The nature of this duty.

    2. What should move to consider this duty.
    3. How and why Satan seeks to prevent the performance of this duty.
    4. How the self-chosen state of the papists is overthrown by this duty.

F. The sixth duty, vv. 9-14a.
    1. Its nature.
    2. The motives to urge us to do this duty.
      a. First motive, v. 9.
      b. Second motive, v. 10.
      c. Third motive, v. 11.
      d. Fourth motive, v. 12.
      e. Fifth motive, v. 13.
      f. Sixth motive, v. 14a.

G. The seventh duty, v. 14b.

H. The eighth duty, v. 15a.
    1. Its nature.
    2. Precaution to be observed.
    3. How the duty is illustrated by two examples.

I. The ninth duty, v. 15b-15c.
    1. Of whom this duty is required.
    2. How to perform this duty against the papists.
    3. The necessity of this duty.
    4. How the Sophists have perverted it.
    5. A precaution to be observed.

K. The tenth duty.
    1. Its nature, v. 16.
    2. The motive that should urge us to do this duty.
      a. The first motive, v. 17. No one should lay a cross upon himself.
      b. The second motive, v. 18.

III. Concerning Christ, vv. 18-22.
A. Of Christ's sufferings.
    1. How Christ in his sufferings is an example for Christians, v. 18a.
    2. The chief attribute in the suffering of Christ, v. 18b.
    3. The nature of Christ's suffering, v. 18c. The condition of Christians at the resurrection.
B. Sermon of Christ to the spirits in prison, vv. 19-21a.
    1. How and why this sermon is difficult to understand, v. 19a.
    2. Characteristics of this sermon, v. 19b. The efficacy of baptism, vv. 20-21a. How men are preserved and saved, v. 21a.
C. The Resurrection of Christ, v. 21b.
D. Christ at the right hand of God, v. 22.

I. Duties of Christian Wives and Husbands (vv. 1-7)

vv. 1-6. In like manner, ye wives, be in subjection to your own husbands; that, even if any obey not the word, they may without the word be gained by the behavior of their wives; beholding your chaste behavior coupled with fear. Whose adorning let it not be the outward adorning of braiding the hair, and of wearing jewels of gold, or of putting on apparel; but let it be the hidden man of the heart, in the incorruptible apparel of a meek and quiet spirit which is in the sight of God of great price. For after this manner aforetime the holy women also, who hoped in God, adorned themselves, being in subjection to their own husbands: as Sarah obeyed Abraham, calling him lord: whose children ye now are, if ye do well, and are not put in fear by any terror.

Peter speaks here especially of wives, who in those days had heathen and unbelieving husbands; and on the other hand, he speaks of believing husbands who had heathen wives. For it often occurred while the apostles preached the Gospel among the heathen, that one hearer was a Christian and another was not. If it then was commanded that the wife should be in subjection to the husband, how much more must it be so ordered now. Therefore it is the woman's duty, Peter would say, to be subject to her husband, although he is a heathen and an unbeliever. And he gives the reason why this should be so.

vv. 1b-2. That, even if any obey not the word, they may without the word be gained by the behavior of their wives; beholding your chaste behavior coupled with fear.

That is, when a man sees that his wife maintains and conducts herself with propriety, then he is drawn toward faith, and he holds the state of a Christian to be truly blessed. And although women are not commanded to preach, yet they should so conduct themselves in their demeanor and conversation that they may thereby encourage their husbands to believe. For example, we read of the mother of Augustine being the means of the conversion of her husband (who had been a heathen) before his death, and then afterward of her son Au-

gustine. This is now only an external matter, which one should
not do to the end that he thereby becomes pious, for obedience does not save one. You may perhaps find an obedient
wife who is unbelieving; but you should do it for this reason,
that you may thereby benefit your husband. For thus has God
ordained, according to Genesis 3:16, when he says to the
woman, "Thy desire shall be to thy husband, and he shall rule
over thee," which is also the punishment he has imposed on
the woman. However this is, I say, the outward conduct, that
belongs to the body and not to the spirit.

But it is a great thing to know while good works we should
do in order to please God; since we should have run far to
secure it, just as we see that the world has run far to secure
that which it has falsely devised. It is a high, noble blessing a
wife may have when she so conducts herself as to be subject
to her husband, in that she is sure that her works please God.
What can be a happier experience for her? Therefore whoever
wishes to be a Christian wife is to reason in this manner: I
will not have a regard as to what sort of a husband I have,
whether he be a heathen or a Jew, righteous or wicked; but I
will have regard to the fact that God has placed me in the
marriage state, and I will be subject and obedient to my husband. Then all her works are golden if she stands in such
obedience.

But for those who will not permit this to move them, nothing else will avail. For you will never succeed by blows in
making a wife pious and submissive. If you knock one devil
out, you will knock two devils in, as they say. Oh! if people in
the marriage state knew this, how uprightly would they walk.
However, no one does cheerfully what God has commanded,
but all run after that which men have invented. God so wished
this command to be carefully observed that he authorized husbands to make void the vows which their wives made if they
were displeasing to them, as we read in Numbers 30:7f, so
that all might go on peacefully and quietly at home. This is
one point. Now the apostle directs further how a woman
should conduct herself toward other people.

vv. 3, 4. *Whose adorning let it not be the outward adorning of
braiding the hair, and of wearing jewels of gold, or of putting on*

apparel; but let it be the hidden man of the heart, in the incorruptible apparel of a meek and quiet spirit, which is in the sight of God of great price.

This treasure, which is within us, should be possessed not only by the wife, but also by the husband. Possibly one may ask whether that which Peter here says of ornaments is commanded or not. We read of Esther (Est. 2:17) that she wore a golden crown, decking herself as a queen; so also of Judith (Judith 10:3f). But in the context it is recorded that she despised the ornament and wore it from necessity (Est. 3:11). Hence we say a wife should be so disposed as not to care for this adorning; yet, inasmuch as people convinced on the subject of ornaments cease not to use them because of their habit and nature; therefore, a Christian wife should despise them. But if the husband require them, or there is a reasonable cause for her to adorn herself, it may be done. But she should be adorned, as Peter here says, be inwardly attired in a meek and quiet spirit. You are beautifully enough adorned when you are adorned for your husband. Christ does not want you to adorn yourself to please others, to be called a handsome prostitute (Bucer: *bella domina*, a pretty mistress). Therefore you are to see to it that you wear in your heart the hidden treasure and the precious adorning, which is incorruptible, as Peter says, and lead a pure, merciful, temperate life.

It is good evidence that there is little of the spirit, where so much is expended on ornaments. But this will be trodden under foot where faith and the spirit are present, and these will say, like Queen Esther: Lord, thou knowest that I regard with aversion the crown which I wear on my head, and that I am compelled thus to adorn myself. If this were not required to be done of me out of love to my king, I would much rather trample it under foot (Est. 3:11). Where the wife is of such a disposition, she will so much the more please her husband. Therefore they are to take this into consideration, says Peter, that they adorn the inward man, where a quiet spirit reigns, one that cannot be ruffled. Not only should they run not to excess, so as to be kept from confusion and shame, but his meaning is that they should beware that the soul remain unruffled and in the true faith, and that this be not forsaken.

Thus is developed a heart that does not break forth and busy itself as to how it shall appear before the world. Such a heart is a precious thing in the sight of God. If a woman were to adorn herself with pure gold, precious stones, and pearls, even to her feet, it would be grand beyond measure. But you cannot put enough on a woman that it shall be preferable to the superior ornament of the soul, which is precious in God's sight. Gold and fine stones are precious in the world's esteem, but before God they are an ill-savor. But she is truly and beautifully adorned in the sight of God who goes forth with a meek and quiet spirit; and since God himself accounts it precious, it must be something glorious.

The adornment of a Christian wife, as was said, is the inner man of the heart, cleansed from all error and stains of the soul. A woman so adorned, who has a pure faith and a quiet, meek spirit, so that she can obey her husband and be to him in word and deed friendly and loving, has all that Christ has.

A Christian soul has all that Christ has, for faith, as we have said (see 1 Peter 1:3), brings us at once all the blessings of Christ. This is a great and precious treasure, and such an ornament as none can sufficiently prize. God himself values it very highly. Hence the husband should draw and dissuade the wife from ornaments, so long as she is inclined to them. When a Christian wife hears that and reflects, she thinks thus: I will not care for bodily adornments, since God does not regard them, but if I must wear them, I will do it to please my husband. Then is she truly adorned and attired in spirit. In this connection Peter now gives us an example of holy women, that he may draw wives to Christian conduct. He says,

vv. 5-6a. *For after this manner aforetime the holy women also, who hoped in God, adorned themselves, being in subjection to their own husbands: as Sarah obeyed Abraham, calling him lord.*

[As these same women adorn themselves, he will say, so do you, follow their example. How then did they adorn themselves? First, by placing their hope in God. Second, by being obedient to their husbands, not of necessity or of constraint, but willingly from the heart, because it was the command and ordinance of God; as Sarah, etc.; translator's note.]

As these women adorn themselves, he would say, so do ye also, just as Sarah was obedient to her husband Abraham and called him her lord. So Scripture speaks in Genesis 18:10-12, where the angel came to Abraham and said: "Within a year shall Sarah have a son;" then she laughed within herself, saying, "After I am waxed old shall I have pleasure, my lord being old also?" This passage Peter has justly noticed and cited here; for she would not have thus called Abraham her lord if she had not been subject to him and had him before her eyes. Therefore he says further:

v. 6b. *Whose children ye now are, if ye do well, and are not put in fear by any terror.*

What does he mean by that? This is what he means. It is usually the nature of women to be troubled and frightened about everything, therefore they are so much occupied with charms and superstitions, which one teaches the other, so that it is indescribable what illusions they have. This should not be the case with a Christian woman, but she should go forward freely and securely and not be superstitious nor should she run about here and there and charm one man here and another there, inasmuch as it becomes her to let God direct and to remember it cannot go ill with her; for as long as she knows her condition, and that her state is pleasing to God, what then has she to fear? Though your child die, though you are sick, it is well if it pleases God. If you are in a state which pleases God, what better can you desire? This, then, is what Peter preaches to wives. Now follows the duty of the husbands:

v. 7a. *Ye husbands, in like manner, dwell with your wives according to knowledge, giving honor unto the woman, as unto the weaker vessel, as being also joint-heirs of the grace of life; to the end that your prayers be not hindered.*

The woman is also God's instrument or vessel, he says, for God uses her to the end that she may bear children, give them birth and nourishment, watch over them, and rule the home. Such work the wife is to do. So she is God's instrument and vessel, created and instructed by God to this end. For this reason is the husband to respect his wife. Therefore, Peter says, Ye husbands, dwell with your wives according to knowledge, not that ye are to rule them with a headstrong will. They are indeed to live, as the husband rules, that what he says and does may be done; but he is also to see to it that he walks soberly and according to knowledge with his wife, so as to give her that respect and honor due her as God's weaker vessel.

The husband is also God's instrument, but he is stronger; while the wife is weaker bodily, as well as more timid and more easily dispirited. Therefore, you are to treat her and live with her, so that she may be able to bear it. You must proceed here just as with other instruments with which you labor. For example, if you wish to have a good sickle, you must not hack upon the stone with it. On this subject no rule can be laid down. God leaves the matter to each individually, to treat his wife according to knowledge, according to the circumstances of each woman. For you are to use the authority you have, not according to your own will, because you are her husband for this very purpose, that you may help her, conserve and support her, and not be her ruin. Hence none can lay down a rule for you with exact limitations; you must understand yourself how you are to proceed according to knowledge.

Thus we have now heard in regard to husbands also, what good works those who please God are to perform; namely, to dwell with their wives, endear themselves to them, and walk soberly with them. Things cannot always go as you would wish. Therefore, see to it that you act like a husband, and have the more discretion when it is lacking in the wife. And, while you are to connive at some matters, tolerate and pardon others, and give to the wife also her honor.

This "honor" has been explained, I hardly know how. Some have interpreted it, that the husband should procure food, drink, and clothing for the wife, and should nourish her. Others have referred it to marriage duties. I hold the meaning to be, as I have said, that the husband should treat the wife as is consistent with her being a Christian, and a vessel or instrument of God. And thus they are both to conduct themselves: the wife is to hold the husband in honor, and on the other hand also the husband is to give to the wife her honor. If matters were thus directed, they would go on harmoniously in peace and love. Yet where this art is wanting, there will be mere disgust in the marriage state. Hence it comes to pass when man and wife marry one another, moved only by lust, and imagine they will have happiness and the gratification of appetite, they experience mere heart-anguish. But if you have regard to God's work and will, then may you live Christianly in marriage; not like the heathen, who know not what God requires.

v. 7b. *As being also joint-heirs of the grace of life.*

The husband is not to dwell on the thought that the wife is weak and frail, but on this, that she also is baptized and has the same that he has, namely, all blessings in Christ. For inwardly we are all alike, and there is no difference between man and woman. But as to the outward condition, it is God's pleasure that the husband rule and that the wife be in subjection to him.

v. 7c. *That your prayers be not hindered.*

What does Peter mean by this? He means that if you do not act with reason, but constantly hum, murmur, and bluster, and self-willed force your way through everything while at the same time you are a frail woman, who neither forgives the other nor considers it for the best, then you will not be in a frame of mind and heart to pray. Here we see that Christians should pray. For, although they are indeed in a state of grace before God, because of Christ on whom they believe; yet Satan never takes a vacation, but walks about as a roaring lion. Hence the world is at enmity with them and persecutes them. Their own flesh also torments them; against all this they have no other defense and weapon than prayer. But in order to have true prayer, you must put away all disharmony, unwillingness and wrath. Otherwise you will never pray well, yes, you feel a hindrance is in the way as soon as you begin to say, "Our Father, who art in heaven...." Therefore, Peter teaches wives to be subject to their husbands, and on the other hand he teaches husbands to dwell with their wives according to knowledge. If they do not, their prayers will be hindered, which will be a sign that they are not Christians—that they do not enjoy the forgiveness of their sins by God because they do not forgive one another. These are now the true, precious, good works we are to do. If that were preached and known, then we all would have our homes full, yes, full of good deeds. Hitherto we have heard how Christians should act in all the vocations of life, and especially in their relations toward others. He further teaches now how Christians are to be and live among themselves, namely, "be like minded," and then how they are to act toward their enemies who persecute them and cause them suffering, namely, they shall not return evil for evil. He says in verse 8:

II. Duties of All Christians (vv. 8-17)

vv. 8a-12. *Finally, be ye all like-minded, compassionate, loving as brethren, tenderhearted, humbleminded (courteous): not rendering evil for evil, or reviling for reviling; but contrariwise blessing; for hereunto were ye called, that ye should inherit a blessing. For, he that would love life, and see good days, let him refrain his tongue from evil and his lips that they speak no guile: and let him turn away from evil, and do good; let him seek peace, and pursue it. For the eyes of the Lord are upon the righteous, and his ears unto their supplication: but the face of the Lord is upon them that do evil.*

This all is said for no other purpose than that we should have mutual love one to another. For here that which the Scriptures sometimes express in few words, is more fully developed. Peter would say, that the summary of all, as to how you are to treat one another in your outward conduct is that ye be all like-minded. The apostles Peter and Paul often use this word, and it means nothing less than that we all should have one mind, one spirit, one thought. What seems to one right and good, let this also seem to another right and good. It is an important, noteworthy theme that should be well understood. Paul particularly has written much upon it.

Not all of us can do the same kind of work, but everyone must labor for himself. A husband works in a different sphere from that of the wife; a servant, in a different sphere from that of the master; and so throughout. And it is foolish to preach that we should all do one work, as those senseless preachers have done who preached the legends of the saints; that these saints have done one work, those, another, and then insist and say we all should do the same. It is doubtless true that Abraham did a good work, highly to be esteemed, when he offered up his son, since this was particularly commanded him of God. When the heathen introduced the same and would likewise sacrifice their children, this was an act of cruelty in the sight of God. So also, King Solomon did well in building the temple, and God justly rewarded him for it. And our blind fools now would also do the same. They preach that we must build churches and temples for God [as St. Peter's at Rome; translator's note), while God has given us no command on that subject. Now it is just the reverse, so that men busy themselves with a single kind of employment, and have many views on it directly contrary to the Gospel. ["to the doctrine of St. Peter," edition of 1539].

But it should be that there be a single aim and many employments, one heart and many hands. Not all should follow one business, but everyone should attend to his own; otherwise unity of mind and heart will not continue. As to external affairs, they must be permitted to remain of a manifold character, so that everyone sticks to that which has been committed to him, and to the work he has in hand. This is a true doctrine, and it is exceedingly necessary that it be well understood; for the devil gives particular care to it and has brought things to such a state that judgment is passed on the employment, and everyone thinks that his own should be counted better than another's. Hence it has come to pass, that men are so disunited one with another, monks against priests, one order against another, for each one has wished to do the best work. Thus they must satisfy themselves, and they have given themselves up to the order and think this order is better than that. There is the order of the Augustinians against that of the Dominicans or the Preaching Monks, and the Carthusians against the Barefooted Friars or the Franciscans. Nowhere is there greater want of unanimity than among the orders.

But if it had been taught that in the sight of God no one employment is better than another, but that through faith all are alike, then all hearts would have remained united, and we all alike would be mutually disposed. We would say: The order or the mode of life which the bishop leads is no greater in God's sight than that which a poor man leads; the mode of life the nun leads is no better than a married woman leads; and the same in respect to all the various stations in life. However, this they will not hear, but everyone maintains that his own rank or calling is the best, and says, Ah! how much better and more important is my state in the order than the state of a common man.

Therefore to "be of one mind" is, that everyone should regard his own employment like that of others, and that the condition of the married woman is just as good as that of the virgin. All are then indeed alike in the sight of God, who judges according to the heart and faith, and not according to the person or his employment. Therefore we also are to judge as God judges, and then are we of one mind, and unanimity continues in the world, and hearts remain unestranged, so that there is no division on account of external condition. All this I hold to be excellent, and I am well satisfied with every man's employment, whatever it be, if it only be not sinful in itself.

On this Paul also speaks in 2 Corinthians 11:3, "I fear lest by any means, as the serpent beguiled Eve in his craftiness, your minds should be corrupted from the simplicity and purity that is toward Christ"; that is, lest the devil beguile you, and pervert and divide the simplicity of aim you have. And he says in Philippians 4:7, "The peace of God, which passeth all understanding, shall guard [keep] your hearts and your thoughts in Christ Jesus." Why does the apostle lay so much stress on the aim of the mind? Yes, all depends upon that. For when I am led to cherish a false aim, everything is already lost. If I were a monk, and had adopted the view that my works are worth more in the sight of God than those of others, and I said; "God be thanked that I have become a monk; my state is now far preferable to the common one of marriage;" then from such a view must spring a proud spirit. It cannot fail that I should count myself more righteous than another and should despise other people and thus deceive myself. For a married woman, if she abides in the faith, is better in the sight of God than I am with the order I belong to. Therefore, if it is understood that faith brings with it all that a Christian ought to have, all of us have one mind and aim, and there is no difference in our works. Therefore we are so to understand this passage of Peter, that he means here the spiritual, not the outward mind, and the inner thought and the mystical feeling, to which belong the things that avail before God. So both the doctrine and the life be one, and I hold that to be excellent which you hold as excellent; and again, that is well-pleasing to you which is well-pleasing to me, as I have said. This sense of things is possessed by Christians, and to this sense we should hold firmly, that it may not be perverted, as Paul writing in 2 Corinthians 11:3, says; for when the devil has corrupted it, he has forced the castle of virgin purity, and all then is lost.

v. 8b. *Be ye compassionate, loving as brethren, tenderhearted, humbleminded [courteous].*

To be compassionate means to share with and have a heart to feel for our neighbor in his need. When misfortune overtakes him if you are compassionate you do not think, Ah! it is right; Ah! it is not too much, he has well deserved it. Where there is love, it identifies itself with its neighbor; and when it goes ill with him, the heart feels as though it were its own experience.

v. 8c. *Be loving as brethren.*

But "to be brotherly," affectionate as brethren, is to regard each other as his own brother. This certainly may be easily understood, for nature itself teaches it; where you see what true brothers are, in that they are united more heartily than any other friends. So ought we as Christians to act; for we are all brethren by baptism; and after baptism even father and mother are brother and sister, for I have the same blessing and inheritance they have from Christ, through faith.

v. 8d. *Be tenderhearted [pitiful,* viscerosi].

This word I cannot explain except by giving an illustration. Observe how a mother or a father acts toward their child; for example, when a mother sees her child enduring anguish, her whole inward being is moved, and her heart within her body. From this is derived the mode of speech that occurs in many places of Scripture, of which we have an example in 1 Kings 3:16-28, where two women contended before King Solomon for a child, each claiming the child. And when the king wished to discover which was the real mother of the child, he had to appeal to nature, when he detects it. He said to the two women, You say that the child is yours, while you say also that it is yours: well, then, bring hither a sword and divide the child into two parts, and give one part to this woman, and another to that. Thus he learned which was the real mother; and the text, 1 Kings 3:26, tells us she was inwardly affected with anxiety for the child, and said: No! no! rather give the child whole to this woman, and let it live." Then the king pronounced his decision and said, That is the true mother; take the child and give it to her. Hence you may understand what this word *tenderhearted* means.

Now Peter will teach by this, that we should conduct ourselves toward one another like those who are truly friends by blood, as with them the whole heart is moved, the life, the pulse, and all the powers. So here also, we should be heartily kind and motherly, and the heart should be thoroughly penetrated. Such a disposition should one Christian bear toward another. But the standard is indeed set high; few will be found who have such a hearty love to their neighbor, when they see there is need to have an affection like a mother has for a child, that it presses through the heart and through every vein. Hence you see what the monks' and nuns' state and life are; how far

they are from such hearty love. If they all were smelted together in one heap, not one drop of such Christian love as this
would be found. Therefore let us look to ourselves and consider whether we can find in ourselves such love. This is a
short sermon and quickly spoken, but it goes deep and reaches
far.

v. 8e. *Be courteous.*

Courteous means "to lead outwardly a gentle, pleasing lovely
manner of life; not merely to sympathize one with another, as
a father and mother for their child, but also to walk in love
and gentleness one with another." There are some' men rough
and knotty, like a tree full of knots; so uncivil that no one likes
to have anything to do with them. Hence they are usually full
of suspicion, and become soon angry; with whom none of
their own choice love to associate. But there are gentle people,
who interpret all for the best, and are not suspicious; do not
permit themselves to be easily irritated; can at least understand some things are well meant; such persons are called in
Latin *"Candidos,"* candid (from which "candidate" comes, one
clothed in white). This virtue Paul names in Greek *chrastotas*
(goodness, Rom. 2:4), and it is often praised by him.

Now consider the Gospel, which portrays the Lord Christ
so distinctly that we may trace this virtue especially in others,
that they might take him; yet he does not suffer himself to
become enraged. And although the apostles often stumble and
act a foolish part here and there, he nowhere assails them with
angry words. Instead he is ever courteous and attracts them
toward himself, so that they remained gladly with him, and
walked with him. This likewise we see among good friends
and associates on earth, where there are two or three good
friends who thoroughly understand one another: though one
acts foolishly, the others can readily pardon him. There is represented in some measure that which Peter here intends, although it is not perfectly set forth; for this courteousness is to
be considered obligatory upon everyone individually. Hence
you see the true nature of love, and what excellent people
Christians are. The angels in heaven live with one another

thus, and so should it indeed also be on earth; but rarely does it take place [but weaknesses and imperfections reign here; edition of 1539].

As Peter has already said, the man servant and the maid servant, the husband and the wife, should so conduct themselves that each may attend to his own business, so would he have us all do generally, one with another. Therefore, if you will be certain and assured that you are doing an excellent work that is pleasing to God, then set yourself in God's name in opposition to whatever has been preached in the devil's name, whereby the world walks and seeks to merit heaven. For how can you be better assured that you are acceptable to God than when you observe, as he here says, the works which a man should do, the conduct which everyone should lead, so that you be compassionate, brotherly affectionate, heartily kind, courteous? In this he says nothing of those fool-works which we have been taught. He says not, build churches, found masses, be priests, wear a cowl, vow chastity, etc. But this is his language: See to it that you be courteous. These are truly precious, golden deeds, precious stones and pearls, well pleasing to God.

But this the devil cannot tolerate, for he knows that thus his interests are thrown to the ground. Therefore he devises what he can in order to suppress such doctrine and to incite monks and priests to cry out, "Do you say: We and our work amount to nothing? That is for you to talk like Satan." But reply to them then: "Do you not know that these must be good works, of which Peter here speaks, to wit, that we be brotherly affectionate, heartily kind, and courteous? If these are the best, as must be confessed, you must indeed be deceived in regard to your works, if you think they are better."

I am really greatly astonished that such blindness could come upon us, for Thomas, the preaching monk, has written and says shamelessly, that monks and priests are in a better state than ordinary Christians. This the high schools have confirmed, and men have been doctorated for doing so. After them the Pope and his multitude have gone ahead and exalted those to be saints, who taught such doctrine.

Therefore understand this now, for as I said, Christ himself and all his apostles have taught, if you would do the best works, and be in the best state in life, you will find them nowhere else than in faith and love; that is the highest state of all. Therefore it must be a falsehood when they say their state is better than that of faith and love. For if it be better than God's Word, it is better than God himself. Therefore Paul has correctly said, in 2 Thessalonians 2:4, that Antichrist should exalt himself against God. So know now therefore how to judge concerning these things; where love and friendship are wanting, there certainly all works are condemned and trodden under foot. Thus we see how Peter has so bravely expatiated on the external character of a truly Christian life, as he taught us above, in a masterly manner, how the inner or spiritual life should be ordered toward God. Therefore this is to be regarded as a truly golden epistle. Upon this it now follows:

v. 9. *Not rendering evil for evil, or reviling for reviling; but contrariwise blessing; for hereunto were ye called, that ye should inherit a blessing.*

This is a still further illustration of love, showing how we should act toward those that injure and persecute us. If any one does you evil, his meaning is, do him good; if any one rails at and curses you, then bless him and wish him well. This is an important part of love. O Lord God! How few such Christians there are!

But why should we render good for evil and bless those who curse us? Because, Peter says, ye are hereunto called that ye should inherit a blessing, which means that instead of children of wrath and enemies of God, ye should become children of grace and friends of God through Christ. Consequently, ye have no reason to revile, but to bless.

You have received a blessing from God, not only for yourselves, but also that you may be a blessing to those who are still held by the curse. In other words you are to pray for them that they may also come to faith through your doctrine, patience, and exemplary manner of living. Is your effort in their behalf lost and they rush ahead injuring and cursing you, then consider how highly God has exalted and honored you; for the blessing you shall inherit is not temporal and pertains not to this fleeting life. It is that you are now in the state of grace with God through Christ, that you enjoy the forgiveness of your sins, that you are rescued from death and the power of Satan, and that you now look for eternal life and salvation. Of this you are sure, for to this end you were baptized and received the Holy Spirit through the word of grace, who assures you of it. Therefore, even if you should lose your head on account of it, what would that be compared with the glory of this salvation? Hence you have more cause to pray for your enemies and to have compassion upon them than to be angry with them, and the like. They are children of wrath and condemnation, and greater punishment they could not have. If they do injustice, it will surely overtake them in time, so that they will weep for it bitterly enough and will have to suffer because of such injustice; if not here in time, then hereafter eternally in the abyss of hell.

In the Scriptures we Christians are called a people of blessing, or a blessed people. For thus said God to Abraham in Genesis 12:3: "In thee shall all the families of the earth be blessed." Since God has now so richly poured this blessing upon us, in that he takes from us all the malediction and the curse which we have brought with us from our first parents, as well as that which Moses suffered to pass upon the disobedient, so that we are now filled with blessing, we ought so to conduct ourselves that it shall be said of us, Yes, that is a blessed people. This then is what the apostle here means: See, God has shown you his favor and has taken from you the curse. Reviling, you have dishonored him. He neither imputes nor punishes, but has bestowed upon you such rich grace and blessing—when we were only worthy of all malediction, because ye reviled God without intermission, for where there is unbelief the heart must ever curse God. Do ye also, as has been done to you; curse not, rail not, do well, speak well, even though you are treated ill, and endure it where injustice is done you. Here then he quotes a passage from Psalm 34:12,13, where the prophet David speaks thus:

v. 10. *For, he that would love life, and see good days, let him refrain his tongue from evil, and his lips that they speak no guile.*

This verse introduced here by Peter from Psalm 34:13 pertains especially to doctrine. But since he is here speaking of the outward life of Christians, he has very beautifully applied it. He teaches by it how they shall prepare for themselves peace and happy days, and says: They shall not plot and strive, like the children of the world, who can have no peace or rest before they take vengeance and cool their rage on those who have caused them grief by hand or mouth. Therefore, if the world and false brethren show you an evil, spiteful spirit, cause you grief or injury, reproach, and curse you, do not let your anger rise, do not wish to take vengeance, do not render evil for evil, one invective for another. Otherwise you will receive a double misfortune instead of one—outwardly injury to your body, honor, and property, and inwardly a restless spirit, an evil conscience, and in addition you will lose your best treasure, the grace and blessing of God, and you will load upon yourself his wrath and everlasting curse. But possess thy soul in patience and establish thy heart in contentment, and remember it is enough that you received injury in body and property or are wickedly reviled. Should I also lose on account of it the peace and joy of my soul, become angry and impatient, in return do evil and curse, which would be the will and joy of the devil? Be that far from me.

Peter calls that, "To refrain his tongue from evil, and his lips that they speak no guile." This is an art that Christians only understand, yes, and are still students in it, for you cannot easily graduate in this fine art. With people who are not Christians, the contrary takes place. If one should punish them and tell them the truth, they would curse him with all the plagues; and if you cause them any suffering or harm, they repay you sevenfold.

That is, whoever would have pleasure and joy in life and would not die the death, but see good days, so that it may go well with him—let him keep his tongue from speaking evil. Let him do this not only in respect to his friends (for that is a small virtue and a thing even the most wicked persons may do, yea, even snakes and vipers), but he says, maintain a kind spirit and keep your tongue silent even against your enemies, though you are incited thereto, though you have cause to rail and speak evil.

Besides, he says, keep your lips that they do not deceive. There are probably many who utter good words and say "good morning" to their neighbor, but they think in their heart, "The devil take you." These are people who have not inherited the blessing; they are the evil fruit of an evil tree. Therefore Peter has introduced a passage that refers to works, even to their root, that which springs from within out of the heart. Furthermore, the passage in the prophet says:

vv. 11-12a. *And let him turn away from evil, and do good; let him seek peace, and pursue it. For the eyes of the Lord are upon the righteous.*

The world considers it to be peace when one person does another injustice, to pound his head real well for it. But in this way we never come nearer to peace, for no king has ever been able to attain peace before his enemies. The Roman empire became so powerful that it struck down all that set itself against it. Despite all that, it could not be preserved. Therefore this method is of no avail in securing peace. For though a man should prostrate and silence one foe, ten and twenty rise up again, till at length he is compelled to yield. But he who seeks true peace, and moreover would also find it, let him restrain his tongue; let him turn from evil and do good: the course is different from that the world pursues. To turn from evil and do good means, that when a man hears evil words, he be able to overlook the wickedness and injustice. Seek thus after peace, so shall you find it; when your enemy has lost his courage and done all he can, if you hear him, rail and rant not back, he has to subdue himself by his own violence. For thus Christ also on the cross subdued his enemies, not by the sword or by violence.

Therefore it is a proverb [Bucer's translation adds "among Germans"] which should be written with gold, "Striking back again produces hatred," and "whoever strikes back again is unjust." Hence it must follow that not to strike back again produces peace. But how can this be? Is it then something not human? Certainly it does not accord with human nature; but if you in this way suffer unjustly and do not strike back again, but let the matter go, it shall come to pass as follows:

v. 11. *And let him turn away from evil, and do good; let him seek peace, and pursue it.*

To turn away from evil and do good signifies that if one hear wicked words, not to render one invective word for another, but a word of blessing. Likewise, not only endure and suffer wrong and injustice, but overcome the evil with the good. Therefore if your enemy cools his rage on you and causes you all the suffering he can; if you then bear it, revile and rage not back, but be a blessing to him and do him all the good you can. In this way you seek peace and also find it, that is to say, keep a good conscience and a friendly, quiet heart, that can with true assurance say: Forgive us, beloved Lord, our debts.

Peter adds not in vain the words: "He seeks peace and pursues it." Only do not think that peace will pursue you; yea, you will indeed feel, when you suffer and are reviled without any cause on your part, that you will be moved to anger, impatience, revenge, that you would gladly render evil for evil; but this is the time when you should stand firmly and conquer yourself, be sorry and pursue peace. This is accomplished when you do not render evil for evil, nor curse in return, but commend the matter to God, and let it comfort you that you are a child of grace and of blessing, and pray that you may not fall into temptation. Now he concludes this exhortation with a promise.

v. 12. *For the eyes of the Lord are upon the righteous, and his ears unto their supplication; but the face of the Lord is upon [against] those that do evil.*

If you do not revenge yourself nor render evil for evil, there is the Lord in heaven above who cannot tolerate wrong; hence he that does not strike back must have his right. These persons God beholds; their prayer reaches his ear; he is our protector and will not forget us; we cannot escape his eye, and this should comfort us. It is this that should induce a Christian to endure all injustice with patience and not return evil. If I properly reflect, I see the soul that does me wrong must suffer forever in hell.

If thou canst confidently believe that the eyes of the Lord neither slumber nor sleep, but behold those who have held their peace outwardly with their mouth and tongue, and inwardly have a friendly spirit toward their enemies, then you will easily stand all kinds of temptations.

This is a very beautiful, glorious consolation for the righteous, the believers in Christ, who are persecuted by the world and must sorely suffer. Yet they prudently restrain themselves, so that they do not render evil for evil. They govern their tongue and lips so as not to curse back, but do good to their enemies and bless them, that the Lord may not turn his countenance from them, as if he were angry with them. They wish that his eyes sleep not nor slumber, as they might think, if they are thus persecuted; but that they graciously look upon them as his dear children and safely protect them. They must suffer much, as the Psalm later says; but God helps them out of all. Moreover, what they pray God for will surely be vouchsafed to them, for his ears, he says, give heed unto their prayer. Is that true, as true it must be without doubt, for the prophet David surely lies not; then he will never forget us nor will he ever let us drop out of his sight. With this we shall comfort ourselves, and this it is that should move a Christian to suffer with patience all the injustice and disgrace that can be laid upon him. For when one rightly reflects, then he sees that the soul of the one who causes him suffering, if he does not repent, must suffer forever in hell. For Peter says further that the face of the Lord is upon them that do evil; he does not behold them with a friendly eye, as he does the righteous, but with an angry countenance. In a person who is very angry one sees how his whole countenance is disfigured and changed; he looks sour, bites his teeth, wrinkles his brow, mouth, and nose, and in general looks he like one who will knock things to pieces with all his might. With such a countenance, Peter says, the Lord beholds those who do evil, so that he will utterly root out their memory from the earth, as all historians testify that he has rooted out many great and mighty potentates, that neither a branch nor a root of them remains. So the final result is that all who persecute the righteous do themselves only harm, lose the blessing and the friendly countenance of the Lord, will not only be uprooted here in time, but will also still possess their guilt yonder; therefore they must be condemned forever.

Because of this, a Christian heart should say: Beloved Father, since our adversaries have so horribly fallen in thy wrath and have cast themselves so lamentably into eternal fire, I pray thou wouldst forgive them, rescue them from thy anger and show them grace, just as thou hast done to me. For, as I said, just as he looks upon the righteous with grace, so he frowns upon the wicked, wrinkles his countenance and in anger turns upon them. Since we therefore know that he looks upon us graciously and upon them ungraciously, we should have mercy and pity upon them, and pray that God would increase our faith to believe that his face is friendly toward us who suffer, and then be cheerful and give understanding to those who persecute us, so that they may believe that God is angry with them, and that they may be terrified and converted. Furthermore, Peter says:

vv. 13-16. *And who is he that will harm you, if ye be zealous of that which is good? But even if ye should suffer for righteousness' sake, blessed are ye: and fear not their fear, neither be troubled; but sanctify in your hearts Christ as Lord: being ready always to give answer to every man that asketh you a reason concerning the hope that is in you, yet with meekness and fear: having a good conscience; that, wherein ye are spoken against, they may be put to shame who revile your good manner of life in Christ.*

If we follow that which is good, namely, do not reward evil with evil, but be heartily kind and courteous, then there is none that can injure us. For though our honor, life and property be taken away, we are still uninjured, since we have a blessing incomparable, one that none can take from us. Those who persecute us have nothing but prosperity on earth, but afterwards, eternal condemnation, while we have an eternal, incorruptible treasure, although we lose a small temporal blessing.

v. 14a. *But even if ye should suffer for righteousness' sake, blessed are ye.*

Not only, he says, can no one injure you if ye suffer for God's sake, but blessed are ye, and ye should rejoice that ye are to suffer, as Christ also says in Matthew 5:11,12: "Blessed are ye when men shall reproach you and persecute you and say all manner of evil against you falsely for my sake. Rejoice and be exceeding glad." Whoever then realizes that it is the Lord who speaks such things, and so tenderly speaks comfort to his heart, he stands well; but to whom this does not bring strength, comfort, and courage, he will indeed remain un-strengthened.

vv. 14b-15a. *And fear not their fear, neither be troubled; but sanctify in your hearts Christ as Lord.*

Here Peter quotes a passage from Isaiah 8:12, 13, where he says: "Neither fear ye their fear, nor be in dread thereof. Jehovah of hosts, him shall ye sanctify; and let him be your support and refuge, in which we may trust, assured that no one can injure us." Let the world terrify, defy, and threaten as long as it will, it must have an end, but our confidence and joy shall never end. Thus we shall have no fear of the world, but shall be courageous. Before God we shall humble ourselves and be in dread.

But how does Peter mean that we should sanctify God? How can we sanctify him; must he not sanctify us? Answer: Thus we pray, even in the Lord's Prayer, "Our Father, hallowed be thy name," that we may sanctify His name, as he himself also sanctifies his name. Therefore it amounts to this: In your hearts, says Peter, ye are to sanctify him; that means, if the Lord our God appoints anything for us, be it good or evil, bring it weal or woe, be it shame of honor, prosperity or adversity, I am not only to consider it as good, but even as holy, and say, this is nothing but a precious blessing, of which I am unworthy, that it should come to me. So the prophet says, Psalm 145:17, "Jehovah is righteous in all his ways, and gracious in all his works." If I give God praise for such things and consider them good, holy, and excellent, then I sanctify him in my heart. But they who resort to books of justice and complain that they are treated unjustly, and say, God sleeps and will not help the just and restrain the unjust, dishonor him, and account him neither just nor holy. But whoever is a Christian should attribute righteousness to God and unrighteousness to himself. He should account God holy and himself unholy, and say, he in all his deeds and works is holy and just. This is what he requires. (So also the prophet speaks in Daniel.)

O Lord, in all that thou hast done toward us, hast thou done in accordance with right and true judgment. For we have sinned; therefore be the shame ours, but the honor and praise thine. If we sing, "*Deo gratias*," "Thanks be to God," and "*Te Deum Laudamus*," "We Praise Thee, O God," and say, "God be praised and blessed," when misfortune overtakes us, that is called by Peter and Isaiah a true hallowing the Lord.

But he does not by this require you to say he did right and well who has injured you, for it is an entirely different judgment between God and me, and between me and thee. I may have in my heart anger, hatred, and wicked lusts, and intend to damage you— while you are yet still uninjured—and have nothing against me; but in God's sight I am unjust; therefore he does right if he punishes me; I have well deserved it. If he does not punish me in that case, he shows me favor, and thus he is right in every way. But it does not therefore follow that he does right who persecutes me. For I have not done injustice to him as I have done in the sight of God. If God sends the devil or wicked people upon you to punish you, he uses them to the end, that they may execute his righteousness; so wicked wretches and injustice itself become a blessing.

Thus we read in Ezekiel 29:18-20 of King Nebuchadnezzar, where God says by the prophet, Knowest thou not that he is my servant, and has served me? Now, says he, I must give him his wages, I have not paid him as yet; well, then, I will give him Egypt, and that shall be his wages. The king had no right to the land, but God had, so that he might punish it through him. For, in order that even wicked wretches might serve him and eat not their bread in vain, he gives them enough, lets them serve him even to this end, that they persecute his saints. Here reason is at fault and thinks God does well and right when he remunerates them only here; gives them plenty of land and does it simply for the purpose to make them his executioners and persecutors of pious Christians. But when you endure and sanctify God, and say, "Just, Lord," then you do well, while he casts them into hell and punishes them because they have done wickedly; but takes you into his favor and gives you eternal salvation. Therefore let him manage them; he will reward justly.

Of this we have an example in holy Job, when all his cattle and all his sons were slain, and his property taken away, he said, Jehovah gave, and Jehovah hath taken away; as it was well pleasing to God, so has it been ordered, therefore blessed be his name (Job 1:21). And when his wife came, deriding him, and railed at him, and said in Job 2:9,10: "See! what hast thou now in thine integrity? Curse God and die," he answered her, "Thou hast spoken like a foolish woman: are we to receive good at God's hands, why should we not also receive evil from him, for he hath done as it hath pleased him? God hath given, and God hath taken away," he does not say: God has given, and God hath taken away, and yet it was the devil that did it. This man truly sanctified the Lord; thereof is he so highly praised and exalted of God. It follows further:

v. 15b. *Being ready always to give answer to every man that asketh you a reason concerning the hope that is in you.*

We must here acknowledge that Peter addressed these words to all Christians—clergy and laity, male and female, young and old—of whatever state or condition they may be. Hence it follows that every Christian should know the ground and reason of his faith, and he should be able to maintain and defend it where it is necessary. But up to this time, the idea that the laity should read the Scriptures has been treated with derision. For in this the devil has hit on a fine trick to tear the Bible out of the hands of the laity; and he has thought thus: If I can keep the laity from reading the Scriptures, I will then turn the priests from the Bible to Aristotle, and so let them gossip as they will, the laity must hear just what they preach; while if the laity should read the Scriptures, the priests would have to study them too, in order that they might not be detected and overcome.

But look now at what Peter tells us all, that we should give answer and show reason for our faith. When you come to die, I shall not be with you, neither will the pope; and if you know but this one reason of your hope, and say: I will believe as the councils, the pope and the fathers believed, then the devil will answer: Yes! but how if they were in error? Then will he have won and will drag you down to hell. Therefore we must know what we believed, namely, what God's Word is, not what the pope and the holy fathers believe or say. For you must not put your faith at all in persons, but in the Word of God.

So when anyone assaults you, and like a heretic asks why you believe you shall be saved through faith, here is your answer: Because I have God's Word and the clear declarations of Scripture for it. As Paul says in Romans 1:17, "The just shall live by faith," and Peter, where he speaks of Christ, the living stone, quotes from the prophet Isaiah, Whosoever believeth on him shall not be confounded; thereon do I build, and I know that the word will not deceive me (Isa. 28:16). But if you speak like other fools, Yes, we will hear how the council decides, and with that we will abide, then you are lost. Therefore you should say, Why do I then ask what this one or that one believes or decides; if they speak not the Word of God, I will not hear it.

Do you say then, It is so confusing that no one knows what to believe, and so one must wait till it is determined what we should hold? Answer: Then you will go to the devil in the meantime. For if it comes to the pinch, and you should die and not know what to believe, neither I nor anyone else could help you. Therefore you must know for yourself and turn to no one else. Cling fast to the Word of God if you would escape hell. And for such as cannot read, it is necessary that they should learn and retain some clear texts of Scripture, one or two at least, and on this foundation abide firmly, as for instance that of Genesis 12:3; 22:18, where God says to Abraham, "In thy seed shall all the nations of the earth be blessed." If you have grasped that, you may stand on it and say: Though pope, bishop, and all the councils stood yonder and said otherwise, yet do I declare this is God's word, that I can depend on, and that does not deceive me. Whoever will be blessed, must be blessed through "the seed," and whoever is blessed is ransomed from the curse, from sin, death, and hell. Therefore it follows from the text, whoever will not be blessed through "the seed" must be lost. So my works or good deeds can avail nothing in securing my salvation.

To the same end also is the passage of Peter, "Whoever believeth on this stone shall not be put to shame" (1 Pet. 2:6). If anyone should now attack you and demand a reason for your faith, reply, There stands the foundation which cannot fail me, and so I ask nothing besides, what popes or bishops teach or decide. Were they true bishops, they would teach the fundamentals of faith that they knew were common to all Christians. Yet they rush on and cry out: The laity dare not be allowed to read the Scriptures.

So if anyone asks you whether you will have the pope for a head say at once, I will hold him for a head, a head of wickedness and profligacy. And for this I have a passage of Paul: "Then shall come the devil's teachers forbidding to marry, and commanding to abstain from meats which God has created" (1 Tim. 4:1-3). That too the pope has forbidden, as is the case now. Therefore is he Antichrist. For what Christ commands and teaches, he transgresses. What Christ makes free, the pope binds; Christ says it is not sin, while the pope rejoins, it is sin.

Thus should one now learn to give a reason and answer for his faith; since it must come to that. If not now, then at death it will come to pass that the devil will come forward and say: Why have you charged the pope of being Antichrist? If you are not prepared and ready to give a reason, then has he won. It is as much as though Peter had said, If ye will now be faithful, ye must henceforth endure much persecution. But in this persecution you must have hope and must look for eternal life. If one asks why you hope for it, then you must have the Word of God on which to build.

But the sophists also have perverted the text, as though one were to convince heretics with reason, and out of the natural light of Aristotle. Therefore they say, It is here rendered in Latin, *Rationem reddere*, as if Peter meant it should be done with human reason. Because, they say the Scriptures are far too weak that we should silence heretics with them. The method by which, according to them, it must be shown that the faith is a right one, must agree with reason and come forth from the brain. But our faith is above all reason, and it alone is the power of God. Therefore, if the people will not believe, then be silent; for you are not responsible for compelling them to hold the Scriptures as the Word or Book of God. It is enough that you give your reason from the Scriptures. But if they take exceptions, and say: You preach that one should not hold to man's doctrine, and yet Peter and Paul, and even Christ, were men. When you hear people of this stamp, who are so blind and obtuse as to deny or doubt that this is God's Word, then be silent, speak no more with them, and let them go. But say: I will give you reasons enough out of Scripture. If you will believe them, it is well; if not, I will give you no others. But do you say, Must God's Word be treated with such shame? Leave that to God. Therefore it is necessary that we thoroughly apprehend this and know how to meet those who now rise up and present such objections. It follows:

v. 15c. *Yet with meekness and fear.*

That is, if you are examined and questioned as to your faith, you should not answer with haughty words and proceed in the matter with contempt and violence, as if you would tear up a tree by the roots. But proceed with such fear and humility as if you stood before God's tribunal and were there to give answer. For if it were not to come to pass that you should be examined before kings and princes, and had well prepared yourself a long time for the occasion with replies, and thus thought with yourself, "Deliberate, I will answer them correctly," then it shall be a happy experience for you. Unless the devil take the sword out of your hand and give you a blow so that you stand in shame and have put on your armor in vain, and he takes out of your mouth the reply you carefully prepared, so that it fails you though you had it fairly well in your mind. For he has beforehand tracked out your thoughts. Even this God suffers to take place, that he may subdue your pride and make you humble.

Therefore if you would avoid such an experience, you must stand in fear, and not rely on your own strength, but on the word and promise of Christ, "But when they deliver you up, be not anxious how or what ye shall speak: for it shall be given you in that hour what ye shall speak, for it is not ye that speak, but the Spirit of your Father who speaketh in you" (Matt. 10:19, 20). It is right, when you are to answer, that you arm yourself well with passages of Scripture; but beware you do not insist on that with a proud spirit, since God will even take the most forcible reply out of your mouth and memory, though you were previously fortified with all your replies. Therefore, fear is proper. And so, if you are summoned, then may you answer for yourself before princes and lords, and even the devil himself. Only beware that it be not the vanity of men, but the Word of God.

v. 16. *Having a good conscience; that, wherein ye are spoken against, they may be put to shame who revile your good manner of life in Christ.*

Of this Peter has already spoken above in 1 Peter 2:12. We cannot disregard it. If we follow the Gospel, then we must be despised and condemned by the world, so that men shall hold us as contemptible rabble. Therefore we shall let nothing disturb us and fear only before God and have a good conscience. So let the devil and all the world rave and rage, let them abuse as they will, they shall at last be made to understand with shame that they have injured and defamed us. This will happen when that day shall arrive, as Peter has said (1 Pet. 2:12), in which we shall be secure, and stand with a good conscience. These are in every respect suitable and forcible replies, which can comfort us and make us courageous, and yet we go on circumspectly with fear.

vv. 17, 18. *For it is better, if the will of God should so will, that ye suffer for well-doing than for evil-doing. Because Christ also suffered for sins once, the righteous for the unrighteous, that he might bring us to God; being put to death in the flesh, but made alive in the spirit.*

It will not be the case that they who reach heaven shall enjoy prosperity on earth, while even those who do not enter heaven may not be prosperous. For that which God said to Adam in Genesis 3:19, 16, is imposed on all men, "In the sweat of thy face shalt thou eat bread;" and to the women: "In pain thou shalt bring forth children." Since now adversity is imposed in common upon us all, how much more must we bear the cross if we would obtain eternal life. Therefore he says, since God will have it so, it is better that ye suffer for well-doing. They who suffer for evil-doing have an evil conscience, and have double punishment. But Christians have only the half of it. Outwardly, they have suffering; but inwardly, comfort. (As Christ says, in John 16:33, "In the world ye have tribulation," but in me peace, etc. Edition of 1539.)

Yet he has here set a limit, as he has said in 1 Peter 1:6, "If need be," by which those were restrained as the Donatists, of whom Augustine writes, who took such passages as spoke of suffering and committed suicide, and threw themselves into the sea. (See *August. de corr. Donatist* (ep. 185) 3; *Contra Gaudentium I.* 28.37.) It is not the will of God that we seek—and even invite—calamity. Go thou on in faith and love. If the cross comes, take it up; if it comes not, seek not for it. Therefore these modern spirits commit sin, in that they lash and beat themselves, or subject themselves to torture, and would thus storm heaven.

This Paul has also forbidden, in Colossians 2:23, where he speaks of such saints as walk in a self-chosen spirituality and humility and spare not their body. We should also restrain the body that it become not too wanton, according to Romans 13:14, yet not so as to destroy it. Also, we should submit to suffer if another sends suffering upon us, but not of our own choice fall into it. That will be the question: "If it be God's will," if he has appointed it, then it is better; while you are also more happy and fortunate in that you suffer for well-doing.

III. Concerning Christ (vv. 18-22)

v. 18a. *Because Christ also suffered for sins once, the righteous for the unrighteous.*

There Peter presents to us again the example of our Lord, and points us always to Christ's sufferings, that all of us should follow his example, so that he need not present a particular exemplar for the condition of every individual. For just as Christ is held forth as an example to everyone in the whole church, so it is the duty of every individual in the church, each for himself, of whatever calling he is, to copy it in his whole life, as occasion may be given. And he will speak after this manner:

Christ was righteous; and for well-doing he has suffered on our account, who were unjust; yet he sought not the cross, but waited till it was God's will for him to drink the cup; and he is our pattern, whom we are to imitate. And Peter cites this one example in particular, to the end that he may thus conclude how every condition in life is to be instructed; and now he will continue to declare more fully the suffering of Christ.

But he says here, in particular, that Christ has suffered once for us; that is, Christ has borne much sin, but he has not done it in such a way as to die for every individual sin; but at one time he has done enough for all. By this he has removed the sins of all who come to him and believe on him, who are now freed from death, even as he is free.

"The righteous for the unrighteous," he says. As though he had said, much rather should we suffer, since we die for the righteous who had no sin. But he has died for the unrighteous, and for the sake of our sins.

v. 18b. *That he might bring us to God.*

This is all said to teach the peculiar nature and end of Christ's sufferings; namely, that he died, not for his own sake, but that he might present us to God. How is that consistent; has he not offered up himself? Answer: It is true he has offered up himself upon the cross for us all who believe in him, but at the same time he offers up us with himself, since all who believe on him must suffer with him, and be put to death after the flesh as he was. However, God has taught us that they are alive in the spirit and yet dead in the flesh, as he afterwards says in 1 Peter 4:6: But we are a sacrifice with him.

As he dies, so we are to die according to the flesh; as he lives spiritually, so do we also live in the spirit.

v. 18c. *Being put to death in the flesh, but made alive in the spirit.*

The word *flesh* is common in Scripture, as is also the word *spirit*, and the apostles usually present the two in contrast. The sense now is: Christ through his sufferings is taken out of this life, which consists of flesh and blood, as a man on earth who lives by flesh and blood, walks and stands, eats, drinks, sleeps, wakes, sees, hears, grasps, and feels, and in brief whatever the body does while it is sensible; to all this Christ has died. This is what Paul calls a natural body, that is, the animal life in 1 Corinthians 15:44; that is, as an animal lives—in the flesh, not after the flesh—that is, in the natural functions that the body exercises, to such a life is he dead. So this life has now ceased with him, and he is now removed to another life and quickened after the spirit, passed into a spiritual and super-natural life that comprises in itself the whole life that Christ now has in his soul and body; so that he has no more a fleshly body, but a spiritual body. In this manner Paul explains it.

Thus shall it be with us at the last day, when spiritual life shall succeed flesh and blood, so that my body and yours will live without food and drink. We will not procreate, nor digest, nor vomit, and the like, but we shall inwardly live after the spirit, and the body shall be purified even as the sun, and yet far brighter, while there probably will be no natural flesh and blood, no natural or corporal labor, like the brutes.

The language of Paul on this point is: "The first man Adam became a living soul. The last Adam became a life-giving spirit" (1 Cor. 15:45). And it follows, "As we have borne the image of the earthly or the natural man, we shall also bear the image of the heavenly or the spiritual man" (1 Cor. 15:49). From Adam we derive all our natural functions like the unreasoning ani-mal as to the five senses. But Christ is spiritual flesh and blood, not according to the outward senses. He neither sleeps nor wakes, and yet knows all things, and is present in all the ends of the earth. Like him shall we be also, for he is the first fruits, the earnest and first born, as Paul says in 1 Corinthians 15:20-

23 and Colossians 1:18, of the spiritual life. That is, he is the first who has risen again and entered upon a spiritual life; that is, he is really man, but has a spiritual body. Therefore we should not here question how we may distinguish flesh and spirit from one another, but we must understand that the body and flesh are spiritual, and the spirit is in the body and with the body. For Peter does not say here that the Holy Spirit has raised up Christ, but he speaks more generally, as when I say the spirit, the flesh, I do not mean the Holy Spirit, but that which is in us, that which the spirit impels, and that which proceeds from the spirit. It follows now:

vv. 19-22. *In which also he went and preached unto the spirits in prison, that aforetime were disobedient, when the longsuffering of God waited in the days of Noah, while the ark was a preparing, wherein few, that is, eight souls, were saved through water: which also after a true likeness doth now save you, even baptism, not the putting away of the filth of the flesh, but the interrogation of a good conscience toward God, through the resurrection of Jesus Christ; who is on the right hand of God, having gone into heaven; angels and authorities and powers being made subject unto him.*

A wonderful text is this, and a more obscure passage perhaps than any other in the New Testament, so that I do not know for a certainty just what Peter means. At first sight, the words read as though Christ had preached to the spirits, that is, the souls who were formerly unbelieving at the time Noah was building the ark; but that I cannot understand and I cannot explain it. And there has been no one who has explained it. Yet if anyone is disposed to maintain that Christ, after he had suffered on the cross, descended to these souls and preached to them, I will not dispute it. It might bear such a rendering. But I am not confident that Peter meant to say this.

Yet the words may well be understood in this sense; that our Lord, after his ascension to heaven, came and preached in spirit, yet so that his preaching was not in the body. For he speaks not with a natural voice; he no longer does what pertains to the natural functions of the body. Therefore it must also follow, as it seems, that inasmuch as he preached to the spirits in that same spiritual body, such preaching must also be a spiritual preaching, so that he did not go there in the body and with oral preaching. The text does not require us to understand that he went down to the spirits and preached to them at the time of his death. For this is his language: "in which"; namely, when he had been put to death in the flesh and made alive in the spirit—that is, when he had unclothed himself of his fleshly existence and had passed into a spiritual being and life, just as he now is in heaven—then he went and preached. Now he certainly could not have descended to hell, after he had taken to himself such a new existence; wherefore we must understand that he has done it after his resurrection.

While the words only require that he be considered as speaking here of spiritual preaching, we may rest in the view that Peter speaks of the office that Christ performs by means of external preaching. For he commanded the apostles personally to preach the Gospel. But with the word preached he comes himself, and is spiritually present there, and speaks and preaches to the people in their hearts. Just as the apostles speak the word orally and in body to the ears, so he preaches to the spirits that lie captive in the prison-house of the devil. Therefore this also should be understood spiritually, like the preaching.

But here the expression follows, "Unto the spirits in prison that aforetime were disobedient [unbelieving]." We should observe, according to the divine account, that in the inner state of Christ's existence at present, those who have lived aforetime and those living now, are alike to him, for his sovereignty extends alike over the dead and the living: and in that life, the beginning, middle and end of the world are all one. But here on earth it is properly measured, so that one age passes on after another, the son succeeds the father, and thus it continues.

Here is an illustration of that: If a high forest lies before you, or you look upon it as it stretches in its length before you, you cannot well see over it. But if it lies near before you, and you stand above it and look down directly upon it, then you have it in full view. So it is here on earth we can form no conception of this life I speak of now, for it passes on, piecemeal as it were, foot by foot, to the last day; but before God it all stands in a moment. For with him a thousand years are as one day, as Peter says in the next epistle, 2 Peter 3:8. Thus the first man is just as near to him as the last that shall be born, and he sees all at once, just as the human eye can bring together two things widely separated at a single glance. So the sense here is that Christ preaches no more in person, but is present with the word and preaches to spirits spiritually in their hearts. Yet you are not to understand that he preaches in this manner to all spirits.

But to what spirits has he preached? To those who aforetime were unbelieving. This is the figure of speech which is called *synecdoche*, which means "from a part the whole" or *ex parte totum*. That is to say, not to these very spirits, but to those who are like them, and are just as unbelieving as they. Thus must we look away from the outward, to that inner life.

That is the best rendering, as I think, of those words of Peter; still I will not insist too strenuously upon it. This at least I can scarcely believe, that Christ descended to those souls and preached to them, because the Scripture is against it and declares that everyone, when he arrives there, must receive according as he has believed and lived. Besides, while it is uncertain what is the state of the dead, we cannot easily explain this passage as one that refers to the dead. But this is certain, Christ is present and preaches in the heart wherever a preacher of God's Word speaks to the ear. Therefore may we safely draw this conclusion: Let him to whom a better understanding is revealed follow the same. The summary of the sense I have given is: Christ has ascended to heaven and preached to the spirits; that is, to human souls. Among these human souls have been the unbelieving, in the times of Noah. Now it further follows:

v. 20. *When the long-suffering of God waited in the days of Noah, while the ark was preparing, wherein few, that is, eight souls, were saved through water.*

Thus does Peter lead us into the Scriptures that we may study them; and he gives us an illustration from them, of the ark of Noah, and he interprets this figure. For it is pleasing to have one bring forward illustrations of such figures, as Paul also does when speaking in Galatians 4:22-31 of the two sons of Abraham and of the two women; and Christ, in John 3:14, of the serpent that Moses erected in the wilderness. Such comparisons, when well drawn, are delightful. Therefore Peter introduces this one here, that we may be able to comprehend faith in a natural picture.

But he would also tell us that as it happened when Noah was preparing the ark, so it takes place at present. As he had regard to himself and was saved in the ark which swam upon the waters, so, it is to be observed, must you also be saved in baptism. Just as that water swallowed up all that was then living, of man and beast, so baptism also swallows up all that is of the flesh and of the corrupt nature, and makes us spiritual. But we sail in the ark, which means the Lord Christ, or the Christian church, or the Gospel that Christ preached, or the body of Christ to which we cling by faith, and are saved as Noah was in the ark. You also perceive how the figure comprises in brief what belongs to faith and to the cross, to life and to death. Where there are now those who cling to Christ, there is surely a Christian church. Where all that springs from Adam and whatever is evil, there is death.

v. 21a. Which also after a true likeness doth now save you, even baptism, not the putting away of the filth of the flesh, but the interrogation [answer or covenant] of a good conscience toward God.

You are not kept and saved by washing away the filth of the flesh, so that the body may be clean, as was the practice of the Jews; such purification has no further value. But you are kept by "the covenant of a good conscience toward God." That is, that you feel your conscience to be rightfully at peace within you, because it stands in covenant with God and can say: He has promised to me that which he will fulfill, for he cannot lie. If you shall rely upon and cleave to his Word, then shall you be preserved. Faith alone is "the covenant" by which we shall be kept; no outward work which you can do will suffice.

v. 21b. *Through the resurrection of Jesus Christ.*

Peter adds this in order to explain the faith which rests on the fact that Christ died, descended to hell, and arose again from the dead. Had he continued subject to death, we would not have been helped. But since he arose and sits at the right hand of God and suffers this to be proclaimed to us that we may believe on him, we have a covenant with God, and a sure promise, whereby we shall be saved as Noah was in the ark. Thus has Peter given to the ark an entirely spiritual significance in which is neither flesh nor blood, but a good conscience toward God, and that is faith.

v. 22. *Who is on the right hand of God, having gone into heaven; angels and authorities and powers being made subject unto him.*

This he says to enlighten and strengthen our faith. For it was necessary that Christ should ascend to heaven and become Lord over all creatures and wherever there is a power, that he may bring us thither and make us conquerors. This is now said for our consolation, that we may know that all powers, whether they be in heaven or on earth, must serve and aid us, even death and the devil, since all must become subservient to and lie at the feet of the Lord Christ. This closes the third chapter. The fourth follows.

1 Peter 4

The Nine Duties Required of Christians.

Outline

I. The First Duty of a Christian, vv. 1-7a.
  A. The nature of this duty, v. 1a. Christ's suffering presented to us in two forms.
  B. The necessity of this duty, v. 1b. What is meant by the word *flesh*. To what purpose does our cross serve.
  C. What should move us to perform this duty, vv. 2-7a.
    1. The first thing, v. 2.
    2. The second, vv. 3-5. What is meant by lasciviousness. Why the life of the Christian is considered by the world as foolish.
    3. The third motive to move us, vv. 6-7a.
    4. The fourth motive, v. 7a.

II. The Second Duty of the Christian, vv. 7b-8.
  A. Its necessity.
  B. Its nature.
  C. What should move us to perform it.

III. The Third Duty of the Christian, vv. 9-10.
  A. Its necessity.
  B. What should move us to perform it.

IV. The Fourth Duty of the Christian, v. 11a.
  A. Its nature.
  B. What should move us to perform this duty.

V. The Fifth Duty of the Christian, v. 11b-11c.
  A. Its nature.
  B. What should move us to perform this duty.

VI. The Sixth Duty of the Christian, vv. 12-13a.
  A. Its nature.
  B. The motive to move us to perform this duty.

VII. The Seventh Duty of the Christian, vv. 13b-14.
  A. Its nature, v. 13b.

   B. What should move us to perform this duty.
      1. The first thing, v. 13b-13c.
      2. The second, v. 14a.
      3. The third, v. 14b.

VIII. The Eighth Duty of the Christian, vv. 15-18.
   A. Its nature, vv. 15-16.
   B. What should move us to perform this duty, vv. 17-18.

IX. The Ninth Duty of the Christian, v. 19.

I. First Duty of a Christian (vv. 1-7a)

vv. 1-3. *Forasmuch then as Christ suffered in the flesh, arm ye yourselves also with the same mind; for he that hath suffered in the flesh hath ceased from sin; that ye no longer should live the rest of your time in the flesh to the lusts of men, but to the will of God. For the time past may suffice to have wrought the desire of the Gentiles, and to have walked in lasciviousness, lusts, wine-bibbings, revelings, carousings and abominable idolatries.*

Peter continues ever in the same strain. Just as he hitherto has admonished in general that we should suffer, if it be the will of God, and has set Christ before us as an example, so he now confirms it more extensively and repeats it again. He says: Since Christ our captain and head has suffered in the flesh and presented us an example, besides that he has ransomed us from our sins, we also should imitate him, and equip ourselves, and put on the same armor. For in the Scriptures the life of the Lord Christ, and especially his suffering, is presented before us in a twofold manner. Sometimes as a gift, as Peter has already exhibited in the third chapter. First, to those who are built upon and instructed in the faith that we are ransomed and our sins are taken away by the blood of Christ. Thus he is given to us and bestowed gratuitously upon us, which none can receive except by faith. Of this he speaks when he says, "Christ also suffered for our sins once" (1 Pet. 3:18). That is certainly the chief doctrine and the most precious one of the Gospel.

In the second place, Christ is set before us and offered to us as an example and pattern for us to follow. For if we now have Christ, through faith, as a free gift, we shall go farther and also do as he has done for us, and imitate him in his whole life and sufferings. In this manner Peter presents it here. But he does not speak here particularly of those works of love that lead us to befriend our neighbor and do good, which are called specifically good works, for he had said enough on this before. But he is speaking of such works as concern our bodies and are of service to us in strengthening our faith, that sin may be put to death in the flesh, and we thereby serve our neighbor better. For if I control my body that it be not lustful, then can I leave my neighbor, his wife or child at peace. So, if I subdue hate and envy, I shall then be better prepared to be kind and friendly toward my neighbor.

We have now repeated often enough that we are justified through faith and have the Lord Christ as our own. Still we must also do good works and show kindness to our neighbor. For we are never entirely purified while we live on the earth, and everyone still finds in his body evil lusts. Faith indeed begins at once to crucify sin and to give us heaven, but it is not yet become perfect and entirely strong. As Christ speaking of the Samaritan says, he, who was not yet healed, was laid under restrictions and directions that he might become healed (Luke 10:33-37). So it is also with us. If we believe, then is our sin or wounds bound up, that is, the disease that we have inherited from Adam, and it begins to heal. But this takes place in one person more, in another less; the more one mortifies self and subdues the flesh, the more his faith increases. Therefore if we have these two attributes, faith and love, then it shall continually be our occupation to cleanse ourselves wholly of sin until our dying breath.

Therefore Peter says, "arm ye yourselves also with the same mind." That is, be of a firm purpose and strengthen yourselves with the mind you received from Christ. If we are Christians, he says, then we must also say my Master has suffered and spilt his blood for me, and has died for my sake. Should I then be so base as not to suffer for him? Since my Master runs upon the spears' points in the conflict, how much more should the servant advance with joy? Thus do we awaken courage to press onward and arm ourselves in our minds so as joyfully to persevere.

The word *flesh* refers in Scripture not only outwardly to the body composed of flesh and blood, bone and skin, but includes all that is derived from Adam. As Jehovah said in Genesis 6:3: "My Spirit shall not strive with man forever, for that he also is flesh;" and in Isaiah, 40:5, "All flesh shall see the salvation of God;" that is, it shall be revealed to all men. So we also make confession in our own form of faith, "I believe in the resurrection of the flesh [body];" that is, that men shall rise again. So the whole man through and through is called flesh, as he lives here in this state of being.

The works of the flesh are carefully named, one after another (Gal. 5:19-21). Not only the gross carnal works, as lasciviousness, are mentioned but also the highest and most reckless blasphemies, as idolatry and heresy, which belong not only to the flesh, but to the reason. We must understand, therefore, that man with his intellectual nature and in respect both to that which is inward and that which is outward, both to the body and the spirit, is called "flesh." With all his faculties, internal and external, he seeks only that which is carnal and serves to gratify the flesh. Peter says here too that Christ suffered "in the flesh," while it is certain that his suffering extended further than merely to the body, for his soul suffered the greatest anguish, as is said by the prophet Isaiah in Isaiah 53:11.

In the same way also you are to understand that which follows in the passage before us: "For he that hath suffered in the flesh hath ceased from sin." This implies not only such things as beheading one and the torture of the body, but all that can work misery to man, whatever he endures through calamity and necessity. For there are many people who are sound in body, and yet inwardly experience much heart-sorrow and anguish. If it come upon us for Christ's sake, it is useful and good. "For whoever suffers in the flesh," says he, "ceases from sin." Therefore the holy cross is profitable, that sin may thereby be subdued; if it appeals to you thus, then lust, envy, hate, and other wickedness vanish. Therefore God has imposed the holy cross upon us that he might urge and constrain us to believe, and to extend the hand of kindness one to the other. Therefore it follows:

v. 2. *That ye no longer should live the rest of your time in the flesh to the lusts of men, but to the will of God.*

We should hereafter, as long as we live upon the earth, take the flesh captive by virtue of the cross and sufferings of Christ, and bring it under control. We do that so we do not live like the unbelievers, who know nothing of God, never inquire for his word, and continue to live in their lusts without any fear of God, as if this life were to last forever and God would never hold judgment and punish their sins. But we should now lead an honorable, holy life as becometh the children of God, and apply ourselves with all earnestness to do the will of our heavenly Father. Not that we may thereby merit anything, for our eternal inheritance Christ has acquired for us without any merit or assistance on our part; but in order that God may thereby be praised and our neighbor served.

We should henceforth, as long as we live, hold the flesh captive through the Cross and by mortifying the flesh so as to do that which pleases God, and not with the idea that we should or could deserve anything by it. "Not in the flesh to the lusts of men," says he; namely, we should not do that to which others tempted us; for we are not to be conformed to this world, as Paul says in Romans 12:2. What the world demands of us we must avoid.

v. 3. *For the time past may suffice to have wrought the desire of the Gentiles, and to have walked in lasciviousness, lusts, winebibbings, revelings, carousings, and abominable idolatries.*

We have already gone altogether too far, that before believing we so shamefully spent our life in accordance with "the will of the Gentiles," which is the same as with the lusts of men. Therefore, as long as life continues, we should see to it that our actions are well pleasing to God. For we have our enemy in our flesh, the one that is the real knave, not gross and coarse ones merely, but more particularly blindness of mind, which Paul calls "carnal wisdom," namely, "the policy or wisdom of the flesh" (Rom. 8:6). If we subdue this depravity, that other is indeed easy to tame. This does our neighbor injury in so secret a manner as not to be observed.

Peter calls "lasciviousness" that which is accompanied with outward gestures or words, by which evil intentions are expressed—though the deed itself be not performed and it is also that which is unchaste to the eye and ear, upon which afterward lust and the act also follow. Then follows such idolatry as is abominable. Therefore we may easily apply all this to ourselves, for when we have lost faith we have certainly lost God also, and may fall into more abominable idolatries than the heathen, if we view the matter aright.

We have already done too much, before we believed, in passing our lives so shamefully after the manner of the heathen in his lasciviousness, lusts, winebibbings, revelings, carousings, and abominable idolatries. Here Peter enumerates vices in which the wild, uncivilized people lived; and now they are common among the people generally, not only among the papists who blaspheme and persecute the Gospel, but also among people who wish to be honored as its friends. But Peter says that where such vices reign among the people, be they called as they may, it is a sign that they fear not God, and that they have no true faith, nor love nor patience. But since they all give themselves up to wantonness, live in their lusts and the like, they are still steeped in their abominable idolatries.

vv. 4, 5. *Wherein they think it strange that ye run not with them into the same excess of riot, speaking evil of you; who shall give account to him that is ready to judge the living and the dead.*

That is: You have heretofore lived like the heathen in abominable idolatries and scandalous sins and vices, as has been said; but now that you have renounced them this seems strange to the heathen. They think you exceptional and wonderful in that you now express your opinion of the same former disorderly life you lived in common with them, and you no longer in company with them slander God's Word and those who believe it. They say, what great fools Christians are to turn from all the joy and pleasure of this life. But let them think you strange and forever slander you, they will indeed have to give an account for that. Therefore commend all to him, who is ready to judge the living and the dead.

vv. 6-7a. *For unto this end was the Gospel preached even to the dead, that they might be judged indeed according to men in the flesh, but live according to God in the spirit. But the end of all things is at hand.*

Here we have, a rare and remarkable text. The words clearly declare that the Gospel is preached not only to the living, but also to the dead, and it adds besides, "in order that they might be judged according to men in the flesh." Now they certainly have not flesh, hence it cannot be understood except of the living only. It is a wonderful passage whichever way it be understood. Whether the text has come to us in its integrity or whether a part has been lost, I do not know, yet my understanding of it is as follows: We are not to be anxious how God will condemn the heathen who died many centuries ago, but only how he will judge those now living; so that the passage should be considered as spoken of men on earth.

But as to the word *flesh,* you are to understand, as I said above, that the entire man is called "flesh," according as he lives; just as he is also called in respect to his whole nature, "spiritual," if he follow after that which is spiritual. Still there is also a commingling of the two with one another, just as I say of a man who is wounded, that he is whole and yet is wounded. And so too, though the sound part is greater than the wounded part; still he is spoken of only with reference to the injured part as wounded. And such also, is the method of the Spirit here. Therefore, he says that they, as to their outward being, are condemned, but inwardly, as respects the spirit, they are saved and live.

But how does it come that he says they live, and yet adds that they are dead? I will explain it as I understand it, yet not so as to limit the Holy Ghost in that he calls the unbelieving "the dead." For I cannot accept the sense that to those who are dead and have perished, the Gospel has been preached; unless Peter meant this, namely, that the Gospel has been freely published and universally spread abroad, concealed neither from the dead nor the living, neither from angels nor yet from devils, and preached not secretly in a corner, but so publicly that all creatures might hear it who have ears to hear, as Christ gave command at the close of Mark: "Go ye into all the world and preach the Gospel to the whole creation" (Mark 16:15). If therefore, it is preached in such a manner, there will be found those who are condemned after the flesh, but live after the spirit.

v. 7a. *But the end of all things is at hand.*

This is also a remarkable passage. Already nearly 1500 years have passed since then. Peter preached that the time is indeed neither near nor brief, yet he says, "but the end of all things is at hand" as John also declares this in 1 John 2:18, "It is the last hour." If it were not the apostle's language, we might say it was contradictory; but by this we must firmly hold that the apostle has the truth on his side. Yet what he means here he shall explain himself in his second epistle, where he tells us why the time is said to be near, and says: "One day is with the Lord as a thousand years, and a thousand years as one day" (2 Peter 3:8), of which I have spoken above. So we must explain it in this manner, that it shall not be as long hereafter to the end of the world as it has been from the beginning to now.

II.   Second Duty of a Christian (vv. 7b-8)

v. 7b. *Be ye therefore of sound mind [temperate] and be sober [watchful] unto prayer.*

Here you perceive the reason we are to be of sound mind and be sober; namely, that we may be prepared to pray for ourselves and our neighbors. Moreover, love cannot be fervent unless you keep the body in subjection, so that love may have place within you. Here Peter has quoted Proverbs 10:12. "Hatred stirreth up strifes, but love covereth all transgressions." And this is what Peter means: Subdue your flesh and lusts. Unless you do it, you will easily offend one another, and not be able freely to forgive one another. Take care therefore, that you subdue the wicked lusts, so that you shall be able to have love one for another and to forgive, for love covereth a multitude of sins.

This passage has been explained to contradict faith, inasmuch as they tell us: You say that faith alone makes us righteous, and that no one through works may be free from sin. Why then do Solomon and Peter, as in this passage, say "love covers sin?" Answer thus: Whoever has hatred toward another, says Solomon, ceases not to stir up strife and bitterness; but where there is love, it covers sins and cheerfully forgives. Where there is wrath, or in other words, where there is an intractable man, reconciliation is not possible; he remains full of wrath and hatred. On the other hand, a man who is full of love is one whom you cannot enrage, however much injury may be done him. He covers it all, but does as though he saw it not. So the "covering" is spoken of as it pertains to our neighbor, and not as it respects God. Nothing shall cover sin before God for you, except faith. But my love covers the sins of my neighbor; and just as God with his love covers my sins if I believe, so too should I cover my neighbor's sins. Therefore he says, Ye should have love one to another, that one may cover the other's sins. And love covers not only one, two or three sins, but all transgressions; it cannot suffer and do too much; it covers up all. Paul also speaks and teaches in harmony with this passage in 1 Corinthians 13:7, "Love beareth all things, believeth all things, hopeth all things, endureth all things." It does the very best to all men, can suffer all, and judge all for the best that is imposed upon it.

Here the apostle exhorts them to prayer and in the same words shows that this duty or office to pray is entrusted to everyone; for the spirit of grace and of supplication is poured upon all believers (Zech. 12:10). Therefore whoever does not pray, has only forgotten that he is a Christian. To be sure true Christians do indeed pray without ceasing, for be they where they may and do what they wish, their hearts are continually overflowing with thoughts like these: O, dear Father, give grace that thy name may be hallowed in all the world through the preaching of the Gospel, that multitudes may be converted, become righteous and be saved, so that the will of Satan and of the wicked world may not be done, but that thy gracious, fatherly will may be accomplished. And besides, Christians pray also at their family altars and in the churches, where the congregations assemble to hear God's Word and to receive the holy communion. Here they are accustomed to pray for the needs of all Christendom and to give thanks with their spirits and with their offerings for all the blessings received. But if prayer is to spring from the heart and be offered in sincerity, then the suppliant must be of sound mind and sober, for a drunkard is never in a fit condition to pray. For how can such a person contend against the devil with faith and earnest prayer; yea, he is verily already swallowed by Satan.

"To be of sound mind" or temperate has reference to the excesses in manners, clothing, ornaments, and all kinds of pomp, that they be not drawn into them but that they conduct themselves modestly as is becoming Christians. "To be sober" means that we eat and drink only sufficient, so that the body may practice abstinence and perform its functions aright; also, that the soul may be watchful and in a state to study and meditate upon God's Word and to pray in sincerity. Eat and drink we must, therefore God gives us the sunshine and rain, lets the corn, wine, and all kinds of fruit grow for us to enjoy with thanksgiving. Hence, debauchery in eating and drinking is forbidden. In Luke 21:34 Christ says, "Take heed to yourselves, lest haply your hearts be overcharged with surfeiting, and drunkenness, and cares of this life." Paul in Galatians 5:21 counts gluttony and drunkenness among the works of the flesh and says, "They who practice such things shall not inherit the kingdom of God."

In the same manner the apostle wishes now to say: I faithfully exhort you to be of sound mind and sober. You are a people called into a state where you must continually be upon the battlefield, warring against sin and the god of this world, Satan. He is thy adversary, and he walks about thee and strives far more eagerly for thy soul than a hungry wolf does for sheep. In order to withstand him, you must not feel too secure and fall asleep, but be of sound mind and sober, and be armed with prayer and spiritual weapons (Eph. 6). And on this subject there should be a great deal of preaching, for we Germans are about sinking in ruin under the shameful vice of overeating and overdrinking.

v. 8. *Above all things being fervent in your love among yourselves; for love covereth a multitude of sins.*

As to thine own person, be of sound mind and sober so that you may pray aright and in sincerity. Then look to those around you and with whom you live that you may love them from your heart. The apostles made diligent use of these words. In Romans 12:9 Paul says, "Let love be without hypocrisy." And in 1 John 3:18: "My little children, let us not love in word, neither with the tongue; but in deed and truth," and 1 Peter 1:22 says, "Love one another from the heart fervently." For everybody complains of hypocritical people, of whom the world is always full, who in their words and manners appear friendly, but do not mean it in their hearts. As the proverbs say: fine words, but nothing back of them. Beware of cats that in front lick you and behind scratch you. And such persons can cover up the rogue to perfection, yea even adorn him, so that, if they act ever so deceitful, they think they have the right and authority to do so. God knows, they say, I wished him everything good, I was even ready to suffer that he might realize his every desire, and where I knew how to help him with personal service and with my means, I shall not fail to do so. However he is too wicked and unthankful; that, though one should show him every kindness, all is in vain and is lost with him.

Such is a false, deceitful love, which indeed the worst wretches on earth have. But you Christians, Peter wishes to say, should exercise true love, which does not glitter and shine like an *ignis fatuus*, yet at the bottom of the heart it is hypocrisy, but a love that possesses such ardor and fire in itself that it springs forth from the heart, and is such a fine and noble virtue that it is never provoked, thinketh no evil, beareth all things (1 Cor. 13:4-7). And as Peter says here, it does not cover one, two, ten, twenty, a hundred sins, but a multitude of sins. For if one person has the right love to another and means it truly and sincerely, he can not represent him as bad. He considers everything relating to him in the best light. He may indeed be angry with him, punish his sin and vice, in harmony with the word of Christ: "And if thy brother sin against thee" (Matt. 18:15-19). But he cannot be his enemy, unless he be a public blasphemer of God and a persecutor of his Word, of whom the Prophet says in Psalm 139:22: "I hate them with perfect hatred."

A pious father indeed loves his son from his heart; but if the son be bad and disobedient, the more the father loves him, the harder he chastises him with words. Yet in deed he even whips him until the blood runs, not because he is his enemy or has pleasure in punishing him and wishes to kill him; but because he is so pained that his son will not be good. All the while, however, he considers him his son and heir and his father-heart remains the same toward him, though at the time his words and actions may appear different. So also a pious mother may have a diseased and scabby child, and yet she does not therefore cast the child away and hate it, but she cares the more for it, and has greater sympathy for, and more worry and labor with it, than with all her other children. She is indeed by no means pleased with the scabs and ulcers, but since it is her child, love blinds her, so that the bad sores dare not be called bad, but they must receive another name to suggest that the child will, after the sores are gone, become very healthy and beautiful. If the child's eyes are squint, then they are called "ogling eyes;" if they are black, then they must be brown and the like. Thus the mother does not only cover the defects of her child, but she beautifies them.

Just so should it be among us Christians. It always happens that at times you do or say something that grieves me, and I do things that do not please you. As example is when as one member of the body injures another, when the teeth bite the tongue, for instance, or the finger is run into the eye. It is not done purposely. Here we should act in harmony with Peter's doctrine, not only one bearing the other's burden, covering his failings and defects, but also excusing and adorning them, as also Paul teaches in 1 Corinthians 12:23: "And those parts of the body, which we think to be less honorable, upon these we bestow more abundant honor; and our uncomely parts have more abundant comeliness."

III.   Third Duty of a Christian (vv. 9-10)

vv. 9-10a. *Using hospitality one to another without murmuring:*

according as each hath received a gift, ministering it among yourselves.

He is said to be "hospitable" who cheerfully acts the part of the host. When the apostles went abroad one with another and preached, and sent their younger brethren here and there, it was necessary that one should entertain the other. It would be well even now, if men preached from one place to another, from city to city, from house to house; and without remaining too long in one place might see to it that where one was weak he should be helped, and where one had fallen he should be lifted up, and things of that kind. Peter directs that this should take place without murmuring; that no one should suffer it to seem too much for him. This is also a work of love, as it follows immediately afterward that we should minister to one another. With what? With the gifts of God, which everyone has received. The Gospel directs that everyone be the servant of the other, and beside, see to it that he abide in the gift which he has received, which God has bestowed upon him; that is, the state or vocation, whatever it be, whereunto he has been called.

God's will is not that a lord should serve his servant, that the maid be as the mistress, and a prince serve the beggar; for he will not overthrow civil and domestic ordinances. But his meaning is that men should serve one another spiritually, with their hearts: although you are a high and great lord, yet should you employ your power to the end that you may serve your neighbor. Thus should everyone consider himself a servant. The lord can still remain lord, and yet hold himself in his own esteem no better than the servant: so that he would even cheerfully become a servant if it were God's will; and the same is applicable to other conditions.

v. 9. Using hospitality one to another without murmuring.

The apostles and disciples of Christ traveled through all countries and kingdoms at the same time and preached the Gospel in the whole world. Wherever they came, they were strangers and guests, possessed nothing of their own, as Christ commanded them to take nothing with them on their journey, but only to be thoughtful and diligent in doing the duties of their calling. For wherever they came, they would find everywhere people who would hear and welcome them, and would provide for their daily bread and their other needs, for a laborer is worthy of his bread and butter. In this connection the exhortation of Peter went forth that Christians should be hospitable to their brethren, and especially gladly receive them, welcome them to their homes and hearts, permit them to eat and drink with them, and show them every kindness, as the teachers of the Gospel, and also do the same to other poor brethren, who were driven into misery because they confessed their Christian faith. And this they were to do without murmuring, that is with joy and gladly from the heart for the sake of Christ, who was received in such persons (Matt. 10:40). To entertain willingly and to be hospitable is one of the virtues that should shine among Christians; but as rare as Christians are, so rare is also this virtue.

Peter comes now into the church, speaks of the gifts of the Holy Spirit, with which Christendom is adorned, by which not the body but the soul is served and helped, and says:

v. 10. *According as each hath received a gift, ministering it among yourselves, as good stewards of the manifold grace of God.*

The world knows no different than to think that the gifts it has, be they wisdom, art, knowledge, power, honor, or riches, it has of itself, and it does not believe that it has received them from God. Therefore it boasts of them, uses them only for its own benefit, and does not serve its neighbor with them; yea, it wishes to be highly honored and praised by those who possess them not. On the contrary, Peter teaches us Christians here that all gifts temporal and spiritual we have are gifts of God, which he gives to us for the purpose that one should serve the other with them; and the more one has received from him, the more he has to give an account for. That is what he means when he said above: "Love one another from the heart fervently," prove the same by being hospitable one to the other; and here: "According as each hath received a gift, ministering it among yourselves;" as if he should say: Gifts you have, which are not innate in you, neither have you inherited them from your mother as an heirloom; but you have received them from God, not to the end that you should puff yourselves up because of them and be considered great and lordly by others; but that you should be faithful stewards of God and of his manifold gifts with which he has adorned you, and use them well, namely, for his praise, honor, and glory and for the benefit and salvation of your neighbor.

However, Peter speaks here especially of the spiritual gifts, of which the world knows nothing, and never inquires about them (for it cares only for one thing, how to fill the stomach). These spiritual gifts the Holy Spirit pours out richly upon his Christendom and decorates and adorns it with them; for to one is given through the Spirit the word of wisdom; and to another the word of knowledge (1 Cor. 12:4-11, Rom. 12:6). Now those who have such gifts, especially those whom is given the office to teach the congregation of God and to feed them with the pure Word, that they use the same as Peter here teaches, namely, to serve them faithfully to whom they minister, that they may come to the right knowledge and faith of Christ and be saved. Paul, after speaking long on such gifts in 1 Corinthians 12, finally strikes as with a powerful thunderclap, and says in the next chapter (1 Cor. 13:1-3): Though one, yea, I myself, spake with the tongues of men and of angels, and had the gift of prophecy, and knew all mysteries and all knowledge, and had all faith so as to remove mountains, and though he bestowed all his goods to feed the poor and gave his body to be burned, and had not love, he would be nothing.

Truly these are very powerful words and terrible to hear. Imagine that one might be a fine, eminent, educated man, possess many beautiful, spiritual gifts, be highly cultured and experienced in the Scriptures, be blessed with strong convictions to others that they could thoroughly understand, grasp, and retain them; yet all will not help him; but with all these glorious gifts, even though they were again as great and glorious, he is nothing and is lost. How does this come to pass? Paul himself explains and says: If he has not love, that is, when such gifts make him proud as if they had grown on him and had not received them, he makes of them an idol, seeks only his own advantage, how he may thereby obtain great honor and high position, that he may be served and adored because of his great intelligence and rare ability; and is not in the least concerned for the honor of God and the welfare and salvation of his neighbor.

These are disagreeable people, and yet they are common in the world, especially among the preachers. As soon as one feels he can do something another cannot—is apt to learn, has a fine voice, or dispatches work quickly—he overdoes it, becomes proud, despises others who cannot equal him, yea, he thinks he knows more than those under whom he studied and suddenly changed from pupil to professor and wishes to make a show before the whole world. If then the public join him and praise and boast of his ability (as such spirits strive for this one thing with all their might), he is then first made a little gentle and is tickled so that he does not know whether he is walking upon the earth or in the clouds. Such characters do the greatest harm to Christianity; what pious orthodox teachers did so well, and planted and built during long years with great care and labor, they break to pieces and ruin in a short time, and consider their ways better and holier, and they must also be honored by such names which suggest that they were seeking the honor of God and salvation of their neighbors.

The apostles had much to do with such scandalous persons, therefore they so faithfully exhort that the spiritual gifts be used aright. But it did not avail anything. How did Paul fare? When he had preached a long time and founded here and there churches with the greatest care and at the risk of his life, he had scarcely turned his back when false brethren were soon upon his heels. They discredited his person and doctrine, and were gifted in speech. They were clever persons, and of finer appearance than Paul himself. Thus they led the people astray and they fell from Paul's teachings as we see clearly in his epistles. Therefore he speaks so strongly against such ambitious spirits and says: If they had yet gifts twice as great, if it were possible that they should speak with the tongues of angels, knew all prophecy, knowledge and mystery of the Scriptures, and besides could raise the dead, yet they are of Satan since they act and believe thus; as Christ also passes terrible judgment on such when he says in Matthew 7:23: "Depart from me, ye that work iniquity;" although they preached in his name, cast out devils, and did many wonderful works; and in Matthew 11:19 he complains that wisdom must be justified of her children.

Therefore this exhortation of Peter is necessary that everyone, however able and learned he may be, should use the gifts he has received to the end that the body of Christ, his congregation, may be edified by them; for to whom much is given, of him much will be required. Therefore in all things, as he says later, God may be praised through Jesus Christ. Whoever now preaches the word of God in its purity, without the addition of any human doctrine, that God out of pure love gave his only begotten son Jesus Christ for the sins of the lost world, seeks not his own, but God's honor, does not like God, rule over you, but serves you with his gifts, points out to you how you may be delivered from your sins and be saved. Whoever does the contrary seeks his own honor and advantage as is the manner and character of all work-righteous persons. Here it would be well to speak of temporal gifts, how they should be rightly used; but it would take too long, besides, I have often considered them in other places.

v. 10b. *As good stewards of the manifold grace of God.*

God has not bestowed upon us all like grace; therefore should everyone inquire to what he has been appointed, and what kind of gifts has been bestowed upon him. When he discovers this, let him use them for the service of his neighbor, as Peter further explains and says:

IV.   Fourth duty of a Christian (v. 11a)

v. 11a. *If any man speaketh, speaking [let him speak] as it were oracles [the word] of God.*

That is, if anyone has the grace that enables him to preach and teach, let him teach and preach. As Paul said in Romans 12:3-6: "To every man, not to think of himself more highly than he ought to think: but so to think as to think soberly, according as God hath dealt to each man a measure of faith. For even as we have many members in one body, and all the members have not the same office: so we, who are many, are one body in Christ, and severally members one of another. And having gifts differing according to the grace that was given to us." And then he said, "Has any one a prophecy, let it be according to the proportion of his faith; has any one a ministry, let him give himself to his ministry: does any one teach, let him give himself to his teaching" (vv. 6-7). He enforces the same doctrine also elsewhere, in his epistles to the Corinthians and Ephesians (1 Cor. 12:12; Eph. 4:7).

For this reason has God distributed various gifts among men. These should be used so that one should minister to another, especially those who are in authority, be it in preaching or in some other public office.

Now Peter says here, "If any man speaketh, let him speak the word of God." This point is worthy of special remark, that no one is to preach anything but what he is sure is the Word of God. Here Peter has closed the pope's mouth; and lo! he will be Peter's successor. And what a fine successor he is! Further:

The apostle considers gifts under two heads, speaking and doing. All the works of those having an office in the church are contained in the two headings, speaking and doing. He means thus to say: Whoever is a steward in the congregation of God either speaks something or does something, and at times he is engaged in both. If he speak, he is to take heed that he speaks the Word of God. Here both teachers and hearers are concerned, that the former teach nothing in the church and the latter hear nothing aside from the Word of God. For here the theme is not how to govern a country or a people, a house or a court, or how to build, and plant. The theme is how may man be delivered from sin, acquire God's grace, and be saved—how God is disposed toward us and the like. This cannot be learned from any jurist, philosopher, work-saint, nor from the pope with his canons; for no one has at any time seen God. However if it is to be made known to you, then you must learn it from the Gospel of Christ, who is in the bosom of the Father and has revealed the Father's will to us in his

Word. Therefore whoever is now called to speak in the church—to preach, teach, and exhort—should speak what Christ has spoken and commanded on subjects relating to our personal salvation. But Christ speaks thus on this point: That he is the good Shepherd, who gives his life for the sheep, who gives unto them eternal life; likewise, if any man will keep his Word, he shall never see death. He is the resurrection and the life, whosoever believes on him though he die, yet shall he live. He is the way, the truth and the life; so that no one can come to the Father, except through him. To the apostles however he says in Matthew 28:20: They shall teach all nations to observe all things whatsoever he commanded them; as Luke says: To preach repentance and forgiveness of sins in his name. And as Mark says: Whoever believes and is baptized shall be saved. Wherever this doctrine goes, there both preacher and hearer are sure, that the former speak the Word of God and that the latter hear that Word. For Christ's sheep hear his voice, and it is done unto them according to his Word. But if the doctrine is different and even proposes another way by which to be delivered from sin than through Christ, the falsity of it appears at once. For such teachers do not speak the Word of God, and the hearers do not hear it; hence theirs is not the true faith, and they cannot be delivered from their sin, nor be saved.

V. Fifth Duty of a Christian (v. 11b, c)

v. 11b. *If any man ministereth [have an office], ministering [let him minister] as of the strength which God supplieth.*

That is, whoever rules in the Christian church and has an office or ministry for the care of souls, he is not to proceed as he may choose, and say: I am sovereign lord, I must be obeyed; what I do shall stand and be established. God requires that we do nothing differently than he directs; also, that it be God's work and order. Therefore a bishop should do nothing unless he is sure that God does it, that it is either God's words or God's work. And besides, inasmuch as God will not permit that we should regard as a game of jugglery what we do with the Christian church, we must stand in the assurance that God speaks and works through us, and that our faith may also say: That which I have spoken and done, God has spoken and done; and on this I will even risk my life. Otherwise, if I have not this assurance, then my faith will rest upon the sand when the devil assails me.

Therefore whoever baptizes, administers the Holy Communion, speaks absolution, or visits and comforts the sick, does it not in his own strength, for thus he would dishonor and blaspheme God; but he does it in the strength of him who commanded it and said, "Go ye into all the world, and preach the Gospel to the whole creation." Likewise Paul also says in 1 Corinthians 11, that he did not institute the Lord's Supper; but the Lord himself was the founder of the ordinance. From him he received it, and he gives it to them from him. Likewise when I lay my hands upon anyone and declare unto him the absolution of his sins, I do it upon the authority of Christ's word, when he said in Matthew 18:18. "Verily I say unto you, what things soever ye shall bind on earth shall be bound in heaven." So now the will of Peter is that nothing be taught in the church except the Word of God, and nothing be done, unless God has commanded and arranged it.

Here it is earnestly forbidden to accept any human commandment, whether of the pope or of a bishop, unless the assurance is given that God does what he does, and he can say: In doing this I have the Word and command of God. Where this is not the case, he is to be looked upon as a liar. For God's order is that our conscience must rest upon the bare rock. Now all this is said of the common government of the church so that no one follows in these matters his own fancy, nor does anything which he is not sure that God wishes to have it as he does it. From this you see how Peter long ago overthrew the government of the pope as it is at present in the world. Wherever the contrary of the saying, "If any man speak, if any man have an office..." is held, you will find that there the very opposite is done. There neither the word nor the work of God have continued in their right use. They have been outrageously perverted, and the poor people have been led to depend upon human doctrines and their own works. It follows:

v. 11c. *That in all things God may be glorified through Jesus Christ, whose is the glory and the dominion for ever and ever. Amen.*

This is the end of the song, the conclusion. Everything that is spoken or done in the church should be directed to the end that God be praised in all things, and that the praise be through Jesus Christ. And this does take place when, by means of the Gospel, God's inexpressible grace and mercy are preached, which he has shown to us in Christ Jesus, whom he offered for our sins, in order that we might have in him the righteousness that avails before God. Wherever that is known, God alone will be praised and thanked, as the one who out of pure fatherly grace, without any assistance on our part, gave such a precious treasure for our sins. This is the true praise and thank offering that is pleasing to God; yet, be it remembered that it is accomplished through Jesus Christ. Without and apart from him, God has no pleasure either in our prayers or in our thanksgiving.

With the words Peter here speaks: "Whose is the glory and the dominion for ever and ever. Amen," he shows that Christ is true God. He ascribes to him even that which he ascribes to the Father, namely, divine glory and dominion, which he has from everlasting to everlasting. This Peter would not have done were Christ not true God. Otherwise, it would have been called robbing God of his glory, which he cannot suffer, as is proclaimed through the prophet Isaiah: "My glory will I not give to another" (Isa. 42:8).

Therefore, he means that you are to be confident that God speaks and does all that you speak and do. For if you perform a work of which you are not sure that God has done it, you cannot praise and give thanks. But where a man is certain of that, then he may praise and thank God for his word and works' sake, though he should be belied and held up to derision. Therefore, it is shameful and ruinous that in Christendom anyone should govern without the word and the works of God. Hence of necessity has Peter subjoined the instruction how governments should be constituted among Christian people. It follows further:

VI.   Sixth Duty of a Christian (vv. 12-13a)

v. 12. *Beloved, think it not strange concerning the fiery trial among you, which cometh upon you to prove you, as though a strange thing happened unto you.*

That is a mode of speech not common in our language. But Peter uses this very phraseology in order to remind us of that concerning which the holy Scriptures speak. For Scripture is accustomed to speak suffering as though it were a furnace full of fire and heat. Peter has spoken in the same manner above in 1 Peter 1:7, "That the proof of your faith, being more precious than gold that perisheth though it is proved by fire." We may also read in the prophet Isaiah, 48:10, where God says, "I have chosen thee in the furnace of affliction;" and Psalm 17:3, "With fire hast thou tried me;" and Psalm 26:2, "Examine me, O Jehovah, and prove me; try my heart and my mind;" and also Psalm 66:12, "We went through fire and through water." Thus the Scriptures are accustomed to call suffering "going through fire," or "a testing by fire." Peter's conclusion is that we should not allow ourselves to be surprised, or to think it strange and wonderful that the heat or fire—by which we are tried just as gold is when melted in the fire—should meet us.

When faith begins, God does not neglect it; he lays the holy cross upon our back in order to strengthen us and make our faith mighty. The holy Gospel is a powerful word, therefore it cannot enter upon its work without opposition, and no one can be sure that it possesses such power, but he who has experienced it. Where suffering and the cross are, there its power may be shown and exercised. It is a living Word, and therefore it must exercise all its energy in the time of death. But if there is no such thing as death and corruption, there is nothing for the living Word to do, and no one can be certain that it possesses such virtue, and that it is stronger than sin and death. Therefore he says that "You will be proved." That is, God appoints for you no flame or heat, in other words, no cross nor suffering, which make you glow as in a furnace, except to test you, whether you rely upon his Word. Thus it is written in Wisdom 10:12, of Jacob, "God appointed for him a severe conflict, that he might learn by experience that divine wisdom is the strongest of all things." Hence the reason God imposes the cross on all believers is that they may taste and prove the power of God that they possess through faith.

v. 13a. *But insomuch as ye are partakers of Christ's sufferings.*

Peter does not say we should experience the sufferings of Christ in order thereby to be partakers with him through faith, but he would say: just as Christ has suffered, so are you to expect to suffer and to be tried. If you do thus suffer, then you have thus fellowship with the Lord Christ. If we would live with him, we must also die with him. If I wish to sit with him in his kingdom, I must also suffer with him, as Paul also says repeatedly (Rom. 6:5; 2 Tim. 2:11).

Do not wonder, Peter wishes to say, that you suffer much, be not angry or sad over it as if God had forgotten and forsaken you, but accept it as a sure sign of his fatherly will toward you. "For whom the Lord loveth he chasteneth and scourgeth every son whom he receiveth" (Heb. 12:6). This he truly proved in Jesus Christ, his only begotten son, and allowed him to become a curse. Therefore rejoice much more that you are promoted to this honor and that since you are now in this like Christ, follow in his footsteps and suffer with him; you shall be well recompensed, as he further says:

VII.   Seventh Duty of a Christian (vv. 13b-14)

v. 13b. *Rejoice; that at the revelation of his glory also ye may rejoice with exceeding joy.*

Even if you were be brought to the torture and the flames of a martyr, you would still be happy. For though there be pain as to the body, there shall yet be a spiritual joy, inasmuch as you are to be happy forever. For this joy springs here from suffering, and is everlasting. Yet whoever cannot bear his sufferings cheerfully, and is dissatisfied, and chooses to contend with God, he shall endure both here and hereafter eternal torment and suffering. Thus we read of holy martyrs, that they submitted cheerfully to torture, thus opening the way to eternal joy. For instance, St. Agatha went as joyfully to prison as though it had been to a dance.

In 1 Peter 1:6-7, he spoke in a similar way and said, "Wherein ye greatly rejoice, though now for a little while, if need be, ye have been put to grief in manifold trials, that the proof of your faith may be found unto praise and glory and honor at the revelation of Jesus Christ." Here he adds a new thought and speaks of his glory, which shall be revealed at that day and which will be beyond the power of the tongue to express or of the mind to comprehend. From this glory we shall have eternal joy and delight, and compared with it all the suffering we meet with in this life, as Paul says in Romans 8:18, is to be reckoned as nothing. Whoever lays hold of this, to him no suffering is too heavy, as we read of certain martyrs, both men and women, who went as cheerfully to the stake as to a banquet. Likewise the apostles departed from the presence of the council and thanked God that they were counted worthy to suffer dishonor for the name of Christ (Acts 5:41).

v. 13c. *At the revelation of his glory.*

Christ does not permit himself as yet to be seen as a Lord, but is still a sharer with us in our labors. So far as he is himself concerned, he is truly such, but we who are his members are not lords as yet. Still we shall be lords when his glory at the last day shall be revealed before all men, brighter than the sun.

v. 14a. *If ye are reproached for the name of Christ, blessed are ye.*

Christ is a hateful name in the eyes of the world; whoever preaches him must endure to have the most esteemed on earth slander and revile his name. But in our times it is worse and more dangerous in that they who persecute us bear also the name of Christ; they say they are Christians and are baptized, yet in fact they renounce and persecute Christ. This is indeed a sad strife. They hold the same name as tenaciously as we do against us. For this reason we greatly need consolation, although the most discreet and pious people follow us, that we may stand firmly and remain cheerful. Why that?

As if he should say: Therefore all depends upon that, should you not believe in and confess this name, then the world would love and esteem you, for there is no name hated more by the world than the name of Jesus Christ. Not that it cannot mention his name or hear it mentioned, yea, the worst and bitterest enemies of this name bear it and boast of it the most. Besides, they call themselves the Christian church and the people of God, but they slander and condemn us as heretics and as the worst enemies of God. Why? Because we do not let this name be considered as an ordinary name, written only with letters as your and my names are. They slander us because we believe, preach, and confess, that Jesus Christ, according to his name, is the only Savior of the world who saves from sin, the only High Priest who reconciles the sinner with God, the only Lord and King who helps out of every need and trouble, and that only those who know him as such, does he deliver from sin and death, and they only obtain grace and eternal salvation. But this the people of the world cannot tolerate.

They indeed grant the name, that he be called Jesus Christ, as I am called Martin; but they will not allow that he should bear his name in reality and in practice, as the angel interprets it in Matthew 1:21: "Thou shalt call his name Jesus; for it is he that shall save his people from their sins" and Luke 2:10f., where the angel said to the shepherds: "Be not afraid; for behold, I bring you good tidings of great joy which shall be to all the people: for there is born to you this day in the city of David a Savior who is Christ the Lord." However, rather than grant that, they condemn his Word, persecute and put to death those teaching and confessing it, and this they did to him also; they put him to death on the cross. For if they grant, that then they must confess that monkery, human righteousness, self-chosen works, and worship and the like do not deliver from sin, nor secure grace and eternal salvation. However, that they will indeed not grant. Therefore, among them the name of Jesus Christ is in the very foundation of truth a hated and cursed name. For whoever does not speak in the Spirit of God, says Paul in 1 Corinthians 12:3, calls Jesus accursed. Paul also

said, "No man can say Jesus is Lord, but in the Holy Spirit."
Beloved, then let me not be a poor doctor of the holy Scriptures, but one who can rightly name the name of Jesus Christ,
even if he has not written or read many books.

v. 14b. *Because the Spirit of glory and the Spirit of God resteth
upon you. On their part he is evil spoken of, but on your part he is
glorified.*

Ye have, he says, within you a Spirit, that is, the Spirit of
God and of glory, such as makes you glorious. But he does
not do this here on earth, but he will do it when the glory of
Christ shall be revealed at the last day. Besides, he is not only
a Spirit that makes us glorious, but one whom we also regard
as glorious in himself. For it belongs peculiarly to the Holy
Spirit to purify and glorify, even as he has made Christ pure
and glorious. Now the same Spirit, he says, rests upon you;
and inasmuch as ye bear the name of Christ, he is slandered
by them. For he must endure to be reviled and slandered, to
the highest degree. Therefore it is not you who receive the
reviling; it is the Spirit, who is the Spirit of glory. Be not
anxious; he will regard it and raise you to honor. This is the
consolation we as Christians have, that we may say, That word
is not mine, this faith is not mine, they are all the work of
God: whoever reviles me reviles God, as Christ says in Matthew 10:40, "Whoever receiveth you receiveth me" and repeats in Luke 10:16. Peter therefore would say, Know that the
Spirit which you have is strong enough to fully punish his
enemies; as God says also in Exodus 23:22, "If thou wilt indeed hearken to my commandments, I will be an enemy unto
thine enemies." And the Scripture often repeats that the enemies of the saints are the enemies of God. If we are now
reviled because we are Christians and believe, we shall not be
ashamed, but the reviling is directed more especially against
God himself. Therefore he says, be ye cheerful and happy, for
that opposition is to the Spirit, who is not yours, but God's.
Now he adds an admonition:

VIII.   Eighth Duty of a Christian (vv. 15-18)

vv. 15-16. For let none of you suffer as a murderer, or a thief, or an evildoer, or as a meddler in other men's matters; but if a man suffer as a Christian, let him not be ashamed; but let him glorify God in this name.

Thus the apostle wishes to say: you have heard how you must suffer and how you are to conduct yourselves in your sufferings; but see to it that you suffer as Christians, who suffer for the sake of righteousness and well-doing, as is said in 1 Peter 3:14; not as murderers, thieves, evil-doers, or as those who venture to do something for which they have no authority, as the fanatical spirits who under the appearance of the truth preach lies and error and stir up rebellion and then must suffer for their evil-doing.

However, if you suffer as Christians, you are not to blush red with shame, but praise God that you are reckoned worthy to suffer dishonor for the sake of his Word and of his name. Thus he makes suffering and martyrdom very glorious and precious, so that it is something so valuable that we should praise God for it, when we come to the point that we are to suffer in this way; as Christ also does, when in Matthew 5:11 he says: "Blessed are ye when men shall reproach you, and persecute you, and say all manner of evil against you falsely, for my sake. Rejoice, and be exceeding glad: for great is your reward in heaven."

v. 17. for the time is come for judgment to begin first at us, what shall be the end of them that obey not the gospel of God?

He here cites two passages from the prophets together in one. As to the first, Jeremiah says, "Lo, I begin to work evil at the city which is called by my name; and if first of all I afflict my dearly beloved children who believe on me, who first of all must suffer and pass through the fire, do ye who are my enemies, ye who do not believe, suppose that ye shall utterly be unpunished?" (25:29). And later he says: "They to whom it pertained not to drink of the cup, shall assuredly drink, and thinkest thou that thou art he that shall not drink?" (49:12).

That is, I strike my beloved, that you may see how I shall treat my enemies. Observe here the force of the words: if God holds his saints in such esteem, yet has been willing to have them judged and exposed with such severity, what will then be done with the others?

So also Ezekiel in 9:6 saw armed men with their swords, who were to slay all, to whom God said, "Begin at my sanctuary." That is what Peter means in this verse. Therefore he says, the time is come, as the prophets have foretold, when judgment must begin with us. When the gospel is preached, God arrests and punishes sin, so that he kills and makes alive. The pious he gently strokes (with a *Fuchsschwanz*, a fox tail), and first of all is the mother rod of kind correction. But what then will become of those who do not believe? As though he had said, if he proceeds with such severity toward his own children, you may infer what must be the punishment of those who do not believe.

v. 18. *And if the righteous is scarcely saved, where shall the ungodly and sinner appear?*

This saying is taken from Proverbs 11:31, where Solomon says, "Behold, the righteous shall be recompensed in the earth: how much more the wicked and the sinner!" Peter frequently thought of the sufferings and tribulations Christians had to endure in this life; for they are not only persecuted by the world, but Satan also terrifies them in their hearts, holds before them their sins and magnifies them, so that they fall into a sad and melancholy state; and they are thus tormented by terror and despair. For here the world cannot judge differently than that Christians are a condemned people, who receive from God neither consolation nor help. Yea, the Christians at times permit themselves to think, since they experience such sadness and melancholy of spirit, that God is angry with them and has forsaken them. Hence the woeful complaints in the Psalms: "I am cut off from before thine eyes" (Psalms 31:22). This is what Peter means when he says here: The righteous can scarcely be sustained, for although they indeed believe and hold firmly to God's promises, yet they have trouble and labor in persevering to the end and in being finally saved, for Satan makes it bitter and hot enough for them; where will then the godless and the sinner appear? If God thus give the believer a shock that he trembles, how can he stand and abide, who is not only without faith, but has despised God's Word and counsel and slandered his saints? Therefore he concludes with the following:

IX.   Ninth Duty of a Christian (v. 19)

v. 19. *Wherefore let them also that suffer according to the will of God commit their souls in well-doing unto a faithful Creator.*

That is, those to whom God sends suffering that they themselves did not seek nor choose, should commit their souls unto their Creator. Such then fare well, they continue in doing good, turn not astray because of suffering, and commit themselves to their Creator, who is faithful. And this is great consolation for thee. God created thy soul without any care or assistance on thy part, when you did not yet have an existence. Therefore, trust him, yet trust in a way that it be done accompanied by good works, that you become not impatient, sad and angry, and be not provoked to take vengeance on those who caused you the suffering. Also, murmur not against God, give him the lie and fall into doubting; but hold fast on both sides, forgive your enemies and pray for them, and give God the glory that he is merciful, true, and faithful, and that he will never forsake thee in thy need, but will graciously help you out of your troubles, although you may at the time feel differently. Not that you are to think: now I will not be afraid to die. You must see to it that you are a true Christian and prove your faith by your works. But if you go on so venturously, it will be wise to examine what will become of you. This is the last admonition Peter gives to those suffering for Christ's sake.

An Exhortation and an Admonition. Conclusion of the Epistle.

Outline

I. The Exhortation, vv. 1-7.
   A. The exhortation to teachers and preachers, vv. 1-4.
      1. The character of those to whom the exhortation is given. Described.
         a. As elders,
         b. As partakers of the glory, v. 1a.
      2. The exhortation itself.
         a. The first part of this exhortation.
            (1) The nature of the first part, v. 2.
            (2) How this part is in no way observed by the pope and his following, v. 2a.
            (3) The foundation of this part.
         b. The second part of this exhortation, v. 2b. Two kinds of false teachers, v. 2b-2c.
         c. The third part of the exhortation, v. 3a.
            (1) The nature of this part.
            (2) How the entire government of the Pope is overthrown by this part of the exhortation.
         d. The fourth part of the exhortation, vv. 3b-4.
            (1) Its nature, v. 3b.
            (2) What should move teachers to observe this part.
            (3) This part of the exhortation is to be found nowhere among the papists. The pope is Antichrist.
   B. The exhortation to the young people, v. 5a.
   C. The exhortation to all christians, vv. 5b-7.
      1. The exhortation itself, v. 5b.
      2. What should move Christians to heed this exhortation, vv. 5c-7.

II. The Admonition, vv. 8-9.
   A. The ground and cause of this admonition, v. 8.

    B. Its nature, v. 9. A short repetition of the subject matter treated.

III. The Conclusion, vv. 10-14, consists:
    A. In a wish, v. 10.
    B. In praise to God. v. 11.
    C. In a reference to the reasons that moved Peter to write this letter, v. 12.
    D. In a greeting, v. 13.
    E. In an exhortation to greet one another, v. 14a.
    F. In praise of peace, v. 14b.

I.   Exhortation (vv. 1-7)

vv. 1-4. *The elders therefore among you I exhort, who am a fellow-elder, and a witness of the sufferings of Christ, who am also a partaker of the glory that shall be revealed: Tend the flock of God which is among you, exercising the oversight, not of constraint, but willingly according to the will of God; nor yet for filthy lucre, but of a ready mind; neither as lording it over the charge allotted to you, but making yourselves ensamples to the flock. And when the chief Shepherd shall be manifested, ye shall receive the crown of glory that fadeth not away.*

Here Peter gives instruction for the conduct of those who are to preside over the people in the spiritual government. He said in the last chapter (1 Peter 4:11), that no one should teach or preach anything, unless he be sure that it is the Word of God, so that our conscience may stand on the firm rock. For this is imperative on us as Christians, that we must be assured as to what is well pleasing to God, or not. Where this is wanting, no one can be a Christian. Afterward he taught us in 1 Peter 4:11, that whatever work or office anyone might have, he should discharge it as though God wrought in it. But the present passage refers particularly to the bishops or pastors as to what their fitness and conduct should be.

But here you must be accustomed to the language and learn the meaning of the words. The expression *presbyter* or *priest* is a Greek word, rendered in German "an elder," just as in Latin they were called "senators;" that is a number of aged, wise men of much experience. So Christ also has called his officers and his council, who bear spiritual rule and are to preach and serve a Christian congregation. Therefore you must not be misled, though they are called at the present day by a different title, "priests." For of those who are now called "priests" the Scriptures know nothing. And the real state of things, as it now is, the Scriptures do not notice. Apprehend the matter thus: When Paul and the other apostles arrived at a city where there were believing people or Christians, they selected there an aged man or two of honorable standing, having wife and children, and being well grounded in the Scriptures; and these were called "presbyters." After this Peter and Paul call them *episcopos*, that is, "bishop." Therefore "priest" and "bishop" are one and the same thing.

Of this we have a fine example in the legend of St. Martin, where an individual, with several companions, arrives in Africa at a certain place and perceives a man lying there in a hovel, whom they took for a husbandman, though they knew not who he was. Afterwards, when the people had come together at that place, this very man arose and preached. They perceived that he was their pastor or bishop; for at that time bishops were not distinguished from other people by their manner, dress, and bearing.

Those elders, says Peter, who are to care for and oversee the people, do I admonish, who am also an elder. Hence you clearly perceive that he calls them elders, who have himself also as an elder. And here Peter humbles himself, does not say that he was a lord over them, although he might have had authority for it, since he was an apostle of Christ and speaks of himself not only as a fellow-elder, but also as a witness of the sufferings that were in Christ. It was as though he should say, I do not merely preach, but am a partaker with Christians, even suffering Christians. By this he shows that wherever there are Christians they must suffer and be persecuted. Such is a genuine apostle. If such a pope or a bishop were to be found among those bearing the title at the present day, we would gladly kiss his feet.

v. 1. *The elders therefore among you I exhort, who am a fellow-elder, and a witness of the sufferings of Christ, who am also a partaker of the glory that shall be revealed.*

Peter speaks thus for the purpose of interesting and moving the elders by his example to tend the flock of Christ faithfully, even if they have to meet great misfortune in doing so in order that they may not despair and forsake the sheep. They are to do as he does, continually preach Christ and suffer for doing it, and to comfort themselves with the assurance of becoming partakers of his glory, which shall be revealed. For it cannot be otherwise than that the sufferings precede and the glories follow (1 Pet. 1:5-6). Therefore he says: I preach not only as you do; but I am also a witness of the sufferings of Christ, namely, I find both in myself and in others that all who believe in Christ and confess him have their fill of suffering; but they are besides also sure of being raised in due time to honor and glory. Now follows what the elders should do.

v. 1b. *A partaker of the glory that shall be revealed.*

This is something still more exalted, and evidently a bishop must not speak it lightly, for here Peter claims to be a saint. He was certain that he should be saved, for he had strong assurance, as when Christ said, "I have chosen you" (Jn. 15:16, 19). However, it cost much pain before the apostles attained it. They had to be first humbled and wickedly derided. Now he knew that he was a partaker of salvation, still he is not proud, neither does he exalt himself, although he is a saint. Now what shall the elders then do? It follows:

v. 2a. *Tend the flock of God which is among you.*

Christ is the chief shepherd, and has many shepherds under him. He also has many herds of sheep, which he has committed to his shepherds here and there in many lands, as Peter writes in this passage. What are these shepherds to do? They are to tend the flock of Christ. This the pope has arrogated to himself, and thus claims that he is sovereign lord, and may dispose of the sheep as he chooses. We know very well what tending is, namely, that the shepherd should lead the sheep to the pasture and set food before them, that they may be fruitful. Besides, they are to guard lest the wolves come and rend the sheep, that is, that they may not assault and destroy them.

Now Peter says particularly, "the flock of Christ," as though he would say: Do not imagine the flock is yours, ye are only servants. But our bishops speak with all confidence the reverse. They say, you are my sheep. But we are Christ's sheep; for so he said before: "Ye are now returned to the Shepherd and Bishop of your souls" (1 Pet. 2:25). The bishops are Christ's servants, and their business is to guard Christ's sheep and feed them. Therefore to tend them is nothing else than to preach the Gospel, by which souls are nourished, made fat and fruitful—since the sheep thrive upon the Gospel and the Word of God. This only is the office of a bishop. So Christ says also to Peter, "Feed my sheep" (Jn. 21:16, 17), that is, the sheep which you are to feed are not yours, but mine. Yet from this they have inferred the doctrine that the pope has external power over all Christendom, and yet none of them preaches to you one word of the Gospel. And I fear that since Peter's day there has been no pope that has preached the Gospel. There has certainly been none who has written and left any writings behind him in which there was any Gospel. Pope Saint Gregory was certainly a holy man, but his sermons are not worth a farthing; so that it would seem the See of Rome has been under the special curse of God. It is very possible that some popes have endured martyrdom for the Gospel's sake; but nothing has been written of them to show that it was the Gospel. And yet they go on and preach that they must feed the flock; and yet they do nothing but bind and destroy the conscience by laws of their own, while they preach not a word of Christ.

It is also probable that among all Christians many might be found, both men and women, as able to preach as those who are thus employed. But certainly among all these multitudes there are many people who have not this ability. And therefore someone must be selected to strengthen them, so that the wolves shall not come and tear the sheep. For a preacher must not only feed the sheep, so as to instruct them how to be good Christians, but, besides this, must guard against the wolves, lest they attack the sheep and lead them astray with false doctrine, and introduce error with which the devil would not find fault. But there are many people to be found at the present day quite ready to tolerate our preaching of the Gospel, if we would not cry out against the wolves and preach against the prelates.

But though I were to preach the simple truth, feed the sheep, and give them good instructions, still it is not enough unless the sheep be guarded and protected, so that the wolves do not come and carry them off. For what is built, if I throw out one stone and see another thrown into its place? The wolf can very readily endure to have the sheep well fed; he had rather have it so, that they may be fat. But he cannot endure the hostile bark of the dogs. Therefore is it a most important matter, if well considered, that we should truly tend the flock, as God has commanded it.

v. 2b. *"The flock,"* he says, *"which is among you."*

There he has expressed, in a single word, what the prophet Ezekiel writes in Ezekiel 34:1f., of shepherds or bishops. And this is the meaning: You are not only to feed them, but also to pay attention and be very faithful where it is called for and there is need. And here he uses a Greek word, *episcopountes,* that is, being bishops, and it comes from the word *episcopos,* rendered in German, an *overseer,* a *guardian,* who is on the watch or look-out, and takes notice of what everyone around him wants. Observe, then, how a bishop and an elder are one and the same person. So it is false, as they now say, that the bishop's office is a dignity, and that he is a bishop who wears a pointed hat on his head. It is not a dignity, but a ministry; so that he who has it should oversee and provide for us and be our guardian. He should know what is generally needed so, that when one is weak and has a troubled conscience, he should then give help and comfort; when one falls, he should raise him up, and things of this sort. In this way the people of Christ may be sufficiently cared for, both in soul and body. For this reason, I have often said that if a proper form of government were to be now established, there must be in one city as many as three or four bishops, who should have the oversight and care of the church, providing for the general wants.

And here Peter touches on two points that might well appall anyone from taking the charge over a people. In the first place, there are some to be found who are truly devoted, yet yield reluctantly to becoming preachers. It is a wearisome office for anyone to have the general oversight as to how the sheep live, so as to direct and help them. There must be oversight and watchfulness night and day, so the wolves do not break in; so that body and life must also be devoted to it. Therefore he says, "you are not to do it of constraint." True it is that no one should force himself uncalled into the ministry; but if he is called and required for it, he should enter it willingly, and discharge the duties his office demands. For they who do it of constraint, and who have no appetite and love for it, will not properly discharge the duties of the ministry.

But the others are worse than these, who stand up before the people and thereby seek their own gain, so as to feed their own stomachs. These men are anxious for the wool and milk of the sheep. They ask no questions about the pasture, just as our bishops at present do, a thing that has become almost everywhere a scandal and a shame, since in a bishop it is especially scandalous. For this reason both the apostles Peter and Paul (Acts 20:33), as well as the prophets, have repeatedly spoken of it. So Moses says, "You know that I have coveted no man's cattle" (Num. 16:15). The prophet Samuel said, "You know that I have taken of you no man's ass or ox" (1 Sam. 12:3). For if he whose duty it is to feed the flock is anxious merely for wealth and gain, he will in a short time become a wolf himself.

v. 2c. *But of a ready mind.*

That is, a bishop should have an appetite and inclination for his calling. This is the character of those who willingly minister and do not seek the wool of the sheep. Thus we have two kinds of false shepherds: the one, those who serve unwillingly; the other, those who do it gladly, but for the sake of avarice.

v. 2d. *But be of a ready mind.*

That is, a pastor should take pleasure in and be inclined to teach, do it cheerfully from his heart and continue to do so with delight, even in poverty and need, and entirely gratuitously for the reason that he is assured that his teaching is well-pleasing to God and that it is the highest benefaction he can do to his neighbor. He seeks not in the pasture of God his own honor, for the sheep committed to him are not for his gain and use; just as Moses, Samuel, and all the pious shepherds have done and still do. Thus we have two kinds of wicked shepherds; the first who do their work unwillingly, avoid the labor, ingratitude and the cross; the second class do their duties willingly, but for the sake of filthy lucre. Those who take the golden mean, do it not of constraint, but willingly; not for the sake of disgraceful gain, but from the depth of the heart.

v. 3a. *Neither as lording it over the charge.*

This is the character of those who rule willingly enough for the sake of honor, in order to rise high and become powerful tyrants. Therefore he admonishes them not to act as though the people were subject to them, so that they might be gentlemen and do as they chose. For we have a master, who is Christ, who rules over our spirits. The bishops are to do no more than tend the sheep. Here Peter has broken down and condemned by one word all that rule which the pope now maintains, and he clearly concludes that they have no power to give one word of additional command, but that they are to be only servants, and say, Thus saith Christ thy master, therefore you are to do it. So Christ also speaks, "The Kings of the Gentiles have lordships over them; and they that have authority over them are called Benefactors. But ye shall not be so" (Luke 22:25-26). Now the pope speaks the very reverse, "Ye shall rule and have authority."

vv. 3b-4. *But making yourselves ensamples to the flock; and when the chief Shepherd shall be manifested, ye shall receive the crown of glory that fadeth not away.*

That is, see to it that you go before them as their leader and conduct yourself so that your life may be an example to the people, and that they may follow you. But our bishops say to the people, Go there and do so and so, and they sit on cushions and play the gentleman, imposing burdens on us which they will not bear themselves (Matt. 23:4), while they will not preach a word, and call others to account if they have not done it for them. But if it should be required of them, they would soon be weary of their dignity.

Therefore Peter does not appoint any temporal reward for bishops. As though he would say: Your office is so great that it never can be rewarded here, but ye shall receive an eternal crown, which shall follow it, if ye truly tend the sheep of Christ. This is the admonition Peter gives to those who are to care for souls. From it you may confidently infer and clearly prove that the pope, along with his bishops, is Antichrist, or an enemy of Christ, since he does nothing of that which Peter here requires, and neither teaches nor practices it himself. He even acts the counterpart and will not only not feed the sheep or let them be fed; but is himself a wolf and tears them, and yet makes it his boast that he is the vicar of the Lord Christ. He certainly is that, for since Christ is not there, he, like the devil, sits and rules in Christ's place.

Hence it is necessary to grasp well these plain texts and others like them, and to hold them up against the Pope's government, so that when anyone asks or questions you, you may be able to answer and say: Christ said and practiced so and so; the Pope teaches and practices directly the opposite; Christ says yes, then the Pope says no. Since they are opposed to one another, one of them must be false; but certainly Christ is not. Whence I conclude that the pope is a liar and the real Antichrist.

In this way must you be armed with Scripture, so that you cannot only challenge the pope as Antichrist, but know how to prove it clearly, so that you could die secure of it and withstand the devil even in death. It follows further:

v. 5a. *Likewise, ye younger, be subject unto the elder.*

This is now the last admonition of the chapter. Peter wishes to establish this order in the Christian church: that the younger should follow the older, so that all may go on harmoniously; those beneath submissive to those above them. If this were now to be enforced, we should not need many laws. He would strictly have it so that the younger shall be directed according to the understanding of the older, as they know best what shall be for the praise of God. But Peter presumes that such elders are to be instructed and established in the Holy Spirit. For should it happen that they are themselves fools, and without understanding, no good government could originate with them. But if they are persons of good understanding, then it is well that they should rule the youth. But Peter is not speaking here of civil, but of church government, that the elders should rule those that are spiritually younger, whether they be priests or even aged men.

Although there is one common doctrine that concerns all men in whatever station they may be; yet the complaint is general that the young people are rough, wild, and ill-bred. Children will not be subject to their parents, pupils to their teachers, nor servants to their masters and mistresses. There is no obedience or discipline any longer among the young people, but only pride and self-will. Everyone does as he pleases, acts the gentleman, is independent and unreproved. In the end God will not let them go unpunished. Now whoever is a Christian, and gives heed, knows that he has no choice as to whether he will be in subjection or not; but he is to do so with good grace and cheerfully. God demands it, and says here through Peter: "Ye younger, be subject unto the elder."

To this end Christ is presented to you as an example, that you be of the same mind as he. Although he existed in the form of God and was equal with God; yet, he was a servant of us all, became obedient unto death, yea, the death of the cross (Phil. 2:6-8). And above in chapter 2 and verse 18 the apostle admonishes servants not only to be obedient and serve their irritable masters with all faithfulness, but also to suffer ingratitude and all evil from them and follow in the footsteps of their Lord Christ, who did no sin. If thou dost now despise the command of God, thy Creator, and art not moved by the example of Christ thy Lord and Savior, then thou art no Christian. Thy baptism, Christ's sufferings and blood, God's grace and favor, avail thee nothing; yea, thou dost bring upon thyself the heavy and unbearable wrath and disfavor of God, who, as Peter says later, resisteth the proud, will overthrow and utterly destroy thee, thou poor worm of the dust, by his powerful hand, with which he casted down to hell the disobedient angels in chains of darkness. Of this divine punishment we not only read in all histories, but also daily experience it. I fear that the disobedience and recklessness of our young people will be soon punished and more terribly than anyone imagines. May God in mercy take his own to himself before that time comes and spare them the sight of such misery!

v. 5b. *Yea, all of you gird yourselves with humility, to serve one another.*

The apostle turns here and modifies his words, teaching that all Christians should be subject to one another. But how does this harmonize, if the elders shall rule and at the same time are to be subject? Are we to overthrow what has been said? No, we will let the words stand, that they were spoken in general of all Christians, that we should be subject to another; the younger to the elder, as I said. On the other hand, the elder is subject to the younger, especially if they are in office and are ready to serve them with their spiritual and temporal gifts every hour and minute if necessary, with comfort, counsel, admonition, help, and punishment. Also for the reason that both old and young have the same spiritual blessings, even the young as well as the old have the word of grace, faith, baptism, hope, the Spirit, Christ, God, life, salvation. There is no difference, there is no young or old, but all are one in Christ. Therefore, whoever is in heart a Christian is at once blessed with the highest gift and is a teacher of others. He humbles himself also before the lowest Christian, for he belongs to Christ just as well as he. Christ redeemed all with the same precious blood; yea, he does not only bear the infirmities and burdens of the weak, but he also covers them, yea, that means to serve and to be in subjection in practice. Often in history the younger are more competent and more highly endowed by God than the older. Therefore Peter wishes that we all serve one another.

Paul also teaches the same in Romans 12:10: "In honor preferring one another," and in Philippians 2:3: "In lowliness of mind each counting other better than himself." Likewise in Luke 14:8-11.

So Christ teaches: "When thou art bidden to a feast, sit not down in the chief seat, lest haply a more honorable man than thou be bidden of him, and he that bade thee and him shall come and say to thee, Give this man place; and then thou shalt begin with shame to take the lowest place. But when thou art bidden, go and sit down in the lowest place; that when he that hath bidden thee cometh, he may say to thee, Friend, go up higher" (Luke 14:8-10). Then he introduces the passage that is found in many places: "Everyone that exalteth himself shall be humbled, and he that humbleth himself shall be exalted" (Luke 14:11; 18:14; Matt. 23:12).

Therefore should the younger be subject to the elder, and yet the elder on the other hand should be so disposed that each one in his heart shall consider himself as the least. Were this done, we should have delightful peace, and all would go well on the earth. This therefore, says he, should we do, exhibit humility.

v. 5c. *Gird yourselves with humility. For God resisteth the proud, but giveth grace to the humble.*

God distributes his gifts among his people according to his good pleasure. He adorns some with temporal blessings, as health, strength, beauty, riches, honor, and power; while others he adorns with spiritual blessings, as wisdom, knowledge of the holy Scriptures, and the like. He does all this to the end, as I said, that they might acknowledge that they received these gifts from him, then thank him for them, and make good use of them for the benefit and happiness of their neighbors. This is here taught by Peter when he says, "Gird yourselves with humility," (or as Luther renders it, "hold fast to humility." Translator), and it is a serious and necessary teaching. For the way of the world is, when one has a little more than another, then he holds up his head, becomes proud and arrogant; as do the rich, the noble, the powerful, the beautiful. Likewise do the learned, the eloquent, and the pious. No one of these characters even remembers that he received his gifts from God. He suppresses all mention of thanks to him for them, and much less does he use them to serve and instruct his neighbors. But he imagines they are a peculiar growth of his own, hence he overestimates himself, no one is good enough for him to associate with, yea, others are even a stench to him. He thus uses what he has, only to despise and injure his neighbor. In the face of all this he wishes his neighbor to do him honor and even to worship him; while in himself there is neither any love nor humility, but mere contempt and pride. Therefore such a person sins not only against the Second Table of the Law, against his neighbor; but also against the First Table, against God, whose grace and mercy he should preach and praise. For his gifts were bestowed upon him to the end that he might not do this very thing; but instead he uses his gifts to seek his own glory and honor. This is surely reviling and slandering the name of God in the most outrageous manner. Therefore the pride that germinates and grows from the gifts of the spirit is a satanic vice and is directly against God's name and God's Word.

However, among you Christians, says Peter, it should not be so; but you should know it is God's will and his earnest command that you, as one body in Christ and members, one of another, should have fervent love to and be subject to one another; since you have the same faith and hope, the same baptism and Spirit, and in short, have like blessings in Christ, in which you are one without any difference whatever. But should one Christian be endowed with more gifts than another, he knows that he received them from God for the purpose of serving others with them, that God may be praised thereby through Jesus Christ. Therefore the higher you are favored, the deeper will you humble yourself, even before the lowest people; while they permit themselves to be taught, directed, reformed, and admonished by you in all humility, in order that you may join hands with one another and hold tightly and firmly to humility, that you all may remain intact and complete, and not be divided and torn by anger, pride, ingratitude, and impatience.

That is, those who will not give place to humility God casts down. On the other hand, he exalts those who humble themselves. This is a common expression, and I would to God that it might become common in our daily lives! However, great earnestness will be required to accomplish this, for humility does not so easily find an entrance into our hearts, neither is it put on like a coat. Hence he says further:

v. 6a. *Humble yourselves therefore under the mighty hand of God.*

Since God requires each to be subject to the other, if it be done willingly and cheerfully, he shall exalt you. But if you do it not willingly, then you must do it of constraint, nevertheless he will humiliate you.

v. 6b. *That he may exalt you in due time.*

It seems, when God suffers his own children to be cast down, as though he would at length desert them. Therefore he says: Do not make a mistake on this point, and suffer yourself to be blinded, but be confident, since you have a sure promise that it is God's hand and that it is his will. Therefore regard not the time, however long it be, that you are brought low. For though he has cast you down, he will yet lift you up.

If however you do the contrary and let not this faithful admonition move you nor allow the spirit of Christ to rule you, but on the contrary you follow Satan who is a proud, arrogant spirit, and does nothing but sow pride in human hearts so that they trust in their temporal possessions, honor, power, wisdom, holiness, and the like, with which they comfort themselves and are not comforted by Christ's sufferings nor concern themselves about God's threatenings and promises; then you may rest assured that you are accumulating to yourself the wrath and enmity of God, who created you and holds your life in his hand. He resisteth the proud who will not humble themselves under his mighty hand. In a moment he can overthrow thee and hurl thee to the abyss of hell, as he has proved from the beginning of the world. One can read about this not only in the Bible but in all histories, and can see daily before his own eyes, if he will only believe it.

Mary, the holy mother of Christ, sings also of the same in her Magnificat and paints forth more in detail this passage of Peter. She says that his mercy is unto generations and generations on them that fear him, that he hath exalted them of low degree, fed and filled the hungry with good things, and finally delivered them out of all need and saved them. On the contrary, he scattereth the proud in the imagination of their heart, hath put down princes from their thrones, and the rich he hath sent empty away, so that they must finally perish forever, as Peter grasps in the few words: "God resisteth the proud, but giveth grace unto the humble." But on both sides, however, they think it should indeed be better. Whatever on the one hand the proud, influential, and rich may will or wish is done, they have every desire of their hearts realized. Hence, they cannot think otherwise than that they have a gracious God, and the last thing they can believe is that God resisteth them and will overthrow them. On the other hand, since the pious must suffer much, as we have heard through this entire epistle, it seems that God is angry with them and resisteth them with all his might. Therefore as it goes so contradictory, Christians should not let that worry them, but hold firmly to the Word of God and be comforted by his promises, as Peter further teaches and says:

v. 7. *Casting all your anxiety upon him, because he careth for you.*

This is a beautiful and comforting passage, one which every Christian should believe and write in his heart, that it may comfort him in every need and temptation. Peter wishes to say: If the world persecute you, the devil terrify and make your heart sad by his fiery darts, if brethren are malicious and treacherous to you, or in any other way attack you, be not angry or impatient, murmur and complain not, even if it continue a long time and there is no end to it. The time will not be so long, for God takes it to heart and he will attend to all. Indeed by becoming angry and impatient we would only give them occasion to tread us entirely under their feet, cause us all suffering and damage, and finally also ruin us. Therefore do not worry in the least, only take care for this, and do not be over anxious as to: How shall I secure money, home, food, and the like? How shall I be delivered from this need or danger? Where will I be when I die? But follow my counsel; let each one do in his calling what God commands him. Does evil befall him while doing his duty, then he endures it and proves thereby his patience and humility and consoles himself besides, that God, to whom he is now reconciled through Christ and whose child he has become through faith in him, is almighty and merciful. On him he calls and casts all his anxiety with confidence upon him, whether temporal or spiritual, for he careth for us. This we should in no way doubt.

The prophet David speaks thus also in Psalm 55:22, from which Peter quotes this passage, where David says, "Cast thy burden upon Jehovah, and he will sustain thee" (he delays, yea, too long, and lets me in the meantime ever stick in my need: Ah! hold fast and persevere), "he will never suffer the righteous to be moved." Many more like passages are found in the Bible. Therefore this doctrine is to be found nowhere else, except in the Holy Scriptures. No philosopher, no legislator teaches man to cast all his cares upon God. Hence the world knows nothing of it, perverts everything, has not only scruples as to what it should do, but it will suffer nothing. Does it happen to the world different than it expected? Then it becomes angry and impatient, and contemplates how to take vengeance. Contrary to the counsel of Peter, it takes the cares upon itself. It should cast upon God, for they are too heavy and it cannot bear them. Consequently we see that in general all people, especially those in high stations, carry and are worried with their cares day and night, can never have any peace, and they pass their lives wretchedly with vain and useless anxieties. And if things do not succeed and prosper as they planned, which is generally the case, they become raging and foolish, also indeed some die largely because of their great suffering. On the other hand if they succeed, that success as a rule means their greatest ruin. Where is the trouble? Here, they follow not Peter's advice and cast all their cares upon God; but retain them to themselves and wish to carry their cares themselves.

But you have such grand promises, through which you are certain that God will not forsake you, but will surely take care of you. Therefore cast all thy anxiety upon him and let him attend to it. These are beyond measure loving words; how could he have made them sweeter and more friendly? But why does he use such strong persuasion? Because no one will cheerfully bend here and let his own opinion go for nought. Therefore he imparts such comfort that God does not only take notice of us, but he cares for us and heartily welcomes us into his friendship. So now everyone does what God has commanded, and if you have well and faithfully accomplished it and thereby secured the world's anger and hatred, for its reward is nothing else, then suffer it only joyfully. Go ever right ahead and let nothing turn you from your calling. Do not be concerned as to how you are to be exalted, but let God take care of that. For thus it is beautifully systematized; the smaller part—the labor and suffering—fall to your lot and it cannot be otherwise; the greater part—the anxiety—God takes upon himself. In this way you can reach your mark in life beautifully, which otherwise would have been impossible, if the care and anxiety had to ever rest upon you. In conclusion he gives a short warning and says:

II. Admonition (vv. 8-9)

v. 8. *Be sober, be watchful; your adversary the devil, as a roaring lion, walketh about, seeking whom he may devour.*

Here he gives us a warning and opens our eyes, and the text is well worthy to be written in golden letters. You perceive here what this life is, and how it is described, so that really we might ever wish we were dead. We are here in the devil's kingdom, just as a pilgrim arrives at an inn, where he knew all in the house were robbers. If he must enter, he will not fail to arm himself in the best way he can devise. He will sleep but little. So are we now on the earth, where the prince is an evil spirit and has the hearts of men in his power, doing with them what he will. It is a fearful thought if we properly consider it. Therefore Peter warns us to take heed to ourselves and act the part of a faithful servant, who know the state of things here. For this reason he says, "be sober," for they who indulge in eating and drinking and are like fat swine, can be prepared for nothing useful. Therefore we must have ever with us such a talisman as this.

"And be watchful," he says, not only as to the spirit, but also as to the body. For a sluggish body, prone to sleep when it eats and drinks to excess, will not resist the devil, since it is difficult to do so even for those who have faith and the spirit.

Why should we then be sober and vigilant? "Because your adversary the devil walketh about as a roaring lion, seeking whom he may devour." The evil spirit sleeps not, is cunning and wicked. He has purposed with himself to assault us, and he knows the right trick to do it. He goes about like a lion that is hungry and roars as though he would gladly devour all. Here Peter gives us a precious admonition, and he forewarns us of our enemy that we may protect ourselves against him; as Paul also says, "we are not ignorant of Satan's devices" (2 Cor. 2:11). That "walketh about" tends to make us heedless, and thereupon follow wrath, hatred, pride lust, contempt of God.

And here observe especially that he says "the devil walketh about." He does not pass before your eyes when you are armed against him, but looks out before and behind you, within and without, where he may attack you. If he now meets you here, he will quickly return there, and attack you in another place. He changes from one side to the other, and he employs every kind of cunning and art that he may cause you to fall. If you are well prepared in one place, he will quickly fall upon another. And if he cannot overthrow you there, then he assaults you somewhere else, and so never gives up, but goes around and around and never lets anyone rest in peace. If we then are fools and regard him not, but go on and take no heed, then has he as good as seized us.

Let everyone now look well to this; surely each shall trace something of it in his own experience. He who has tried it knows it well. Therefore it is so sad for us that we go about so heedlessly. If we rightly considered it, we should cry out, death rather than life. Job says, "Man's life on earth is nothing but an encampment, a mere conflict and strife" (Job 7:1). Why then does God thus leave us in life and misery? In order that faith may be exercised and grow, and that hastening out of this life, we may have a desire to die and be anxious to depart.

Satan is by nature such a wicked and poisonous spirit that he cannot tolerate anything that is good. It pains him that even an apple, a cherry, and the like grow. It causes him pain and grief that a single healthy person should live upon the earth, and if God would not restrain him, he would hurl everything together in ruin. But to nothing is he a more bitter enemy than to the dear Word; because, while he can conceal himself under all creatures, the Word is the only agency that can disclose him and reveal to everybody how black he is. Since then you have God's Word, Peter says, and you cleave by faith to it, you should know beforehand that Satan will be your enemy; and you should know that he is not only a wise, cunning, but also a very wicked, poisonous, and powerful spirit. He rules and dominates the whole world. Therefore, Christ also calls him in John 14:30 the Prince, and Paul in 2 Corinthians 4:4 and Ephesians 6:12, the God and Ruler of this world.

If now Satan, thy adversary, were far from you, and would let you alone in peace, he would do little harm. But he will not do that. He is not a thousand miles from you, but he encircles you and stands by your side, so close to you that he cannot come closer. He does not lie upon a cushion, and sleep and snore, but he walks about without ceasing day and night. He does not do so that he may joke and play with you, nor because he wishes to see what you are doing; but he is angry and furious, and hungrier than a wolf or lion, and seeks not how to appease his hunger with thy possessions or to do you harm in other ways such as inflicting wounds upon your body, or beating you with a club, or burning your house and court. His only purpose is to swallow you whole. He walks about, tries and seeks everything, until at last he causes you to fall; now he attacks you and stirs you to adultery and anger, then to avarice and pride. If he succeeds not in this way, he tries with terror and unbelief, to persuade you to let go of the Word of God and to doubt his grace. He can even aside from temptation appear to you as an angel of light, so that one thinks all he instills into you and disputes with you is surely God's Word from the Scriptures and the pure truth. And you would indeed swear and die by it, and yet it is nothing but error and falsehood. So cunningly and wickedly does he plot for you Christians; for the godless he has already taken captive by his snares, so that they must do, speak and think as he wills (2 Tim. 2:26). Peter warns us in 2 Corinthians 2:11, "We are not ignorant of Satan's devices," and Paul says in Ephesians 6:12, "For our wrestling is not against flesh and blood."

v. 9a. *Whom withstand steadfast in your faith.*

Sober you should be, and vigilant, but to the end that the body be kept in a proper frame. Yet with all this, the devil is not routed; this only suffices to afford the body less occasion to sin. The true sword is that ye be strong and firm in the faith. If you in heart lay hold on the Word of God and maintain your grasp by faith, then the devil cannot gain the advantage, but will be compelled to flee. If you can say: This has my God said, on this I stand, then shall ye see that he will quickly depart, and ill-humor, evil lusts, wrath, avarice, melancholy, and doubt will all vanish. But the devil is artful and does not readily permit you to understand this, and so he assaults you in order to take the sword out of your hand. If he can make you lazy, so that your body is unguarded and inclined to wantonness, then will he quickly wrench the sword from your grasp. Thus he served Eve: she had God's word. Had she continued to depend on it, she would not have fallen, but when the devil saw that she held the word so indifferently, he tore it from her heart, so that she let it go and he triumphed (2 Cor. 11:3; Gen. 3:4,13).

Thus Peter has sufficiently instructed us to contend with the devil. It requires not much running hither and thither; it is besides a work that you can do, yet no longer than you depend by faith on the Word of God. If he comes and would drive you into despondency because of sin, only seize hold of the Word of God that speaks of the forgiveness of sin, and exercise yourself in that. Then will he be compelled quickly to let you alone.

But as to how we are to oppose Satan in this life and guard ourselves against his attacks Peter teaches and says: First you are to be sober and watchful, not merely as to the body, but much more as to the soul, and bestir yourself with all earnestness that you be not drunken and sleepy, but sober and watchful, in other words, that you may always take pleasure in God's Word, remember it, meditate upon it and diligently cling to it, thank God for it, and pray that you may understand it better and lay hold on it more firmly. Where that is done, the body remains in a fine sober and watchful state and you gladly go to church, hear God's Word, and let nothing keep you away. And you continue temperate. But if the body be surfeited, sluggish, and lazy, it is a certain sign that the soul before was drunken, that is, secure, weary and tired of the Word, and besides sleeps and snores. Therefore Satan takes special pains to intoxicate us spiritually so that in time our love for and pleasure in the Word may leave us and we acquire a distaste for it. We become enemies of the preachers of the Word when they chastise us for our vices and threaten us with God's judgment, or when on the other hand through his fanatical or quack preachers Satan perverts and falsifies the Word, ye with such a show that those, who hear it and are not well posted, do not know otherwise than that it is the pure truth; as we have experienced during late years with the Sacramentarians, Anabaptists, and other sects. Thus are lost both the true doctrine and the true faith, and there is no longer any resistance offered to the devil.

v. 9b. *Knowing that the same sufferings are accomplished in your brethren who are in the world.*

Shortly before the denial of Christ by Peter, the Lord showed Peter that Satan would sift him and bring him to the point that he would thrice deny his Lord. He said further in Luke 22:32, "But I made supplication for thee, that thy faith fail not; and do thou, when once thou hast turned again [art converted], establish thy brethren." What the Lord commanded him at that time he does in this passage especially, namely, comforts or establishes his brethren, the Christians, who are plagued and tempted by Satan; he will now say: I have preached to you of the devil and painted him forth in his true colors, that he neither sleeps nor recreates, but watches and walks about without tiring and the like. This you will surely experience for yourselves.

Now the temptations of the Christian are twofold, spiritual and bodily. The spiritual, set forth in the first table of the Law, are the higher and harder; the bodily temptations, set forth in the second table, are of a lower order and lighter. The degree of suffering is according as persons are strong or weak in faith. Some are tempted by coarse sins; as unchastity, anger, and impatience, which cause pain to the pious, Christian hearts, and they would gladly be free from such temptations, but they cannot. They must however battle and slay the works of the flesh by the Spirit. Hence they persevere in the inner man and go right ahead, otherwise they are not Christians, and will die the eternal death (Rom. 8:13). Satan attacks others harder, so that they are persecuted and banished for the sake of God's Word, robbed of their possessions, and a portion of them martyred for confessing the truth: These have severer suffering than the first. Yet since they suffer for the sake of a good cause, for the sake of Christ and the truth, it is great consolation. Therefore, though they outwardly suffer anxiety and need, yet, their heart is contented and in favor with God through Christ.

Moreover Satan attacks certain Christians especially hard, as the highly enlightened and experienced classes, with strong spiritual temptations, and puts at times terrible and wicked thoughts into their hearts, so that they cannot see, acknowledge, or hold God to be gracious, true, faithful, and patient, but imagine the very opposite of him. Hence they hate his judgment and are in no way pleased with his government. They lose both God and his promises, and they can neither pray nor call upon him. Yea, they rage and murmur terribly against him. That is a very perilous and irresistible temptation. If it continue long, it consumes our marrow and bones, of which the Psalter often complains and likewise Job, Jeremiah, and others. I imagine Peter also experienced a large share of it, since he denied Christ. Had the Lord not prayed for him before and graciously looked upon him soon after his fall, and permitted peace to be spoken to his soul, and had he himself not later comforted him, he would have had to doubt, and be ruined and lost in sin and thus have followed Judas.

Therefore what he speaks he speaks from his own experience to console and strengthen all Christians, who suffer or are tempted; as if he should say: No one among you who suffers or is tempted in soul or body, even in the highest and severest degree, should imagine that he suffers something special, new or rare, or as if no one before him or contemporary with him had ever experienced and endured such hard and terrible temptations; no, you are not alone. Your suffering and temptation cannot be so great, severe and exceptional, that your brethren before you or your contemporaries have not experienced the same and indeed even greater and worse temptations; if you will not believe this then you may learn it from me as a living example. I was so bold that I did not only resolve to stand by my Lord and Master, even if all the others forsook him, but also to accompany him to prison and to death. I was so certain that I had given the dear Lord the lie about the matter, when he said to me, that very night I would not only along with the others be offended at him, but that I would do worse than they, namely, deny him thrice. What happened? Christ was found true, but he found in me that I was not only a liar and shamelessly denied him; but that I perjured myself and swore terribly that I never knew him. That was suffering and temptation, good and strong.

Therefore has Christ the Lord commanded, that when I am again restored to the right path after my fall, I shall strengthen and comfort my brethren. So I say as an apostle of Christ, as one who has a special commission, and also as he who has experienced it, that no suffering or temptation so high, rare, and wonderful can take place or meet you that others were not tempted and tried like you or even worse. Not only God's dear children, your brethren, who lived before you from the beginning of the world, but also those, who now live, in your day, scattered here and there in the world as far as Christ's name is known and published, they all meet the same that you meet; for they have the devil as their adversary who walks about them also and seeks to swallow them as well as you.

Hence whoever is a Christian and earnestly desires to remain so, let him not feel too secure, be idle and lazy, but watch, teach, practice the Word faithfully, persevere in prayer, be prepared for temptation and suffering, and remember that he is called thereto, as the apostle said in 1 Peter 2:21. For Christ himself speaks in Matthew 16:24 thus: "If any man would come after me, let him deny himself, and take up his cross, and follow me;" and in John 16:33 he said, "In the world ye have tribulation." In Acts 14:22 Paul said, "Through many tribulations we must enter into the kingdom of God." And notice 2 Timothy 3:12, "Yea, and all that would live godly in Christ Jesus shall suffer persecution." Therefore if you come so far that you are tempted and must suffer as a Christian, take it as a sign of grace, for whom the Lord loveth he chasteneth, and scourgeth every son whom he receiveth. And remember you do not suffer alone, but all Christendom with you, and it cannot be so wonderful and exceptional with you that others have not experienced the like, yea, indeed even in a higher and severer degree.

What tribulations and misery were endured by the great saints, as the prophets, apostles, and especially the patriarchs who lived so long, is indescribable, yet, a part of these tribulations, noticed only in the briefest manner, will remain unthought and unexpressed until we see face to face on that great day. It was the hardest for Adam and Eve because they had no example before their eyes, with which they could comfort themselves. We have before us all the Scriptures, where we can see how it has gone with all the saints, and the head and Lord of all the saints. In brief the sense is this: In this we should be resigned, that we must suffer here for a short time and follow our Lord Christ, yet we should be confident of the eternal life and glory; not because of our suffering, but because they are promised by God and acquired by Christ.

That is, be not surprised that you must meet opposition from the devil; but comfort yourselves, inasmuch as ye are not alone, but there are others besides you who must endure such suffering, and reflect that you have brethren who share with you in this strife.

This is now the epistle in which you have sufficiently heard the true Christian doctrine; in what a masterly manner he has described faith, love, and the holy cross; and how he instructs and warns us as to how we should contend with the devil. Whoever comprehends this epistle has doubtless enough, so that he needs nothing more; except that God may teach him from the abundance of the same truth that overflows in the other books of the Bible. But that is in no way different from this; for here the apostle has forgotten nothing necessary for a Christian to know.

Finally, he does what every faithful preacher should do, in that he not only takes heed to feed the sheep, but also cares and prays for them; and concludes with a prayer that God may give them grace and strength to understand and retain the word.

III.   Conclusion (vv. 10-14)

v. 10. *And the God of all grace, who called you unto his eternal glory in Christ, after that ye have suffered a little while shall himself perfect, establish, strengthen you.*

That is the wish with which he commits them to God. God, who alone bestows grace, and not a single part of grace, but all grace richly in one, who has called you through Christ that ye might have eternal glory, not through any worthiness of your own, but through Christ. If ye have him, ye have through faith—without your own merit—eternal glory and salvation, which will prepare you, that you may be strong, grow, and stand, and that ye may be able to accomplish much; and to the end he will strengthen and establish you, that ye may be able to bear and suffer all things.

v. 11. *To him be the dominion for ever and ever. Amen.*

This is the sacrifice of praise that we Christians should offer to God. Since he does all to commence and to complete our salvation—gives us his beloved Son, sends us the Holy Spirit, who strengthens and comforts us through all our lives, and sustains us by the pure doctrine—it is right and proper that the honor and praise be his, whose are the work and the power. Therefore let him be praised in eternity, Amen.

v. 12. *By Silvanus, our faithful brother, as I account him, I have written you briefly, exhorting, and testifying that this is the true grace of God: stand ye fast therein.*

Although I well know, he would say, that you have heard this before and know it well, so that you do not need that I should teach it to you, yet have I written this to you, as true apostles should do, that I might also admonish you to abide therein, since you are tried and exercised. You are not to imagine that I preach in any way different than you have already heard.

v. 13a. *The church that is in Babylon saluteth you.*

Such was the custom of writing the farewell in the epistles. "The church at Babylon," says he, "greets you." I suppose, but am not fully confident, that he here meant Rome, for it has been generally supposed that the epistle was written from Rome. Still, there were two Babylons; one in Chaldea, the other in Egypt, which is now Al Cair. But Rome is not called Babylon, except figuratively; in the sense, as was said before under 1 Peter 4:4, of "excess of rioting" or "disorderly life." Thus *Babel* means in the Hebrew "confusion." So perhaps he has called Rome confusion, or Babel, since in it there was also such disorderly conduct and a confused multitude of all kinds of shameful practices and vices; and whatever in the whole world was scandalous had drifted together there. In this same city, he says, a congregation is gathered of such as are Christians, who greet you. But I will readily leave everyone to hold it as he may, for no importance is attached to it.

v. 13b. *And so doth Mark, my son.*

Some say that he here means Mark, the evangelist, and calls him his son, not literally, but spiritually, as Paul calls Timothy and Titus his sons (1 Tim. 1:2; 2 Tim. 1:2; Titus 1:4). He says to the Corinthians that he has begotten them in Christ (1 Cor. 4:14, 15; 2 Cor. 6:13).

v. 14a. *Salute one another with a kiss of love.*

This custom has now passed away. In the gospel we read distinctly that Christ received his disciples with a kiss (Mat.

26:49), and such was then a practice in those lands. Of this kiss Paul also often speaks (Rom. 16:16; 2 Cor. 13:12).

v. 14b. *Peace be unto you all that are in Christ Jesus.*

That is, those who believe in Christ. This is the *adieu* with which he commits them to God. Thus we have explained this first epistle. God grant his grace, that we may grasp it and keep it. Amen.

INTRODUCTION TO SECOND PETER

The reason Peter wrote this second epistle was that he saw how the true, pure doctrine of faith was being corrupted, obscured and suppressed. He wished to meet two kinds of error that sprang from a false understanding of the doctrine of faith and to guard it on both sides, namely: that we attribute not to our works the power to justify us and make us acceptable to God, which belongs to faith alone; and in the second place, that no one should think that faith exists without being accompanied by good works. For if we preach concerning faith that it justifies and makes us righteous without any assistance of our good efforts, the people reply: Then we need do no good works, as is seen in our daily experience. But if we emphasize good works and extol them, then faith is laid aside and neglected, so that in this it is very difficult to keep the golden mean where the preachers are not true and faithful.

Now we have constantly taught that all is to be ascribed to faith, that it alone justifies us before God and sanctifies us. Consequently, if faith be present, from it good works will and must proceed; since it is impossible that we should go through this life entirely idle and should do nothing at all.

This is what Peter will teach also in this epistle and meet those who may have perhaps wrongly understood the first epistle, that faith would be sufficient even if they did no good works. And against this especially the first chapter is directed, that believers should prove themselves by their good works and thus become assured of their faith.

The second chapter is against those who immediately commence with good works and suppress faith. Therefore he warns against the future false teachers, who would root out and utterly exterminate the true faith by human doctrines. For he evidently saw what a horrible falling away there would yet be in the world; as it had already at that time commenced, as Paul said in 2 Thessalonians 2:7: "For the mystery of lawlessness doth already work." Thus this epistle was written for a warning that we prove our faith by our good works and yet, that we do not trust in our good works.

THE SECOND EPISTLE OF PETER

2 Peter 1

Peter's Greeting. A Description, an Exhortation, a Consolation and an Instruction.

Outline

I. The Greeting of Peter, vv. 1-2.
   A. He who gives the greeting, v. 1a.
   B. Those who are greeted, v. 1b.
   C. The greeting itself, v. 2. What it is to know God. Faith should manifest itself in good works.

II. The Description, vv. 3-4.
   A. The power which believers received.
      1. The nature of this power, v. 3a.
      2. The way and means by which believers receive this power, v. 3b.
   B. The promise which is given to believers, v. 4.
      1. This promise in general.
      2. This promise in particular.

III. The Exhortation, vv. 5-9.
   A. The exhortation itself.
      1. The first part of this exhortation, v. 5a.
      2. The second part, v. 5b.
      3. The third part, v. 6a.
      4. The fourth part, v. 6b.
      5. The fifth part, v. 6c.
      6. The sixth part, v. 7a.
      7. The seventh part, v. 7b.
   B. The reason of this exhortation, v. 8.
      1. The first reason, v. 8a.
      2. The second reason, v. 9. Good works should follow faith.

IV. The Consolation, vv. 10-11.
   A. Its nature. The more a Christian exercises his spiritual

power, the stronger it becomes. In what way should we
treat the foreknowledge of God?

B. The reason and cause of this consolation, vv. 10b-11.

V. The Instruction, vv. 12-21.

    A. What moved Peter to give this instruction, vv. 12-15.

    B. The instruction itself, vv. 16-21.

        1. The first part of this instruction, vv. 16-18.

           a. Its sense and meaning.

           b. Its use.

           c. An objection, that may here be raised, and the
answer.

        2. The second part of this instruction, v. 19.

           a. Its sense and meaning.

           b. An objection, that may be raised here, and its
answer.

           c. How this part of the instruction is to be used
against human doctrines.

        3. The third part of this instruction, vv. 20-21.

           a. Its sense and meaning.

           b. Its use. A short review of the matter discussed.

I. The Greeting of Peter (vv. 1-2)

v. 1. *Simon Peter, a servant and apostle of Jesus Christ, to them that
have obtained a like precious faith with us in the righteousness [God
gives] of our God and the Savior Jesus Christ.*

In these words we have the subscription and the superscription of this epistle in order that we may know who wrote
it and to whom it was written, namely, to those who have
heard God's Word and live in faith. But what kind of faith is
it? Peter said, "In the righteousness of God," the righteousness that God gives. Here he gives the righteousness of faith
alone, as Paul also said in Romans 1:17: "In the Gospel is
revealed a righteousness that avails before God, which springs
from faith;" as it is written in Habakkuk 2:4, "The righteous
shall live by his faith." By these words Peter wishes to admonish them to be thoroughly armed and not to let the doctrine of faith be overthrown, which they have laid hold of and
thoroughly understand.

And moreover in that he added, "in the righteousness, which
God gives," he excludes all human righteousness. For through

faith alone we are justified before God; and therefore faith is called the God-righteousness, for it avails nothing before the world, yea, it is even condemned by the world.

v. 2. Grace to you and peace be multiplied in the knowledge of God and of Jesus our Lord.

This is the greeting that in former times it was the custom to insert at the beginning of letters, and it has this significant meaning: Instead of my presence and service I wish that you would increase in grace and peace and grow richer and richer, which grace springs from the knowledge of God and of our Lord Jesus Christ; or in other words, which grace no one can have except he has the knowledge of God and of Jesus Christ.

This knowledge of God the apostles and also the prophets are continually setting forth in the Scriptures, as in Isaiah 11:9, "They shall not hurt nor destroy in all my holy mountain; for the earth shall be full of the knowledge of Jehovah, as the waters cover the deep." That is, so abundantly will the knowledge of God break forth, as when the waters overflow, gush forth and flood a whole country; and from this such peace will follow that no one will then cause another any injury or suffering. But that is not called knowing God, when you believe as the Turks, the Jews, and the devil believe, that God created all things; also even, that Christ was born of a virgin, suffered, died, and rose again. The true knowledge is when you instead hold and know that God is your God and Christ is your Christ; which Satan and false Christians cannot believe. Thus this knowledge is nothing more nor less than the true Christian faith. For if you know God and Christ thus, then you will also trust in Him with your whole heart, and confide in him in fortune and misfortune, in life and death. Such confidence evil consciences cannot have, for they know not God beyond that he is the God of Peter and of all the saints in heaven; but as their own personal God they know him not. Instead, they consider Him to be their taskmaster and their angry judge.

To have God is to have all grace, all mercy, and everything that can be called good. To possess Christ is to possess the

Savior and Mediator who has brought us even to the truth, that God is ours and has obtained all grace for us with God. Thus you must twist into one another that Christ is thine and thou art Christ's, and then you will have this true knowledge. A woman unmarried may indeed say that is a man, but she cannot say that he is her man or husband. Just so we all can truly say that this is a God, but we all cannot say that he is our God. For we are not all trusting in him nor are we all confronted by him. To this knowledge belongs also what the Scriptures call *faciem et vultum Domini*, "the face and countenance of the Lord," of which the prophets often speak. Whoever does not see the face of God, knows him not, but sees only his back, that is, he sees an angry and ungracious God (compare Jer. 18:17).

And thus you see that the aim of Peter here is not to write especially of faith, since he has done that sufficiently in his first epistle; but he will give the believers an admonition, that they are to show forth their faith by their good works. For he will not have faith without its good works, nor on the contrary good works without their accompanying faith; but first of all faith and then the good works to follow upon and spring from the faith. Therefore the apostle now adds:

II.   The Description (vv. 3-4)

v. 3a. *Seeing that his divine power hath granted unto us all things that pertain unto life and godliness.*

This is the first of the blessings Peter has commenced to describe, which we have received of God through faith, namely, that to us (seeing we know God by faith) is given "all divine power." But what kind of power is that? It is the power that serves us in securing eternal life and in godly living here that is, if we believe, we then gain so much that God himself does it. He is in us strong, powerful, almighty, even if we are about to suffer and die, and are weak in the eyes of the world. There is no power nor virtue in ourselves if we have not this God-power.

But this power of God that is in us, Peter will not have so understood, that we also can create heaven and earth, and do miracles like God did; for how could we be helped by that? But we have God's power at our disposal in so far as it is useful and necessary for us. Therefore the apostle inserts and says, "All things that pertain unto life and godliness," that is, we have such power of God that we are favored with an overflow of his grace, to do good and to live forever.

v. 3b. *Through the knowledge of him that called us.*

Such power of God and such rich grace come from no other source than from this knowledge of God. For if thou dost hold him to be God, then he will also deal with you as God. The same is taught by Paul in 1 Corinthians 1:5-7: "In everything ye were enriched in him, in all utterance and all knowledge; even as the testimony of Christ was confirmed in you; so that ye come behind in no gift." This is now the greatest thing of all, the noblest and the most needful that God can bestow, in exchange for which we would not take all that is in heaven and upon earth. For what would it benefit you, if you could go even through fire and water and do all kinds of wonderful works, and you had not this power of God? And yet many people who do such wonderful deeds shall be condemned. But it is the wonder of wonders that God bestows upon us such power by which all our sins are forgiven and blotted out, and death, Satan, and hell vanquished and swallowed up; so that we have an unharassed conscience and a happy heart, and we fear nothing.

v. 3c. *By his own glory and virtue.*

How then did that all take place, through which we are called by God? Thus: God permitted his holy Gospel to go forth in to the world and to be made known. Consequently, no human being had ever before labored to secure it, or sought after it or prayed for it. But before man ever thought of it, God offered, bestowed, and shed forth such grace richly beyond all measure, so that he alone has the glory and the praise for it, and we ascribe the virtue and the power to him alone, for it is not our work but his alone. Therefore, seeing the calling is not of us, we should not exalt ourselves as if we did it, but praise and thank him, because he gave us the Gospel and in it bestowed upon us power and might against Satan, death, and all evil.

v. 4a. *Whereby he hath granted unto us his precious and exceeding great promises.*

Peter inserts this clause for the purpose of explaining the nature and character of faith. If we know him as God, then we have through faith eternal life and divine power to triumph over death and Satan, but we see it not and we grasp it not, though it is promised to us. We indeed have it all, though it does not yet appear; but at the day of judgment we shall see it present before our eyes. Here it begins in faith, though we have it not in its fullness; but we have the promise that we shall live here in the power of God and then be saved forever. Whoever now believes this, has the promise; whoever does not believe it, has it not, and must be forever lost. How great and precious this now is, Peter paints more fully and says:

v. 4b. *That through these ye may become partakers of the divine nature, having escaped from the corruption that is in the world by lust.*

This we have, Peter says, through the power of faith, namely, that we are partakers of and enjoy the fellowship and communion with the divine nature. This is a passage the like of which is not found in the New and Old Testaments; although it is a small matter with unbelievers that we should have fellowship with the very divine nature itself. But what is the nature of God? It is eternal righteousness, wisdom, eternal life, peace, joy, and happiness, and everything good that can be named. Now whoever becomes a partaker of the nature of God receives all this, namely, he lives forever, possesses endless peace, pleasure and joy, and is sincere, pure, just and almighty against Satan, sin and death. Therefore Peter will say: As impossible as it is to separate eternal life and eternal truth from the nature of God, just so impossible is it to separate them from you. Whatever one does to you, he must do to him, for whoever will crush a Christian must crush God.

All this is contained in the words, "the divine nature"; and Peter chose these words for the purpose to include all in them; and it is truly a great thing if one believes it. But, as I said above, this is merely instruction in which Peter does not lay the foundation of faith; but paints forth what great and rich treasures we receive through faith; therefore he says, all that will you possess, if you so live as to prove your faith by your life, that you have escaped from worldly lust.

III.   The Exhortation (vv. 5-9)

v. 5a. *Yea, and for this very cause adding on your part all diligence, in your faith supply virtue.*

Here Peter now considers the admonition that they should prove their faith by their good works, seeing such great blessings are bestowed upon you through faith. He would say that you truly have all that God is, do this now besides; be diligent, and not sluggish; "in your faith supply virtue;" that is, let your faith break out before the people, that it may be zealous to serve, busy, powerful, active, and accomplish much; do not continue idle and unfruitful. You have a good inheritance and a good field, but take heed and let not the thistles and tares grow in it.

v. 5b. *And in your virtue knowledge [discrimination].*

This *knowledge* or *discrimination* means in the first place that one should direct his outward life and the virtue of his faith in harmony with reason. For we should subdue and tame the body so far that we may remain sober, vigorous, and prepared to do good; not that we are to torture and mortify ourselves as some whimsical saints have done. For although God is likewise an enemy to the sins remaining in the flesh, yet he does not wish that you should therefore destroy the body; you should guard against its viciousness and caprice, yet you are not for that reason to ruin or injure it; but give it food and whatever it needs that it may remain healthy and lively.

In the second place discrimination means also that we lead a beautiful and modest manner of life and act with discretion in external matters, as in food and things of that kind; and that we be not in these matters unreasonable, nor offend our neighbor.

v. 6a. *And in your knowledge, self-control [temperance].*

Temperance does not apply only to eating and drinking, but it means moderation in all our being and in all our doing, in our words, works, and manners, that we live not too expensively and avoid excess in ornaments and clothing, that we break not forth too proudly and make too lofty a show. But here Peter will not fix any rule, measure, or mark, as the orders were bold enough to do, who wished to apprehend everything by rules and framed commands and rules on these things, which had to be rigidly observed in every detail. It is something that cannot be tolerated in Christendom, that men should require by law that there be a common rule or command relating to self-control or temperance; for people are unlike one another, one being of a strong, another a weak nature; and no one is in all things and at all times situated like another. Therefore each person should study himself, how he is disposed and situated, and what he can bear.

v. 6b. *And in your self-control patience.*

Thus Peter would say: If you lead a temperate and discreet life, you should not imagine that it will be without conflict and temptation. For if you believe and lead a good Christian life, the world will not let you alone, it will have to persecute and hate you; and in this you must show patience, which is a fruit of faith.

v. 6c. *And in your patience, godliness.*

The sense here is that in all our outward life, whatever we do or suffer, we should so deport ourselves so that we serve God in it, and seek not our own honor and gain. Thereby God alone may be glorified; and others may take knowledge that we do all for God's sake.

v. 7a. *And in your godliness brotherly kindness.*

By these words Peter puts us all under obligation to extend to one another a helping hand, like brethren, and one to protect the other, and none to hate or despise or injure another. This is also a proof of faith, by which we show that we possess the godliness of which he has spoken.

v. 7b. *And in your brotherly kindness, love [charity].*

This love extends to both friend and enemy, even to those who do not show themselves friendly and brotherly to us. Thus Peter has here comprehended in few words whatever pertains to the Christian life, and whatever are the works and fruits of faith, as discretion, temperance, patience, a God-fearing life, and brotherly love; and be kind to everybody.

v. 8. *For if these things are yours and abound, they make you to be not idle nor unfruitful unto the knowledge of our Lord Jesus Christ.*

That is, if you do such works then you are on the right way, then you possess true faith, and the knowledge of God is active and fruitful in you. Therefore take heed that you do not neglect this knowledge; control your body, and do to your neighbor even as you know Christ did to you.

v. 9. *For he that lacketh these things is blind, seeing only what is near, having forgotten the cleansing from his old sins.*

Whoever has not this supply of the fruits of faith, gropes like a blind man here and there. He leads such a life that he knows not what his real state is. He has no true faith, and of the knowledge of Christ has nothing more than that he can say how he has heard it. Hence he goes along and gropes like a blind man on the road, in an unconscious life, and forgets that he was baptized and his sins were forgiven, is unthankful, and is an idle, negligent man, who takes nothing to heart, and neither feels nor tastes such great grace and blessing.

This is the admonition which Peter gives to us who believe, to agitate and perform those works by which we shall in this one conviction, namely, that faith alone justifies. Where this then is present, there works must follow. The next verses aim to strengthen our faith.

IV.   The Consolation (vv. 10-11)

v. 10a. *Wherefore, brethren, give the more diligence to make your calling and election sure.*

The election and eternal foreknowledge of God in themselves are indeed sufficiently settled and man does not need to make them more so. The calling is also effectual and certain. For whoever hears the Gospel, believes it, and is baptized, is called and saved. Since we then are also now thereunto called, we should apply great diligence, says Peter, that our calling and election may be assured with us also, and not only with God.

This is now a mode of scriptural expression that Paul also uses in Ephesians 2:12, "Ye were strangers from the covenants of the promise, having no hope and without God in the world." For although there is no man, neither bad nor good, over whom God does not reign, since all creatures are his, yet Paul says he has no God who does not know, love, and trust God, although he has his being in God himself. So here, although the calling and election are effectual enough in themselves, yet with you it is not yet effectual and assured, since you are not yet certain that it includes you. Therefore Peter desires that we make our calling and election sure by good works.

Thus you see what the apostle attributes to the fruits of faith. Although they are due to our neighbor, that he may be benefited by them, still the fruit is not to be wanting, that faith may thereby become stronger, and ever do more and more good works. Besides, this is quite another kind of power than that of the body, for that grows weary and wastes away if one member of the body is used and exercised too much; but as to this spiritual power, the more it is used and worked the stronger it becomes; and it suffers injury if it be not exercised. For this reason God introduced Christianity at first in the manner he did, driven and tried by the wrestling of faith, in shame, death, and bloodshed, that it might become truly strong and mighty, and the more it was oppressed the more it prospered. This now is Peter's meaning that we should not let faith rest and lie still, since it is ordained that it ever becomes stronger and stronger by trial and exercise, until it is assured of its calling and election. It cannot fail.

Here a limitation is set as to how we should treat the foreknowledge of God. There are many lightminded persons who have felt but little of the power of faith, who when they meet this subject stumble, take offense and, worry themselves at first with it, and would satisfy themselves by their own reason as to whether they are elected, so that they may be assured where they stand. But desist from this quickly; it is something that cannot be grasped by the mind. However, if you will become assured, then the only way is that marked out for you here by Peter. If you choose another way for yourself, then you have failed already, and your own experience must teach you. If faith be well exercised and tried, then you will finally be assured of the fact, so that you cannot fail, as now further follows:

v. 10b. *For if ye do these things, ye shall never stumble.*

That is, ye are to stand immovable, not stumble nor sin; but succeed in all difficulties and ever prosper, and everything will adjust itself aright. On the other hand, if you wish to adjust matters with your own reason, the devil will soon hurl you into despair and hatred of God.

v. 11. *For thus shall be richly supplied unto you the entrance into the eternal kingdom of our Lord and Savior Jesus Christ.*

This is the road on which we enter the kingdom of heaven. Therefore no one should propose to enter by the dreams and thoughts of faith he has invented in his own heart. We must have a living, well-disciplined, and approved faith. God help us! How have our deceivers written, taught, and spoken against this text. Yet whoever has even the least measure or only a spark of faith, shall be saved when he comes to die. If you however put off believing and in this way think to attain such faith quickly and suddenly, you will then have waited too long. Yet you are to understand well, that they who are strong have enough to do, although we are not to despair even of such as are weak. For it may indeed easily happen that they shall endure to the end, yet it will be difficult and hard, and will cause much worry. But whoever carefully sees to it in his life that his faith be exercised and strengthened by good works, he shall have an abundant entrance. With a calm spirit and confidence, he will enter upon the future life, so that he will die comfortably, despise this life, and go on, even triumphantly, and with gladness be ushered into the eternal kingdom. But those who take another road shall not enter thus with joy: The door shall not stand open to them so wide; moreover, an entrance shall not be supplied so richly unto them. But it shall be narrow and hard for them, so that they tremble, and would rather their whole life should be spent in weakness than that they should die even once.

V.   The Instruction (vv. 12-21)

v. 12. *Wherefore I shall be ready always to put you in remembrance of these things, though ye know them, and are established in the truth which is with you.*

That is the same as we have often said. Although God has now let such a great light go forth by the revelation of the Gospel, so that we know what true Christian life and doctrine are, and so that we see how all Scripture insists upon it, yet this light we are not to neglect. We are to use it daily, not for the sake of doctrine, but for the sake of putting us in remembrance. For there is a twofold office in the Christian church, as Paul says in Romans 12:7-8: "He that teacheth, let him give himself to his teaching; or he that exhorteth, let him give himself to his exhortation." "To teach," is to set forth the fundamental principles of faith to those who have no knowledge of faith. But to "exhort," or as Peter says, "to remind," is to preach to those who know and have heard the doctrine already, so that they are seized by it and awakened, in order that they should not be heedless, but go forward and grow. We are all overburdened with the old sluggard load, with our flesh and blood that ever chooses the byroads and keeps us ever subject to its load, so that the soul easily falls asleep. Therefore we are continually to urge and shake it, as a master urges his servants, lest they become sluggish, although they know very well what they should do. For since we must pursue this course for the sake of our temporal support, far more must we do it here in spiritual matters.

v. 13. *And I think it right, as long as I am in this tabernacle, to stir you up by putting you in remembrance.*

Here Peter calls his body a tabernacle wherein the soul dwells. It is a phrase like that in 1 Peter 3:7, where he speaks of the body as a vessel or an instrument. So Paul also speaks in 2 Corinthians 5:1-2: "For we know that if the earthly house of our tabernacle be dissolved, we have a building from God, a house not made with hands, eternal in the heavens. For verily in this we groan, longing to be clothed upon with our habitation which is from heaven." "For indeed we that are in this tabernacle do groan" (v. 4). There the apostle Paul speaks also of the body as a house, and makes two homes, and two sojournings. So Peter speaks here of the body as a tabernacle wherein the soul rests, and he makes it mean enough. He will not call it a house, but a hut or tent-house, such as shepherds occupy. Great is the treasure, but small is the house in which it lies and dwells.

vv. 14-15. *Knowing that the putting off of my tabernacle cometh swiftly, even as our Lord Jesus Christ signified unto me. Yea, I will give diligence that at every time ye may be able after my decease to call these things to remembrance.*

Here Peter testifies of himself that he has become assured

of eternal life, and to him God revealed beforehand when he should die. But this took place for our sake and for the sake of our faith. There must have been some such persons as knew assuredly that they were elected, who should found and establish faith, that we might know that they preached not the doctrine of men, but the Word of God. But before they came to such assurance, God thoroughly proved them and purified them. Thus Peter now says: I will not only remind you with the living voice, but set such things also in writing, and charge you through others, that ye ever hold them in remembrance during my life and after my death, and not let them slip. Notice here how great anxiety the apostle had for souls. But, alas! It did not help any.

vv. 16-18. *For we did not follow cunningly devised fables, when we made known unto you the power and coming of our Lord Jesus Christ, but we were eyewitnesses of his majesty. For he received from God the Father honor and glory, when there was born such a voice to him by the Majestic Glory, This is my beloved Son, in whom I am well pleased: and this voice we ourselves heard borne out of heaven, when we were with him in the holy mount.*

There Peter refers to the history written in Matthew 17:1-13. Then Jesus took to himself three of his disciples, Peter, James, and John, and led them up into a high mountain. He was glorified or transfigured before them, his face did shine as the sun, and his garments become white as the light. There appeared unto them Moses and Elijah talking with him, while a bright cloud overshadowed them, and a voice out of the cloud said, "This is my beloved son, in whom I am well pleased; hear ye him." When the disciples heard it, they fell on their face and were sore afraid. And Jesus came to them and touched them and said, "Arise, and be not afraid. And lifting up their eyes, they saw no one save Jesus only. And as they were coming down from the mountain, Jesus commanded them, saying, Tell the vision to no man, until the Son of Man be risen from the dead" (vv. 7-9).

So Peter would now say: That which I preach to you of Christ and of his coming—this Gospel that we preach—we have not drawn it from our fingers nor devised it ourselves nor taken it from cunning writers of fables, who know how to speak brilliantly of everything (such as at that very time the Greeks were). For it is mere fable and fancy and idle babbling that they cunningly give forth, and in which they would be wise. Such we have not heard, nor have we followed them. That is, we preach not the nonsense of men, but we are sure that what we preach is of God and has become so through our eyes and ears. That is to say, When we were with Christ upon the mountain, we saw and heard his glory. For his glory was that his face did shine as the sun and his garments became white as snow. Besides we heard a voice from the highest Majesty: "This is my beloved Son; hear ye him."

So confident now should every preacher be, and not doubt, that he possesses and preaches God's Word, that he could even die for it, since it is worth life to us. Now there is no man so holy that he needs to die for the doctrine he has taught concerning himself. Therefore one concludes from this that the apostles had assurance from God that their Gospel was God's Word. And here it is also proved that the Gospel is nothing else than the preaching of Christ. Therefore we should hear no other preaching, for none other pleases the Father. "This is my beloved Son," he says; "hear ye him," he is your Doctor or Teacher; as though he had said: When ye hear him, then ye have heard me. Therefore Peter now says: We have preached Christ and made him known to you—that he is Lord and rules over all things and all power is his. And whosoever believes on him has likewise his power. Such things we ourselves have not devised, but we have seen and heard them through God's revelation, who has charged us that we should hear Christ.

But why does Paul separate from one another the power and the coming or presence of Christ? The power consists, as we have heard above in verse three in that he is mighty over all things; that all must lie at his feet; and that this shall continue as long as the world stands. While we are flesh and blood, and live upon the earth, so long shall Christ's kingdom flourish, even to the day of judgment. Then shall come another period, when he shall give up the kingdom to God the

Father, of which Paul speaks in 1 Corinthians 15:23-24: "Christ the first fruits; then they that are Christ's, at his coming. Then cometh the end, when he shall deliver up the kingdom to God, even the Father." In verse 28 he says, "And when all things have been subjected unto him, then shall the Son also himself be subjected to him that did subject all things unto him."

How is then the kingdom not God the Father's now? Is not all subject to him? Answer: Paul explains himself in verse 28, and says: "That God may be all in all." That is, whatever anyone shall need or should have, that God will be; as Peter has told us above, in verse 4, that we should be partakers of the divine nature. Therefore we shall have all that God has, and all that is needful for us we shall have in him. This includes wisdom, righteousness, strength, and life. This is a truth that we now believe and grasp merely with the ear and possess in the Word of God. But then shall the Word cease, when our souls shall be enlarged and we shall indeed see and feel all as a present reality.

Both Paul and Peter teach that the power of Christ's kingdom is now in motion. Now he rules by means of his Word made flesh, and thereby through his humanity he reigns over the devil, sin, death, and all things. But at the last day this shall be made clear. Therefore, although God ever rules, still it is not yet manifest to us. He clearly beholds us, but we behold him not. Consequently Christ must deliver up to the Father the kingdom, so that we also shall see it, and then we shall be Christ's brethren and God's children. Thus Christ received from God honor and glory, Peter here says, when the Father made all things subject to him, and made him Lord, and glorified him by this voice, in which he says, "This is my beloved Son, in whom I am well pleased" (Matt. 17:5).

By this Peter would confirm his doctrine and preaching, that it might be known whence he received his doctrine. But nothing more happened to him than that he had heard this and was enabled to preach it. But the Holy Spirit had also to come and strengthen him, that he might believe in it, and preach and confess it cheerfully. The former belongs only to the office of the preacher, not to the soul; but the latter belongs to the Spirit.

v. 19. *And we have the word of prophecy made more sure; whereunto ye do well that ye take heed, as unto a lamp shining in a dark place, until the day dawn, and the day-star arise in your hearts.*

Here Peter grasps right hold of his theme and would say at least this much: All that I preach is to subserve the end, that your conscience may be assured, and your heart may stand firm in this teaching, and not let itself be torn from its faith. Thus both you and I may be certain that we have God's Word. For it is an important matter as respects the Gospel that we should receive and hold it in its integrity and purity, without addition and without false doctrine. Therefore Peter begins henceforth to write against human doctrines.

But why does he say: "We have a sure word of prophecy?" Answer: I hold indeed that we will have no more prophets, such as the Jews had in former times under the Old Testament. But a prophet eminently should he be who preaches Jesus Christ. Therefore, although many prophets in the Old Testament have foretold things to come, yet they came and were sent by God for this reason especially: that they should foretell of Christ. Those then who believe on Christ are all prophets, for they have the true central article of faith that the prophets had, although they have not the gift to foretell things to come; f. For just as we, through the faith of our Master, are Christ's brethren, and are kings and priests, so are we all through Christ also prophets. For we can all decide as to what belongs to salvation and God's honor and to a Christian life. Besides, we know as much of future things as is necessary for us to know. We know that the day of judgment shall come and that we shall rise from the dead. Besides, we understand the whole Scriptures. Of this Paul also speaks in 1 Corinthians 14:31: "Ye can all prophesy, one by one."

This now is what Peter says: We have such a word of prophecy as is sure in itself; see to it only that it be sure to you; "whereunto ye do well that ye take heed." As though he should say: It will be necessary for you to hold firmly to it. For it was given even to the end to serve the Gospel. It is as though one were imprisoned in a house in the midst of the night, when it was pitch-dark, and it was necessary that one should kindle a light till the day came when he could see.

Eminently such is the Gospel in the midst of the night and the darkness. For all human reason is mere error and blindness, while the world is even nothing else but a kingdom of darkness. In this darkness has God now kindled a light, even the Gospel, whereby we may see and walk, while we are on the earth, till the morning dawns and the day breaks.

Thus this text also strongly opposes all human doctrine; for since the Word of God is the light in a dark and gloomy place, the conclusion follows that all besides it is darkness. For if there were another light besides the Word, Peter would not have spoken as he did. Therefore look not to how gifted with reason they are who teach any other doctrine—however grandly they set it forth. If you cannot trace God's Word in it, then doubt not that it is mere darkness. And let it not disturb you at all that they say they have the Holy Spirit. How can they have God's Spirit if they do not have his Word? Wherefore they do nothing else but call darkness light and make the light darkness, as the prophet Isaiah says, in Isaiah 5:20.

This is God's Word, even the Gospel; that we are ransomed by Christ from death, sin, and hell: Whoever hears that, has this light and has kindled this lamp in his heart, even that by which we may see the one that enlightens us, and teaches us whatever we need to know. But where this is not, there we rush on, and by principles and works of our own device would find out the way to heaven. Of this you can judge and see by your light, that it is darkness. Therefore since they have not the light, neither wish to receive it, they must remain in darkness and blindness. For that light teaches us all we ought to know and all that is necessary to salvation, a thing which the world by its wisdom and reason knows not. And this light we must still have and depend upon, even to the day of judgment. Then shall we have no more need of the Word, just as we put out the lamp when the day breaks.

vv. 20-21. *Knowing this first, that no prophecy of Scripture is of private interpretation. For no prophecy ever came by the will of man: but men spake from God, being moved by the Holy Spirit.*

Here Peter takes up the subject of false doctrine. Since ye know, he says, that we have the Word of God, abide in the same and suffer yourselves never to be drawn from it by others who teach falsely, though they come and affirm that they have the Holy Spirit. For ye should know first of all, the second matter he will speak of later, that no prophecy of Scripture is of any private interpretation. By this be directed, and do not think to explain the Scripture by your own reason and wisdom.

In this, the private interpretation of Scripture by all the fathers is overthrown and rejected, and it is forbidden to build upon such interpretations. Though Jerome, or Augustine, or any one of the fathers has explained it of himself, yet we will not have it from him. Peter has forbidden you to explain it by your own reason. The Holy Spirit will explain it himself, or it shall remain unexplained. If now any one of the holy fathers can prove that he draws his explanation from the Scriptures, which prove that it should be so explained, then it is right. Where this is not the case, I for one shall not believe him.

Thus Peter lays hold on the boldest and best teachers; therefore, we should rest assured that none is to be believed who expounds the Scriptures by interpreting and explaining them with his own powers. For the true sense cannot be obtained by private interpretation. Here have all the teachers and fathers who have explained the Scriptures stumbled, so far as they are extant to us. For instance, when they refer the passage of Christ in Matthew 16:18: "Thou art Peter, and on this rock will I build my church," to the pope; that is a human, self-invented explanation. Therefore no one is to believe them. For they cannot prove out of the Scriptures that Peter is ever spoken of as pope. But we can prove that the rock is Christ and faith, as Paul says. This explanation is the right one; for of this we are sure, it has not been invented by men, but drawn from God's Word. Now what is found written and foretold in the prophets says Peter, that men have not discovered nor invented; but holy and pious men have spoken it from the Holy Spirit.

This is now the first chapter in which Peter has taught us what good works really are, whereby we are to give proof of our faith. In the second place, he has taught that in Christendom nothing should be preached but God's Word alone. The

reason why it should be so is no other, as we have said, than
that men should preach the Word that shall remain forever,
whereby souls may be saved and live forever. Now there follows a faithful admonition, which Christ and Paul and all the
apostles have also given, that each should look out for himself
and guard against false teachers. It is especially necessary for
us to observe it carefully, so that we may not suffer that right
and authority which all Christians have to be torn from us;
that is, to judge and decide on all doctrines; and that we may
not let it come so far as to wait till the Councils determine
what we are to believe, and then follow that. This we wish
now to consider.

A Picture of False Teachers in Their Sins, and the Punishment Connected With Those Sins.

Outline

I. This Picture in General, v. 1a.
  A. The aim of this picture.
  B. How this picture is little esteemed in the papacy.
  C. How this picture is found here and there in the Holy Scriptures. Of the high schools of the papists and their teachers.

II. This Picture in Particular, v. 1b-22.
  A. The first part of this picture, where we find:
    1. The sins of the false teachers.
      a. The first sin, v. 1b.
      b. The second sin, v. 1c.
    2. The punishment, v. 1d.
  B. The second part of this picture, where we find:
    1. The sins of the false teachers.
      a. The first sin, v. 2a.
      b. The second sin, v. 2b.
      c. The third sin, v. 3a.
    2. The punishment.
      a. Its nature, v. 3b.
      b. Its certainty, which becomes clear.
        (1) From the punishment that came upon the angels, v.4.
        (2) From the punishment that came upon the antediluvian world, v. 5.
        (3) From the punishment visited upon Sodom and Gomorrah, v. 6.
      c. Like punishment will be visited upon the institutions of the papacy, vv. 6-7.
      d. The righteousness of this punishment, vv. 9-10.
  C. The third part of this picture, where we find:
    1. The sins.
      a. The first sin, v. 9.

        b. The second sin, vv. 10-11.
        c. The third sin, v. 12.
    2. The punishment, vv. 12-13.
  D. The fourth part of this picture, to which belong:
    1. The sins.
        a. The first sin, v. 13b.
        b. The second sin, v. 13c.
        c. The third sin, v. 13d.
        d. The fourth sin, v. 14a.
        e. The fifth sin, v. 14b.
        f. The sixth sin, v. 14c.
        g. The seventh sin, v. 14d.
    2. The punishment, v. 14e.
  E. The fifth part of this picture, where we find:
    1. The sins.
        a. The first sin, v. 15a.
        b. The second sin, v. 15b-16.
        c. The third sin, v. 17a.
    2. The punishment, v. 17b.
  F. The sixth part of this punishment, where we find:
    1. The sins.
        a. The first sin, v. 18a.
        b. The second sin, v. 18b.
        c. The third sin, v. 19.
    2. The punishment, vv. 20-22.
  G. The conclusion.

I.   The Picture in General (v. 1a)

v. 1a. *But there arose false prophets also among the people, as among you also there shall be false teachers.*

This is what Peter would say: All prophecy must proceed from the Holy Spirit, even to the end of the world, just as it has gone forth from the beginning of the world, so that nothing shall be preached but God's Word. Yet it has ever so happened that close upon the true prophets and the Word of God there have been false teachers, and so also it shall continue. Therefore, since ye have God's Word, ye should take heed to yourselves that ye do not have in addition also false teachers. This is sufficient admonition, and it cannot fail—where the Word of God is preached in its purity—that close upon it false teachers also should arise. The reason is that not everyone lays hold of the Word and believes it, although it is preached to all. They who believe it follow it and hold fast to it, but the greater part—they who do not believe—receive a false understanding of it. Therefore they become false teachers.

We have not seriously considered, nor have we attended to, this warning. Instead, we have gone astray, and whatever has been preached we have done. There we have stumbled and fallen and been led away by delusions, as though the pope, with his priests and monks, could not err. Thus those that should have been on their guard against such things have been the first to urge them upon us. So we are not free from blame, though we have a wrong belief and follow false teachers. It will not help us that we have not known, since we were warned beforehand. Besides, God has bidden us that we should each judge what this or that one preaches and give account of it. If we do not, then are we lost. Therefore it concerns everyone's own soul's salvation to know what God's Word is and what false doctrines are.

Such warnings against false teachers are moreover very frequent, here and there, throughout the Scriptures. In Acts 20:29f, Paul gives just such an admonition in his preaching, when he blesses them of Ephesus and bids them his farewell, where he speaks in this manner: "I know that after my departing grievous wolves shall enter in among you, not sparing the flock; and among your own selves shall men arise, speaking things, to draw away the disciples after them." Christ proclaims it also in Matthew 24:23-24: "Then if any man shall say unto you, Lo, here is the Christ, or, Here; believe it not. For there shall arise false Christs and false prophets, and shall show great signs and wonders; so as to lead astray, if possible, even the elect." And again, Paul says in 1 Timothy 4:1: "but the Spirit saith expressly that in later times some shall fall away from the faith, giving heed to seducing spirits and doctrines of demons, through the hypocrisy of men that speak lies...." As forcefully as such admonitions have now gone forth, so careful should we have been; yet they have been of no avail. The admonitions have been kept silent, and thus we have wandered and suffered ourselves to be led astray.

Now let us see who those false teachers may be of whom Peter speaks. I think God ordained by special counsel that our teachers should have been called doctors, that it might be seen whom Peter means. For he as much as uses the word here: false doctors. That is, false teachers, he says, not false prophets or false apostles. In this he hits even the high schools, where this class of men is created, and whence all the preachers have come forth into the world; so that there is not a city under the papacy which does not have such teachers turned out from its high schools. For all the world thinks they are the fountain, the streams of which are to teach the people. This is a desperate error, so that no more cruel thing has ever come upon the earth than has come from the high schools. Therefore Peter says such vain, false teachers are to appear.

II.   The Picture in Particular (vv. 1b-22)

v. 1b. *Who shall privily bring in destructive heresies.*

He calls them destructive heresies, sects, or classes and orders, because whoever is persuaded into them is already lost. These they shall secretly bring in, he says, not that they shall preach that the Gospel and the Holy Scriptures are false, for that would work quite against them. But they still hold the names, God, Christ, faith, church, baptism, and sacrament. But under these names they bring forward and set up something entirely different. For there is a great difference, whether I say a man preaches against this doctrine or privily introduces other ideas along with it. When I preach, for example, that Christ is the Son of God and true man, and whoever believes on him shall be saved, that is right preaching and true Gospel. But if one preaches that Christ is not the Son of God, nor true man, moreover that faith does not save, it is in plain contradiction to it. Of this Peter does not speak, for this is what our high schools, priests, and monks do not attempt. But he speaks of those associate doctrines which they introduce through the true doctrine. As when they speak thus: It is true that Christ is real God and real man; that he died for our sins, and no one can be saved who does not believe him, but that belongs only to the common state of ordinary Christians. We wish however to set up a more complete order, in which men shall vow chastity, poverty, and obedience, as well as fast, endow institutions, etc. Whoever does this shall go full tide up to heaven. Where men now preach and hear such things as that there is nothing better and more saving than virginity and obedience, and that the monk and the priest are in a higher and more perfect calling than the ordinary Christian person, there is nothing said against the pure Christian doctrine directly, nor are faith and baptism denied, nor that Christ is the Savior. But they privately introduce such doctrines along with these as to lead men away from the right path, that they build upon themselves and their works, and hold nothing more in regard to Christ than these words: We believe that Christ is the Son of God, and man; that he died and rose again; that he is the Savior of the world. But they repose no trust and confidence in him, for if they did that they would not rest an hour upon themselves. Thus they have also preached and said among the people: Ye are indeed Christians, but that is not enough. Ye must also do such and such works, build churches and cloisters, found masses and vigils. The great multitude has tumbled into this notion, and thought it is right. This Christendom is divided and separated into as many sects almost as there are states and people.

But men should have preached and taught: Ye are Christians indeed, and just as well as those a hundred miles away, ye have all of you one Christ, one baptism, one faith, one spirit, one Word, one God; so that no work man can do helps to make a Christian. Thus the people would have been held in a common faith. There would be no difference before God, but one would be like another. This unity they have rent asunder, in that they say: You are a Christian, but you must do certain works in order to be saved; and thus they lead us away from faith to works. Therefore Peter says, if we explain it rightly, it amounts to nothing but this: There shall come high schools, doctors, priests, and monks, and all classes of men, who shall bring in ruinous sects and orders, and shall lead the world astray by false doctrines. Such are those whom he means here, for they all hold to the notion that their calling and order save them, and they cause men to build and trust on that notion. For where men do not hold to this view, they carefully keep clear of entering them.

v. 1c. *Denying even the Master that bought them.*

Oh! say they, we do not deny the Lord at all. But if anyone says: Since you are ransomed by Christ, and his blood blots out your sin, what will you blot out by your doings? Then they say: Ah! faith does not do it alone, works must also aid toward it. Thus they confess the Lord Christ indeed with their mouth, but with their hearts they entirely deny him.

See how admirably Peter expresses it: "They deny even the Master that bought them." They should be under him as under a master whose own they are; but now, though they believe indeed that he is a master and has purchased the whole world by his blood, yet they do not believe that they are bought, and that he is their master; and they say: He has indeed bought and ransomed them, but then this is not enough, we must first by our works expiate sin and make satisfaction for it.

But we say, if you yourself take away and blot out your sin, what has Christ then done? You certainly can never make two Christs who take away sin. He should and must be the only one to take away our guilt. If that be true, then I cannot understand how I am myself to cancel my own sin. If I do it, I can neither say nor believe that he takes it away. And that is called denying Christ; for, although they hold Christ to be their master, they deny that he has bought them. They believe indeed that he sits above in heaven and is Lord; but that which is his peculiar office, to take away sin, they do not grant him, but ascribe it to their own works. Thus they leave to him nothing more than the name and title; but his work, his power and his office they appropriate to themselves. Therefore Christ truly said in Matthew 24:5, "Many shall come in my name, saying, I am the Christ; and shall lead many astray." For they are really those who do not say: I am called Christ; but those who say: I am Christ, for they seize to themselves the office that belongs to Christ, thrust him from his throne, and seat themselves in his place. We see before our eyes that it is going thus and no one can deny it. Therefore Peter calls them damnable or destructive heresies, for they all run straight to hell; so that I suppose that among a thousand hardly one is saved.

For whoever among them shall be saved must say at least: My obedience, my chastity, do not save me; my works do not take away my sin. But how many there are who have these views and remain in their condemned state!

v. 1d. *Bringing upon themselves swift destruction.*

That is, their condemnation shall quickly overtake them; although it is plain that God forbears long, yet he will come soon enough. But it does not take place visibly as respects the body, that we should be able to see it with our eyes, but just as Psalm 55:23 says, "They shall not live out half their days"; that is, death shall seize upon them before they themselves expect it, so that they shall say, like Hezekiah in Isaiah 38:10: "I said in the noontide of my days I shall go into the gates of Sheol;" as though they should say: O Lord God, is death already here? For those who do not live in faith are never weary of life. The longer they live, the longer they wish to live. The holier they appear to be, the more terrible will death be to them, especially to those who have scrupulous consciences and cruelly urge and vex themselves by works. For it is not possible to vanquish death by human powers; where faith is wanting, the conscience must tremble and despair. Where faith is strong, death delays too long. On the other hand, it comes to the unbelieving always too soon, for there is no end to their thirst and love of life.

Now this is what Peter means here: These people who start such sects and so deny Christ must meet death with the greatest unwillingness, trembling, and despair. For they can have no other thought but this: Who knows whether God will be gracious to me and will forgive my sins? And they remain forever in such doubt: Who knows it—who knows it? And their conscience will never be happy. The longer they thus continue, the more terrible is death to them. For death cannot be subdued before sin and an evil conscience have been taken away. Thus will their condemnation come upon them quickly, and they will have to abide in eternal death.

v. 2a. *And many shall follow their lascivious doings.*

It is now apparent before our eyes that it has come to pass just as Peter years ago declared. There has not been a father or mother who wished not to have a priest, monk, or nun from their children; thus one fool has made another. For when people have seen the misfortune and misery that are found in the marriage state and have not been taught that it is the more blessed state, they wished to do the best for their children—to help them to a happy life and freedom from wretchedness. Therefore Peter has foretold here nothing else than that the world should become full of priests, monks and nuns. Thus the youth, and the best in the world, have run in multitudes to the devil; so that Peter says—alas! only too truly—that many shall follow their lascivious doings.

v. 2b. *By reason of whom the way of truth shall be evil spoken of.*

This also is a fact that is apparent before our eyes. To *blaspheme* is "to libel, condemn and curse;" as when one condemns the Christian life as error and heresy. If one now should preach and say that their course is against the Gospel because they lead men away from faith to works, then they go about and cry: Thou art cursed, thou leadest the world astray; and blaspheme indeed yet more, in perverting what Christ has said, and saying no to it (compare Matt. 5:20f.) This happens when they make nothing but a story out of what Christ has commanded; likewise, that they forbid what Christ would have left free, and make that sin which he does not, besides condemning and burning whoever preaches against them. The way of truth is a well-ordered life and walk, in which there is no fraud nor hypocrisy, such as that faith is in which all Christians walk.

v. 3a. *And in covetousness shall they with feigned words make merchandise of you.*

This is really the way of all false teachers. They preach concerning avarice in order that they may fill their belly; just as we see that not one of them has ever held a mass of vigil gratis. So neither has a monastery or an institution been erected for which sufficient tax or tribute could be levied. There is also not a cloister in the world that serves the world for God's sake. It is all done merely for money. But if anyone really preaches true faith, that does not bring in much money. For then all pilgrimages, indulgences, cloister, and monasteries— to which more than half the wealth of the world has been devoted and given—must cease. From that no one has any benefit except the priests and monks only.

But how do they work it to draw the gold into their own hand? "With feigned words," says Peter, "shall they make merchandise of you." For they have selected words for this very purpose by which to make money of the people. As when they say: If you give the dear Virgin, or this or that saint, so many hundred florins, you do a great and excellent good work, and merit so much indulgence and the forgiveness of sins; and you rescue many souls from purgatory.

These and like words are chosen and devised merely for the purpose to shave us of our money. For in them there is truly no merit and no grace, neither any blotting out of sin. Yet they explain all the noble words of Scripture to the end that they may make annual merchandise with them for money. So also the holy and very gracious sacrament has become nothing more than an annual fair or market. For they use it for nothing more than to smear the people's mouths and flay them of their money. Therefore see now whether Peter has not judged them and painted them according to life:

v. 3b. *Whose sentence now from of old lingereth not.*

They shall not do this long, nor carry it out, he would say; for when they urge it most strongly, their sentence and condemnation shall fall upon themselves. Even now it begins; they shall not escape it, as Paul also says in 2 Timothy 3:9: "Their folly shall be evident to all men," so that they shall be put to shame. God grant that they may be converted and come out from their dangerous state when they hear and understand it. For, though there are some who have not been seduced into this state, yet it is in itself nothing but a mere pernicious sect.

Thus Peter has commenced to describe the shameful, godless life that should follow the genuine doctrines of the Gospel, which the apostles preached. Now he goes further and sets before us three terrible examples; of the fallen angels, of the whole flooded world, and of Sodom. He speaks of how God condemned them.

v. 4. *For if God spared not angels when they sinned, but casted them down to hell, and committed them to pits of darkness, to be reserved unto judgment.*

With these words Peter terrifies those who live so gay and secure as those who cleave to whatever the pope has enacted, being so daring and shameless that they would tread everyone under foot. Therefore he would say this much: Is it not great presumption on their part that they go on so eagerly, and would accomplish everything with their own head, as though God should yield to them, and spare them, who yet spared not the angels? As though he had said: These examples should justly terrify even the saints when they see such a severe sentence. God has not spared those high spirits and noble beings who are far shrewder and wiser than we, but has thrust them into chains of darkness. Such is the severe sentence and condemnation to which he ordained them and in which they are held bound and imprisoned, so that they cannot flee away out of the hands of God. They have been cast into outer darkness, as Christ says in Matthew 25:30; 22:13.

And here Peter also shows that the devils have not yet their final punishment, but still go about in a hardened, desperate state, and look every moment for their judgment. They go about like a man who is condemned to death—perfectly desperate, hardened, and becoming more and more wicked. Their punishment has not yet overtaken them, but they are now only bound and reserved for it. This is the first example. Now follows the second:

v. 5. *And spared not the ancient world, but preserved Noah with seven others, a preacher of righteousness, when he brought a flood upon the world of the ungodly.*

This is also a fearful example, the most horrible one in the Scriptures. One might almost despair in view of it, even if he were strong in faith. For when such language and judgment of God go to a man's heart, and he thinks of it, that so he too shall die. He must tremble and fear if he is not well armed, since among so many in the whole world no one but these eight only were saved. But how did they deserve it, that God by such a severe sentence should have drowned all together in one mass, husband and wife, master and servant, young and old, beast and bird? Because they led such a wicked life. Noah was a pious man and a preacher of righteousness, and he had already lived five hundred years before the flood. Then God commanded him to build an ark, on which he worked a hundred years. All the while he led a uniformly godly life.

Whence you may judge what a cross he had to bear, and in what care and anxiety the pious man stood, when he had to show by words and works that he was a Christian. For it cannot be possible that faith should conceal itself and not break out before men in words and well-doing. So this man was a lonely preacher—perhaps long before God bade him build the ark and spread the word of God not in one place, but doubtless through many lands. Therefore he must have greatly suffered and been severely persecuted, inasmuch as he is specially, as Peter says, sustained and kept by God, or he would soon have been overwhelmed and slain. For he had to bear much envy and hatred and make even many high, wise, and holy people his enemies. But it did not help, for the world despised God's word and continually grew worse.

When they had now carried on their wickedness a long time, Jehovah said, "My Spirit shall not strive with man forever, for that he also is flesh: yet shall his days be a hundred and twenty years" (Gen. 6:3). Also, "I will destroy man whom I have created from the face of the ground; both man and beast; and creeping things . . ." (v. 7). These words he preached and enforced daily, and he began to build the ark as had been commanded him. He labored on it a hundred years. But the people laughed at him and were only so much the more obstinate and hardened. But what the sin was for which God destroyed the world, Genesis 6:2-4 tells us "the sons of God," that is, those born of holy parents and were instructed and brought up in the faith and in the knowledge of God, "saw the daughters of men, that they were fair; and they took them wives of all that they chose; of whom came mighty tyrants." They did everything they chose after their own caprice; therefore God punished the world and destroyed it by the flood.

v. 6. *And turning the cities of Sodom and Gomorrah into ashes condemned them with an overthrow, having made them an example unto those that should live ungodly.*

This is the third example, drawn from the destruction of those five cities in Genesis 19:24-25, of which also the prophet speaks in Ezekiel 16:49, addressing the city of Jerusalem: This was the sin of Sodom thy sister, pride, fulness of bread, luxury, and idleness, and that to the poor they did not extend a helping hand, and have exalted themselves, and have wrought such shameful cruelty before me that I have even destroyed them. For Sodom was a land, like the garden of Jehovah, as Moses says in Genesis 13:10. It was a rich mine of costly oil and wine and all things, so that everyone would think, here dwells God. Therefore they were secure, and they led such a shameful life as Moses describes. Nothing brought this sin upon the people other than the false assurance that they had enough to eat and drink and to spare. And added to this was their idleness. Just as we still see, the richer cities are, the more shamefully do the people in them live; but where there is hunger and grief there the sins are fewer. Therefore God permits his faithful ones to obtain their food with difficulty, so that thereby they continue to be pious.

These are the three fearful examples of which Peter threatens those that are godless. And as he applied it to them, we must hold that this is its importance. And it is spoken especially of the spiritual orders; pope, cardinals, bishops, priests, monks, and nuns, and all who follow them. These are, as it were, angels in the apostles' stead, appointed to this very end, that they should preach and make known God's words. For an angel is a messenger, or one sent, who discharges his message by word of mouth, for which reason preachers are called in Scripture angels, that is, messengers of God. Such angels should our clergy be. But as these angels of old fell from God, set themselves above God, and wished to be their own masters, so these do also. They have nothing but just the name of messengers, as those have the name alone of angels. So these also, as they have fallen from God, shall be held in chains of darkness and reserved to condemnation; as he has said in verse 3, that their sentence does not linger, nor their damnation slumber, although punishment has not as yet overtaken them.

In the second place, they are like the former world, who, although they heard the prophets and the word of God, yet blasphemed and reviled them. As Moses writes in Genesis 6:4, took to themselves wives according to their pleasure, whomsoever they would, and became great and powerful tyrants. Observe then whether all that Moses wrote of them is not now taking place. These are the great scamps that live in revelry, oppress the world by their tyranny, and no one dare reprove them. Whom they will, they take for a wife or daughter, in spite of anyone's complaining. For if anyone finds fault with it they are themselves judges, and there is no one who can win his case with them. Accordingly whatever they can devise to bring into their hands by oppression or fines, that they also execute. And if anyone should tax it, they then say: It is the spiritual possession of the church; it is exempt, and no one dare lay hands on it. And as to those who preach God's Word, they punish them even to death, and declare God's sentence on those that laugh at them. They will not hear the word, and they persecute the very preachers of righteousness. Then remaining great and mighty lords, they retain their title, that they may be called spiritual, like those that are God's children. Yet they rule with full power in all obstinacy; but they must at last be subdued and destroyed. The others who preach God's Word shall be kept and sustained.

Third, as the land where the cities of Sodom and Gomorrah were located was a fertile country, and all had enough of whatever the earth could bear, the people became indolent, glutted themselves with food and drink, and to none of the poor did they reach out the hand. Such is the case also with our spiritual leaders, who possess generally the best land, the best castles and cities, and the greatest drink. Besides, there is not a more indolent class of people on the earth, that lives without any care of labor, and is fed by the sweat of the poor. But what indolence brings with it we see before our eyes. The pope forbids them to take a married wife, so that if they then keep their concubines and have children they must give money to the bishop for every child, whereby they smooth the thing over and cancel the sin. I will not here speak of other secret sins which one dare not indeed name.

The summary is, you see, that Peter does not consider the state of the clergy to be different from that of Sodom and Gomorrah. For they are all characters who are a benefit to no one, they lend no one a helping hand, but seize to themselves all they can under the pretense, affirming that what is given to them is given to God, and they let no one be helped, though he suffer want. Therefore just as those were overthrown and turned to ashes, so shall these also be destroyed at the last day.

v. 7. *And delivered righteous Lot, sore distressed by the lascivious life of the wicked.*

Was it not a great aggravation that they rushed publicly and shamelessly not only into whoredom and adultery, but also into sins that dare not be mentioned, insomuch that they did not even spare the angels who came to Lot? And they rushed on thus in their course, both young and old, in all the corners of the city. Against this, righteous Lot daily preached and warned them. But it was all in vain, except that he is silenced by them, so that he had to cease preaching and he could not help the evil, just as is the case with us at present. For there is now no more hope to reform or help this grievous course of life that the world leads.

v. 8. *For that righteous man dwelling among them, in seeing and hearing, vexed his righteous soul from day to day with their lawless deeds.*

Here Peter describes the cross which this holy man must

have borne while he preached to the people and brought up his daughters in faith; and so with them was saved by God. Now Peter concludes by stating how the godless are reserved for punishment at the day of judgment.

vv. 9-10. *The Lord knoweth how to deliver the godly out of temptation, and to keep the unrighteous under punishment unto the day of judgment; but chiefly them that walk after the flesh in the lust of defilement.*

This is certainly deep passion and earnestness on the part of the apostle. If God spared not, says he, the young, new world, how much more severely and fearfully will he punish now, after that the Gospel has been revealed and preached, and formerly no such great light had gone forth; as Christ also declares this in Matthew 11:23, 24: "Woe to thee, Capernaum, shalt thou be exalted unto heaven? Thou shalt go down unto Hades: for if the mighty works had been done in Sodom which were done in thee, it would have remained until this day. But I say unto you that it shall be more tolerable for the land of Sodom in the day of judgment than for thee." But such threatening is in vain; and the godless do not turn because of it.

"To walk in the lust of defilement" is to live just like an unreasoning beast, according to mere sense and every kind of lust. So everything is ordered by the laws of the Pope, as it has pleased him, and all must subserve their caprice and tyranny; and they have warped and explained all just as they pleased, and moreover said that the holy See at Rome cannot err. And there is not one who has preached anything of faith or love; but they have taught nothing except what they have themselves devised.

vv. 10b-11. *And despise dominion [government]. Daring, self-willed, they tremble not to rail at dignities: whereas angels, though greater in might and power, bring not a railing judgment against them before the Lord.*

Kings, princes, and lords and all civil governments he calls "Dominions." But not the Pope and bishops, for these are not to be lords at all, since Christ in the New Testament instituted only servants, so that one Christian is to serve another, and hold him in honor. Therefore this is Peter's meaning: they should be subject and obedient to the civil government; as the sword is introduced by God's ordinance, stand thou in fear. Yet they do the very reverse of this. They have excepted themselves, and they say they are not subject to the civil government. Yea, they have not only excepted themselves, but have even subjected the civil rulers to themselves and have trampled on them with their feet. They permit themselves shamelessly to be called lords, even by kings and princes, just as the pope writes of himself that he is a lord of heaven and earth, and has in his hand both the civil and spiritual sword, and that everyone must fall at his feet.

Besides, Peter says, "They tremble not to rail at dignities." For it has become to the pope a small and mean thing to put kings and princes under ban, to curse them, and depose them. Also, he excites mischief among them and stirs the princes up one against another. And those who resisted he has quickly overthrown and trodden upon, not because they have done anything against faith or love, but only because they have not been willing to be subject to the See of Rome or kiss the foot of the pope, because his power was as much greater than that of secular princes as the sun is than the moon, or as the heaven is higher than the earth, as they blaspheme and lie; while they themselves are under obligation to be subject and obedient to them, and bless them and pray for them, as Christ our Lord subjected himself to Pilate, and gave to the Emperor the penny tribute. They ought therefore to tremble for railing against the rulers and dignities; yet they are unafraid and presumptuous in regard to it. They revile with all zeal and recklessness, whereas angels, though greater in might and power, bring not a railing judgment against them before the Lord. Yet they are hardened, and blaspheme and curse the very thing from which they cannot escape. How then will these wretched people endure it?

vv. 12-13a. *But these, as creatures without reason, born mere animals to be taken and destroyed, railing in matters whereof they are ignorant, shall in their destroying surely be destroyed, suffering wrong as the hire of wrong-doing.*

Peter identifies them, as though they had within them not a spark of hunger for the Spirit, perform no duties of the spiritual office they should administer, but live like the swine and are drowned in their carnal life.

But in that he says, "they are born mere animals to be taken and destroyed," it may be understood in a two-fold manner: first, as of those that take and destroy, such as the wolf, lion, bear, the sparrow-hawk, and eagle; so these grasp to themselves and tear away from others all they can, goods and honor. Second, of those that shall be taken, crushed, and destroyed at the judgment of the last day.

v. 13b. *Men that count it pleasure to revel in the day-time.*

See how indignant Peter is! I must not chide the young gentlemen so grievously. They think if they only live well and have good times, then they have enough of everything, and are right well fixed. This one can easily trace in their spiritual claim, when they say that whoever touches them as to their property or their belly, is of the devil. They themselves cannot deny that their whole system is framed to the end, that they may have lazy and idle times, have sufficient of everything, they will burden themselves with no trouble or labor, but every person has to do enough for them, and they pretend they must go to the choir and pray. God commanded all men to eat their bread in the sweat of their face (Gen. 3:19), and he imposed trial and anxiety upon all. Meanwhile, these young masters would slip their heads out of this noose and recline upon their cushions. It is, however, the greatest blindness that they are so hardened, as to hold that such a shameful life is right and praiseworthy.

v. 13c. *Spots and blemishes.*

They know no different than that they adorn Christianity, as the sun and moon do heaven, and are the noblest and most precious jewels, like gold and precious stones; yet Peter calls them spots of shame and blemishes. The true Christian life develops from faith, serves everyone in love, bears the holy cross, which is the true badge, ornament, jewel and honor of

the Christian church; but these have, in place of the cross, lust
and luxury. Instead of love to their neighbor, they seek their
own interest, snatch all to themselves, and let nothing go to
another for his advantage; moreover, they know nothing at all
of faith. Therefore they are nothing but the spots and stains
which Christianity must have as its shame and derision. That
is, I think, chiding enough, for our spiritual lords.

v. 13d. *Reveling in their deceivings while they feast with you.*

What was given at first out of Christian love to procure a
common fund for widows and worthy persons and also for
the poor, so that no one among the Christians need suffer
want or beg—property of this kind is now all devoted to monasteries and cloisters. From these places our ecclesiastics cram
their stomachs, living upon it most luxuriously, and passing
their days in pleasure. To this end they say it belongs to them,
and no one dare reprove them for it. The Holy Spirit will not
permit that the servants of the Church should lead an easy, ef-
feminate life from other people's labor; moreover, it is indeed
kept from the day laborers and from the common man with
his wife and child.

v. 14a. *Having eyes full of adultery.*

Such must always follow when the body is crammed with
food and drink, one goes about idly, as was said above in
verse 13b. But why does Peter say not, they are adulterers but,
"They have eyes full of adultery?" It is as much as though he
should say: They think ever on nothing but fornication, and
can never restrain their roguery, nor be satisfied and quiet.
This is the cause of their continual gluttony and revelry, so far
as they can drive it, and thus they are suffered to live at large
and to be unpunished, just as they like; as follows:

v. 14b. *And that cannot cease from sin.*

The pope has forbidden any prince or secular magistrate to
punish ecclesiastics, and where they venture to do it, he puts
them under the ban; but it is committed to the bishops. How-

ever, since they are knaves themselves, they wink at it or look at it through their fingers. Thus they have exempted themselves from subjection to civil government and the sword, so that no one dares to restrain them in their caprice, and they all live to their own lusts, like those of old before the deluge.

v. 14c. *Enticing unsteadfast souls.*

With such great show as they exhibit in their knavish life, as saying mass, begging, singing, etc., do they allure and draw light-minded and unstable souls who are without faith, to imagine that everything is spiritual and that all is shaped to that end. For it is thought that in their position everyone shall have enough, and good times besides, and moreover, that he shall also reach heaven. Yet all is done only to the end that they may fill their bellies and their lazy pockets.

v. 14d. *Having a heart exercised in covetousness.*

This vice is so gross and open among the clergy that even the common people have complained of it. Yet he says not, they are covetous, but, "They have a heart penetrated with covetousness," and especially exercised with it. This may be seen in the fact that they have invented so many swindling and cunning stories that it is impossible to count them, by which they draw all the world's wealth to themselves. All that this class practices and pursues is simply pure covetousness, and all must be worth high prices. They show it also most plainly in how they are equipped and prepared on all sides to draw the money from the people; so Peter here told the truth.

v. 14e. *Children of cursing.*

That is in the Hebrew as much as to say, they are cursed children, subject to the curse of God. Before God they have no favor or salvation, and they become only more wicked from day to day and are continually greater blasphemers of God; so that they surely laden themselves heavily with the wrath and terrible judgment of God. That is surely spoken severely and fearfully enough; since it is high time that whoever can flee and run, should flee and run from this cursed state. Should we bear such a title, then it is certainly pitiful. For if the high Majesty also arraigns, curses, and condemns, who will endure it?

v. 15a. *Forsaking the right way, they went astray.*

They should have taught the right way, how we must cleave to Christ and come to God through faith and through love to our neighbor. Then we bear the holy cross and endure whatever meets us in doing so. But they preach no more thus; for they go hither and thither, become monks and priests, found churches, masses, etc., etc.; and lead the people from faith in Christ to their own works, which are of no use to their neighbor.

vv. 15b-16. *Having followed the way of Balaam the son of Beor, who loved the hire of wrong-doing; but he was rebuked for his own transgression: a dumb ass [beast of burden] spake with man's voice and stayed the madness of the prophet.*

Here he introduces an illustration from Numbers, chapters 22, 23, and 24. When the children of Israel had journeyed out of Egypt and had come into the land of the Moabites, king Balak sent to a prophet in Syria, by the name of Balaam, and besought him to come and curse the Jewish people, that they might become weak and that he might slay them. Then God appeared to Balaam, and forbade him to curse the people; therefore the prophet declines to comply with the request of Balak. Thereupon the king sent to him once more, and promised to give him large wealth. Then God permits him to go to him, yet he was to say nothing except what he should direct him to say. Upon this he arose and mounted an ass. The angel of God came and walked in the way, and stood before him with a drawn sword. The ass saw it, and turned aside out of the way, at which the prophet struck her, that she should walk in the way. Then the angel went to a narrow place where the ass could not turn aside, and when she presses against the wall and bruises the prophet's foot, she is forced to fall under him upon her knees; this grieved him so that he became angry and he struck the ass with his staff. Then God opens the mouth of the beast to speak with the voice of a man, and she said, What have I done to you that you should strike me so? And he said: Ah! if I had now a sword in my hand, I would slay you. Then the ass answered and said, Am I yet the ass upon which thou hast ridden continually even to this day, and have done the like of this never before? Then were the eyes of the prophet opened, so that he saw the angel with the drawn sword, at which he was affrighted and would have turned back. The the angel bade him go on, but thereupon forbade him to speak anything except what he should say to him.

When now the prophet was come to the king, he takes him up to a height from which he could see all the people of Israel. The prophet bade him erect seven altars, and on each offer a sacrifice. Then went aside and asked the Lord what he should say. And God gave him his word in his mouth. And he rose up to bless and glorify the people of Israel with fair words; and this he did three times, one after another. Then was the king filled with wrath, and said, Did I not call thee that thou shouldst curse mine enemies? And instead thou hast blest them now these three times. I had thought that I should honor thee, but the Lord hath turned thee away from honor. Balaam answered and said, Yet I told thee at first, though thou shouldst give me thine house full of silver and gold, still I could speak nothing else but what God should say to me.

Yet the prophet afterward gave the king counsel how he should manage the people, because he was not allowed to curse them and overcome them by force, so that they should sin against God. Then the king sets up an idol, by name Baal-Peor, and causes that the Moabite women, daughters of lords and princes, should ensnare the people to themselves, to sacrifice to their gods. When they had brought them to themselves, they made supplication to the idol with meats and drinks, and committed sin with the women. Then was God angry, and commanded the chief of the people to be hung upon the gallows, and he permitted four and twenty thousand men to be overcome in one day. Such was this prophet Balaam's advice, for the sake of money.

Of this Peter here speaks and would say that our ecclesiastics are especially Balaam's children and scholars. For just as he gave evil counsel to set up an idol so that the children of Israel should be brought to sin and provoke God that they should be slain, so have our bishops also set up an idol, in God's name, to wit, their human doctrines of their own works. They let faith go and lure to themselves Christian souls whom they injure, and thereby provoke God to anger, so that he has punished the world with blindness and stupidity. For all this we may thank our spiritual masters.

Thus Peter compares especially these false teachers to the prophet Balaam, since they, just like Balaam, purely for the sake of money, set up such idolatry and ruin souls. With this his true name agrees; for Bileam or Balaam is called in Hebrew, a *swallower* or *swiller*, like one who gapes his throat open and swallows and devours all. This shameful name he had to bear, because he brought so many people into sin, when they were destroyed and overcome. Such Balaamites are our bishops and ecclesiastics, who are the throat of the devil, by which he draws so many souls to himself and swallows them. But the surname of this prophet is, the son of Bosor, which means "flesh," or as Moses says, son of Beor, that is, son of a fool. A fool is his father. So are these also, blind, dull, and foolish people, who must themselves indeed rule. Such people the flesh produces, for the spirit makes men of another stamp. So God has given these in the Scriptures their own name, and by their name they are so painted that we may know what estimate to put upon them.

Now "the dumb beast of burden," the ass, signifies the people that lets itself be bridled and ridden, and goes as it is led. They are like the ass, that was forced and beaten cruelly when she went out of the way into the ditch. It could neither give place before the angel in the way so long as possible, nor turn aside, and hence it had to fall down. For in the same way have these seducers also urged on the people, until they at last have become sensible that it is not to be endured and that they have been unfairly dealt with. Therefore they have wished to turn aside from the way. But the power has been too great by which they have overwhelmed and deafened the people, that at length God has opened our lips and given words to our mouths, that even the children speak of it; thus their folly is made plain, and they must be ashamed.

In like manner we ought to meet them when they go about and publish that it is out of place for the laity to read and hear the Scriptures. And when they say, we must hear what the Councils decide. For then you may answer, Has not God spoken even by an ass? Be content that we confess that ye in times past preached the Word of God. But now ye have become fools, and are possessed by avarice, what wonder is it that now the common people have been roused and impelled by God to speak the truth, though it has been burdened and oppressed like a dumb beast of burden. This is their likeness, taken from the prophet Balaam. Now Peter says further of these false teachers:

v. 17a. *These are springs without water, and mists driven by a storm.*

In like manner Solomon presents us a comparison from Proverbs 25:14. He says, As when a great cloud and strong wind go forth, and yet no rain follows, so is a man who greatly boasts of himself, and does not make good his words. Thus Peter says here, "These are springs without water, and mists driven by a storm;" that is, they make great show, and have nothing beside. They are like the dry, false, and exhausted wells, although they have the fame and title of being true wells. For Scripture calls those who teach, wells, as the ones from whom should flow that wholesome doctrine by which souls are quickened. To this office are they annointed and set apart. But what do they do? Nothing. For everywhere there is nothing more than the bare name, just as they are called shepherds, and yet are wolves.

Besides, they are "the mists driven by a storm," not like the thick, black, and lowering clouds that are wont to give us rain, but like those fleecy ones that move about and fly high in the air, and are very light—which the wind drives wherever it will, and from which no rain can fall. So our teachers also sweep about and move high in Christendom, like clouds in the heavens, but permit themselves to be driven about wherever the devil chooses, to whom they are ready to yield in all kinds of lusts. But yet they in no way preach the Word of God like true teachers and preachers, who are called clouds in Scripture. For example, Isaiah 5:6, as all things that give forth water signify preachers in the Scriptures:

v. 17b. *For whom the blackness of darkness hath been reserved.*

They live now at their ease, and things go with them just as they would have them. But eternal darkness shall come upon them, although they do not believe nor apprehend it.

v. 18a. *For uttering great swelling words of vanity.*

If you ask how they can be called wells without water and clouds without rain, despite filling the whole world full of their preaching, Peter answers: They rain and preach, alas! altogether too much. But they are only vain, swollen, and puffed-up words, by which they blow the poor people's ears full, so that they think it is something fine; and yet there is nothing in all they preach. Just as the monks, with high, bold words, set forth their obedience, poverty, and chastity, and people think they are a holy people. Yet it is nothing but mere trickery, and not the least faith nor love can be found among them. Like this, also, is their pretense that the life of bishops is more perfect since they do nothing but ride about pompously on their fine horses, and now and then consecrate churches and altars, and baptize bells. The whole fabric of the pope is through and through full of such swollen and pompous words.

v. 18b. *They entice in the lusts of the flesh, by lasciviousness, those who are just escaping from them that live in error.*

This is what these wells and teachers do, so that they who were almost escaped must fall into the snare of wickedness, and for the first time be truly captured. A child that has been baptized, rescued from all sins, snatched from the devil and transplanted from Adam into Christ—when he begins to reason, he is soon entangled and led away into error. The people should be taught of faith, and love, and the holy cross; but our clergy go their own way, exalt their own works whereby they fall back again into error, even though they had escaped it. But how does this come to pass? Thus: in that by guile they entice the people in the lusts of the flesh. Their strongest enticement is in their saying that priests, monks, and nuns should not marry, and they pledge themselves to maintain chastity. By this they do no more than allure to unchastity, so that the wretched people must perish in their wicked lusts, and there is nothing to help them.

Here you clearly see that Peter speaks of none other than teachers who rule in Christendom, where people are baptized and believing. For among the Turks and heathen, no one has thus escaped. It is only among Christians, where they have the chance to lead souls astray and bring them into the snare of the devil.

v. 19. *Promising them liberty, while they themselves are bondservants of corruption; for of whom a man is overcome, of the same is he brought into bondage.*

They set up orders by which a man is to be saved, as Thomas the monk preacher has shamelessly written, that when a man enters into one of these orders, it is as though he had just come forth from his baptism. Then they promise him freedom and forgiveness of sins by virtue of their own works. Such blasphemy must we hear, while they set their human fancies and ludicrous conceits, destitute of faith, on a level with faith and baptism that God has established and that are peculiarly his work. Who is to endure this and still keep silent? Such stories have the monks gotten up, and crammed into the young; and such teachers men have set up as saints. But the other saints, who were truly saints, they have burnt to ashes.

v. 20. *For if, after they have escaped the defilements of the world through the knowledge of the Lord and Savior Jesus Christ, they are again entangled therein and overcome, the last state is become worse with them than the first.*

Here Peter proves why they are the servants of corruption.

"To acknowledge Christ" is to know what he is, even our Savior, who forgives us our sins from pure grace. By thus acknowledging Christ, we escape the vice and are delivered from the pollution of the world. But though they have now been delivered from sin in baptism, they shall afterwards be plunged again into sin, in that they have turned from faith to their own works. For where there is no faith, the Spirit is absent; but where the Spirit is absent, there is nothing but flesh, so nothing at all pure can be there. Thus it has gone hitherto in Christendom. Rome first heard the pure Gospel, but afterward went back and fell away to human doctrines, until all abominations have come even upon herself. And now her last end has become worse than her first, in that she is far more hopeless in her heathenism than she ever was before she heard the Word of God.

vv. 21, 22. For it were better for them not to have known the way of righteousness, than, after knowing it, to turn back from the holy commandment delivered unto them. It has happened unto them according to the true proverb, The dog turning to his own vomit again, and the sow that had washed to wallowing in the mire.

This proverb Peter has taken from Proverbs 26:11, where Solomon says, "As a dog that returneth to his vomit, so is a fool that repeateth his folly." By baptism they have cast out unbelief, and have been washed from their polluted life, and have entered upon a pure life of faith and love. Then they fall from it again into unbelief and their own works, and defile themselves again in their filth. Therefore we are not to apply this proverb to works; for little is accomplished by one saying and directing after confession: Thou shalt henceforth be chaste, meek, and patient. But if you will be righteous, pray God that he may give you a real faith, and see to it that you forsake your unbelief. When you shall then have attained faith, good works will afterwards take care of themselves, and you will live purely and chastely. Moreover you will not be able to defend yourself with any other means; and although you can conceal the rogue in your heart for a time, yet at last he will come out.

This is the second chapter of this epistle, in which Peter speaks especially of our former teachers, how shamefully we have been misled by them. We have indeed had warning enough, but we have not given heed to it. Therefore, the fault is ours that we have not laid hold on the Gospel and that we have by our lives deserved such anger of God. We all hear it generally with gladness, when someone assaults and upbraids the pope along with his priests and monks; but yet, no one will draw advantage to himself from it. It is not such a trifling matter of sport that one dare laugh at it, but of such seriousness that the heart should fear and tremble before it. Consequently we should lay hold of it with seriousness, and pray God to turn from us his anger and such plagues. For this calamity has not come upon us unforeseen, but it is sent upon us by God as a punishment, as Paul says in 2 Thessalonians 2:10-12: "Because they received not the love of the truth, that they might be saved. And for this cause God sendeth them a working of error, that they should believe a lie." For had the punishment gone only so far that the false teachers alone were lost, it would have been a little thing compared with the fact that they have been the rulers and have carried all the world with them to hell. Consequently there is no help for the evil except that we lay hold of it with godly fear and humility, confess our guilt, and pray God to turn away the punishment from us. By prayer we must storm the false teachers, otherwise the devil will not let us win.

The Preparation of Christians for "The Day of the Lord."

I.   Why Peter Wrote His Second Epistle, vv. 1-10.

II. Of the Last Day.
    A. Of the signs of the last day, vv. 3-4.
    B. Of the certainty of the last day, vv. 5-6.
    C. What will take place at the last day, vv. 7-10.

III. How a Christian Should Prepare Himself for the Last Day, vv. 11-18.
    A. Should he expect the last day with joy and hasten to welcome it? vv. 11-12. Of the new heaven and the new earth, v. 13.
    B. Should a Christian despise vanity, and live a blameless life? v. 14.
    C. Should a Christian esteem the long-suffering of God as gain? v. 15. The witness of Peter to Paul's doctrine, v. 16.
    D. Should a Christian beware of false teachers? vv. 17-18.

I.   Why Peter Wrote His Second Epistle (vv. 1-10)

vv. 1, 2. *This is now, beloved, the second epistle that I write unto you; and in both of them I stir up your sincere mind by putting you in remembrance; that ye should remember the words which were spoken before by the holy prophets, and the commandment of the Lord and Savior through your apostles.*

Here Peter now comes to us again and warns us in this chapter to be prepared and to look every moment for the last day. He says first that he has written this epistle, not in order to lay the foundation of faith, which he had done before, but to awaken, remind, restrain, and urge them not to forget the same, and to abide in the clear sense and understanding which they have of a true Christian life. For it is the preacher's office, as we have often said, not only to teach, but also continually to admonish and restrain. For since our flesh and blood ever cling to us, God's Word must be valiant and vigilant in us, that we may not give room to the flesh, but strive against it, and subdue it.

II.　The Last Day

vv. 3, 4. *Knowing this first, that in the last days mockers shall come with mockery, walking after their own lusts, and saying, Where is the promise of his coming? for, from the day that the fathers fell asleep, all things continue as they were from the beginning of the creation.*

Yet men are swayed hither and thither by a book concerning Antichrist, in which is written that before the day of judgment the people shall fall into such error that they shall say, there is no God, and shall scoff at all that is preached of Christ and the judgment day. That is true, whencesoever it has been taken. But we are not so to understand it that the whole world shall say and hold such things, but the greater part. For that time is already now at hand, it shall prevail yet more when the Gospel shall be better spread among the people. Then the people will stir themselves in grand style, and the secrets of many hearts shall break forth, which are now hidden and not revealed. There have even already been many who have altogether rejected the idea of the coming of the day of judgment.

Of such scoffers Peter warns us, and he tells us beforehand that they must come and rush into this hazardous condition and live as they wish. In Rome and Italy this word was long ago fulfilled, and they who come hence, bring such delusions also with them. Therefore as the people have long perplexed themselves in this false notion, so the people also must drive it out.

And even though the day of judgment were now before the door, such people must appear in order that the words of Christ in Matthew 24:37-39, shall be fulfilled! "And as were the days of Noah, so shall be the coming of the Son of Man. For as in those days which were before the flood they were eating and drinking, marrying and giving in marriage, until the day that Noah entered into the ark, and they knew not till the flood came and swallowed them all; so shall be the coming of the Son of Man." Also in Matthew 24:44 says, "In an hour that ye think not the Son of Man cometh." Likewise notice Luke 21:35: "For so shall it come upon all them that dwell on the face of all the earth." And once more, Luke 17:24: "As the lightning, when it lighteneth out of the one part under the heaven, shineth unto the other part under heaven; so shall the Son of Man be in his day." That is, so quick and unforeseen and sudden shall he break in upon it—while the world shall be living most securely and while it shall be throwing God's Word to the winds.

Therefore this shall be a sign of the day of judgment that it is near, when the people shall live as they desire, according to all their lusts, and such talk is heard among them as this: "Where is the promise of his coming?" The world has stood so long and continued to abide, is it now for the first time to be otherwise? Thus Peter warns us that we should not be surprised, and that we have a sure sign that the day will soon come. It follows further:

vv. 5, 6. *For this they wilfully forget, that there were heavens from of old, and an earth compacted out of water and amidst water, by the word of God; by which means the world that then was, being overflowed with water, perished.*

Such people they are, he says, as show not enough diligence to read the Scriptures, but obstinately refuse to consider and take warning that so also it was of old. When Noah built the ark, the world which existed and was made through the water and in the water, was destroyed by water, and the people were yet so secure and certain that they thought, surely there is no danger; yet they were all alike destroyed by water. As though he should say: If God did then destroy the world by water, and showed by an example that he can sink it, how much more will he destroy it now since he has promised to do it.

But here Peter speaks a little in detail of the creation. The heaven and the earth stood fast aforetime; they were made of water and existed in the water by the Word of God. Heaven and earth have a beginning; they have not been forever; the heaven was made from the water, and there was water above and beneath. The earth is made and exists in the water, as Moses writes, to whom Peter here refers. All is sustained by God's Word, as it also was made by the same, for it is not their nature, that they should so exist. Therefore if God did not sustain it, it would all soon fall and sink in the water. For God spoke a word of power when he said in Genesis 1:9, "Let the waters under the heavens be gathered together unto one place and let the dry land appear." That is, let the water put itself aside and give room for the earth to come forth, whereon man might dwell; yet naturally the waters should spread themselves over the earth. Therefore this is one of the greatest miracles that God works at the present day.

Now Peter would say: So obstinate and stupid are these scoffers that they will not do honor to the Holy Spirit. They read how God holds up the earth in the water, whence they should be convinced that all rests in the hands of God. Therefore, since God at that time drowned the earth, so he will deal also with us. For that example should certainly convince us that, as in that case he did not lie, so he will not lie now.

v. 7. *But the heavens that now are, and the earth, by the same word have been stored up for fire, being reserved against the day of judgment and destruction of ungodly men.*

At that time, when God destroyed the world by a flood, the water pressed down from above, up from beneath and from all sides, so that nothing could be seen but water only. The earth, as its nature was, must have sunk in the water. But now he has promised and given the rainbow in the heavens for a sign, that he will no more destroy the world by water. Therefore he will now destroy it and let it perish by fire so that here it shall be fire only, as there it was water only. Of this Paul in 2 Thessalonians 1:7f., says, "At the revelation of the Lord Jesus from heaven with the angels of his power in flaming fire." Also notice 1 Corinthians 3:13: "Each man's work shall be made manifest; for the day shall declare it, because it is revealed in fire." So when the day of judgment breaks and bursts in on the world, it will in a moment be fire only; what is in heaven and in earth shall be turned to dust and ashes, and all things must be changed by fire, as that change took place by water. This rainbow shall be the sign that God will keep his Word.

vv. 8-10. *But forget not this one thing, beloved, that one day is with the Lord as a thousand years, and a thousand years as one day. The Lord is not slack concerning his promise, as some count slackness; but is longsuffering to youward, not wishing that any should perish, but that all should come to repentance. But the day of the Lord will come as a thief; in which the heavens shall pass away with a great noise, and the elements shall be dissolved with fervent heat, and the earth and the works that are therein shall be burned up.*

With these words Peter meets those of whom he has just spoken, who say: The apostles have said much more about the day of judgment coming quickly, and yet so long time is past, and still all continues as heretofore. And he has quoted this passage from Moses, in Psalm 90:4, where he says, "For a thousand years in thy sight are but as yesterday, when it is past." Hence there are two views of things: one as God views them, the other as the world views them. So also this present life and that to come are different. This life cannot be that, since none can reach that but by death, or by ceasing from this life. Our present life is only to eat, drink, sleep, digest, and rear children, in which all moves on successively, hours, days, years, one after another. If you wish now to apprehend that life. You must banish out of your mind the course of this present life; you dare not think that you can so apprehend it, then it will all be one day, one hour, one moment.

Since now in God's sight there is no reckoning of time, a thousand years must be with him, as it were, a day. Therefore the first man, Adam, is just as near to him as he who shall be born last before the day of judgment. For God sees not time lengthwise but obliquely—just as when you look at right-angles to a long tree which lies before you, you can fix in your view both place and parts at once—a thing you cannot do if you only look at it lengthwise. We can, by our reason, look at time only according to its duration; we must begin to count from Adam, one year after another, even to the last day. But before God it is all one; what is long with us is short with him; and again, with him there is neither measure nor number. So when man dies, the body is buried and wastes away. It lies in the earth and knows nothing. But when the first man rises at the last day, he will think he has lain there scarcely an hour, when he will look about and become assured that so many people were born of him and have come after him, of whom he had no knowledge at all.

Peter's meaning is: the Lord does not delay his promise as some scoffers imagine, but is long-suffering. Therefore, should ye be prepared for the last day—for it will come soon enough to everyone after his death, in that he will say, "Lo! I have but just now died!" But it comes upon the world all too soon, when the people shall say, "there is peace, no danger threatens." It shall break forth and come upon them, as Paul says in 1 Thessalonians 5:3. And with so great a noise shall the day tear its way and burst forth like a great storm, that in a moment all must become a waste.

III. How a Christian Should Prepare Himself for the Last Day (vv. 11-18)

vv. 11-12a. *Seeing that these things are thus all to be dissolved, what manner of persons ought ye to be in all holy living and godliness, looking for and earnestly desiring the coming of the day of God.*

Since ye know this, that all must pass away, both heaven and earth, consider how ye shall be prepared to meet this day—by a holy and godly life and conversation. For Peter describes this day as one that is to come even now, so that men should be prepared for it, to hope for it with joy, and even hasten to run to meet it, as that which sets us free from death, sin, and hell.

vv. 12b-13. *By reason of which the heavens being on fire shall be dissolved, and the elements shall melt with fervent heat? But, according to his promise, we look for new heavens and a new earth, wherein dwelleth righteousness.*

God has promised by the prophets, here and there, that he would create new heavens and a new earth, as he says in Isaiah 65:17-18: "Behold, I create new heavens and a new earth, wherein ye shall be glad and rejoice for ever in that which I create." Also notice Isaiah 30:26: "Moreover the light of the moon shall be as the light of the sun, and the light of the sun shall be sevenfold, as the light of seven days, in the day of Jehovah." And Christ said in Matthew 13:43, "The righteous shall shine as the sun, in the kingdom of their Father." How that is to pass away we cannot know, except that the promise is that such a heaven and earth are to exist. Therein no sin, but righteousness only, and the children of God shall dwell. Paul also says, there shall be pure love, pure joy, and nothing but God's kingdom (Rom. 14:17).

Here some may disquiet themselves as to whether the saints shall exist in heaven or on the earth. The text seems to imply that man shall dwell upon the earth, yet so that all heaven and earth shall be a paradise where God dwells, for God dwells not only in heaven, but in all places. Wherefore, the elect shall be also even where he is.

v. 14. *Wherefore, beloved, seeing that ye look for these things, give diligence that ye may be found in peace, without spot and blameless in his sight.*

Since ye have escaped such misery, he says, and have come to so great joy, ye should suffer yourselves to be persuaded to despise willingly all that is upon the earth and to suffer cheerfully whatever duty requires. Therefore be diligent, that ye may live a peaceful and blameless life.

v. 15a. *And account that the longsuffering of our Lord is salvation.*

In that he so spares and delays, and does not come to speedy judgment, consider this as designed for your benefit. He had good reason to be angry and to punish, yet out of his grace he does it not.

vv. 15b-16. *Even as our beloved brother Paul also, according to the wisdom given to him, wrote unto you; as also in all his epistles, speaking in them of these things; wherein are some things hard to be understood, which the ignorant and unsteadfast wrest, as they do also the other scriptures, unto their own destruction.*

Here Peter bears testimony for the apostle Paul in respect to his doctrine, which shows plainly enough that this epistle was written long after Paul's epistles. And this is one of the passages that might be adduced to maintain that this epistle is not Peter's, as also there was one before this in this chapter, where he says, "The Lord wishes not that any should perish, but that all should come to repentance" (v. 9). For it falls some little below the apostolic spirit. Still it is credible that it is nonetheless the apostle's, for since in it he is writing not of faith but of love, he lets himself down somewhat, as the manner of love is, inasmuch as it humbles itself to its neighbor, just as faith rises above itself.

However, he saw that many unstable spirits had confused and perverted the words and doctrines of Paul, inasmuch as some things in his epistles are hard to be understood. For instance, when he says thus, "that no one is justified by his works, but by faith alone" (Rom. 3:28); or that the law is given to make sin more manifest (Gal. 3:19); or "where sin abounded, grace did abound more exceedingly" (Rom. 5:20); and other like passages. For when men hear this they say, if that is true, we will go on indolently, and do no good, and so be righteous, as even now it is said that we forbid good works. If they so perverted Paul's own words, what wonder is it that they should in like manner pervert ours?

vv. 17-18. *Ye therefore, beloved, knowing these things beforehand, beware lest, being carried away with the error of the wicked, ye fall from your own steadfastness. But grow in the grace and knowledge of our Lord and Savior Jesus Christ. To him be the glory both now and for ever. Amen.*

Since ye know, he says, all that has been said above, and since you see that many false teachers must come—people to lead the world astray and since scoffers as pervert the Scripture and will not understand it—take care of yourselves. Guard against them with diligence that ye fall not from your faith by reason of the doctrines of error. And grow, so as to become stronger from day to day by the steadfast practice and preaching of the Word of God. Here observe how great care the apostle shows for those who have come to faith, those who urged him even to write these two epistles, in which is fully comprehended what a Christian should know, besides also that which is to come. May God give his grace, that we also may lay hold of and retain it. Amen.

THE EPISTLE OF JUDE

A Picture of False Teachers, in Their Sins and Punishments.

Outline

I. He Who Paints the Picture, vv. 1-2.

II. The Occasion and Cause of This Picture, vv. 3-4a. Of faith and love, v. 4a.

III. The Picture Itself, vv. 4b-16.
   - A. The first part of this picture. where we find:
     - 1. The sins.
       - a. The first sin, v. 4b.
       - b. The second sin, v. 4c.
     - 2. The punishment, vv. 5-7.
   - B. The second part of this picture. where we find:
     - 1. The sins.
       - a. The first sin, v. 8a.
       - b. The second sin, v. 8a.
       - c. The third sin, vv. 8b-9. The contention about the body of Moses, v. 9.
       - d. The fourth sin, v. 10.
       - e. The fifth sin, v. 11a.
       - f. The sixth sin, v. 11b.
     - 2. The punishment, v. 11c.
   - C. The third part of this picture. where we find:
     - 1. The sins.
       - a. The first sin, v. 12a.
       - b. The second sin, v. 12b.
       - c. The third sin, v. 13a.
       - d. The fourth sin, v. 13b.
     - 2. The punishment, vv. 14-15b.
   - D. The fourth part of this picture, vv. 15c-16.

IV. How Several Admonitions are Attached to This Picture, vv. 17-23b.
   - A. The first admonition, vv. 17-19.

I.   He Who Paints the Picture (vv. 1, 2)

vv. 1-2. Jude, a servant of Jesus Christ, and brother of James, to them that are called, beloved in God the Father, and kept for Jesus Christ: Mercy unto you and peace and love be multiplied.

The authorship of this epistle is attributed to the holy apostle Jude—the brother of the two apostles James the Less and Simon. They were his brothers by the sister of the mother of Christ, who is called Mary (the wife) of James and Cleopas, as we read in Mark 6:3; 16:1. However, this epistle does not seem to be from one of the first apostles; for in it the author speaks of the apostles, as if he were their junior, having lived long after them. In it is nothing special except it refers to the Second Epistle of Peter from which it has taken nearly all its words, and on the whole it is nothing else than an epistle against our clergy, bishops, priests and monks.

II.   The Occasion and Cause of This Picture (vv. 3-4a)

v. 3. Beloved, while I was giving all diligence to write unto you of our common salvation, I was constrained to write unto you exhorting you to contend earnestly for the faith which was once for all delivered unto the saints.

That is to say: I am constrained to write you in order that I may remind and admonish you to press forward and hew a clear path for your feet in the faith that has once already been preached to you. It is as if Jude should say: It is necessary that I admonish you to be on your guard and continue in the right way. Why it is necessary, however, he states, and says:

v. 4a. *For there are certain men crept in privily, even they who were of old written of beforehand unto this condemnation.*

The reason I wish to remind you is that you may continue in the faith you have heard. There is already a beginning, and preachers are at hand, to advocate other doctrines besides faith, by which the people are gently and unsuspectingly led astray from the true way. Peter in his second epistle, called attention to the same thing: "There shall be false teachers, who shall privily bring in destructive heresies" (2:1). and the like. Upon these false teachers the sentence of judgment, he says, was announced already long ago, namely, that they are condemned.

This we understand now very well, since we have learned that no one can become righteous or be justified by his own works, but alone through faith in Christ; also, that he must rely upon the work of Christ, as his chief good and only support. Then after faith is present, whatever man does should all be done for the benefit of his neighbor. One should guard against all works that are not done with the intention to benefit his neighbor, for example as the orders of the priests and monks are at the present time. Therefore where anyone now secretly introduces anything else than this doctrine of faith relating to such orders and their works, he misleads the people so that they will be condemned along with him.

III.   The Picture Itself (vv. 4b.-16)

v. 4b. *Ungodly men, turning the grace of our God into lasciviousness.*

The sermon that is preached to us on the grace of God and holds before us Christ—how he is offered and given unto us with all that he has, that we are free from sin, death, and all misfortune—such grace and gifts offered through the Gospel—they use only to lead corrupt lives. That is, they call themselves Christians and praise the Gospel, but they lead such lives themselves—in which they work their wantonness in eating and drinking and in their villainous ways—that as they boast and say: We are not in a secular but in the spiritual state, and include in that name and claim all good, honor, and luxury. That has already commenced, says Jude. For we read that it began already a thousand years ago, that the bishops wished to be lords and to be considered of a higher order than the common Christians. We see this in the epistles of Jerome.

v. 4c. *And denying our only Master and Lord, Jesus Christ.*

Peter also mentioned this same thing in his epistle; but this denying, as we have heard, is not done by the mouth, for they confess that God is Lord. But they deny the Lord Christ in fact and by their works, and they consider him not as their Lord—but themselves as their own lord. For when they preach that fasts, pilgrimages, church institutions, chastity, obedience, and poverty, are the way to salvation, they lead the people astray by their own works. And they keep silent about Christ. It as much as if they said: Christ is of no account to you. His works help you nothing, but you must merit salvation by your own works. Thus they deny the Lord, who has bought us with his own blood, as Jude says:

vv. 5-7. *Now I desire to put you in remembrance, though ye know all things once for all, that the Lord, having saved a people out of the land of Egypt, afterward destroyed them that believed not. And angels that kept not their own principality, but left their proper habitation, he hath kept in everlasting bonds under darkness unto the judgment of the great day. Even as Sodom and Gomorrah, and the cities about them, having in like manner with these given themselves over to fornication and gone after strange flesh, are set forth as an example, suffering the punishment of eternal fire.*

Here Jude introduces three examples, as Peter did in his epistle. But in addition to those, he adds a new one: How God permitted the children of Israel, whom he had led out of Egypt by many miracles, to be overthrown and defeated, when they believed not, so that of the 600,000 of 20 of age and above, not more than 2 were found to have survived when they were numbered. This example he gives to warn and terrify them, as if he would say, let those be on their guard who are called Christians and under this name turn the grace of God into wantonness lest it go with themselves as it did here with the

Israelites. And it is true that since the time the papacy was set up, and the Gospel has been silenced in the whole world, one plague after another has continually been visiting the world, with which God punished the unbelievers and casted them into the throat of the devil.

v. 8a. *Yet in like manner these also in their dreamings defile the flesh.*

These teachers are here called "dreamers." It is just as when a person lies in a dream and is occupied with images. He thinks he has something, but when he wakes up nothing is there. For then he sees that it was a dream, and he gives it no further attention. So also it is with what these teachers say. It is nothing more than a pure dream. When their eyes are once opened, they will see that it is nothing. As when they go about pretending that their tonsure and cowl, obedience, poverty, and chastity are well-pleasing to God. These they have before their eyes, but before the eyes of God they are nothing but a pure dream. Thus he gave them truly a becoming name, that they are occupied with dreams by which they deceive themselves and the world. But the apostles ascribe the vice of living unchaste lives especially to the clergy. God long ago foretold that they would not enter the married state. Now it is scarcely possible that God does as many miracles as there are priests; therefore, they cannot all be chaste. In like manner the prophet Daniel says of the pope's rule: "Neither shall he regard the desire of women" (in marriage, 11:37). Thus their outward characteristic, like their inward one, proves that they are dreamers.

v. 8b. *And set at nought dominion, and rail at dignities [glories].*

The third characteristic is that they will not be subject to the civil authority. We have taught that as long as we live upon the earth we are under obligation to everyone to be subject and obedient to those in authority. The Christian faith does not do away with the civil rule; therefore, no one can exempt himself from it. And because of this, the pope's decree concerning the freedom of the church is a mere devil's law.

v. 9. *But Michael, the archangel, when contending with the devil he disputed about the body of Moses, durst not bring against him a railing judgment, but said, The Lord rebuke thee.*

This is one reason why this epistle was formerly rejected, because an example is cited here that is not found in the Scriptures: That the archangel Michael and the devil contended with one another about the body of Moses. And that could have taken place for the reason that so much is written about Moses in Deuteronomy 34:6, how God buried him, and yet no one knows his sepulcher. And the Scriptures bear witness in Deuteronomy 34:10 that no prophet has arisen since in Israel like unto Moses, whom Jehovah knew face to face. Hence it is said in reference to the same text that his body was left concealed in order that the Jews might not practice idolatry with it. And therefore the angel Michael contended with Satan, who desired that the body be disclosed so that the Jews might worship it. And although Michael was an archangel, says Jude, yet he did not make so bold as to curse the devil himself. Yet these scoffers trample underfoot the authority ordained by God, and curse in seven, eight, and nine degrees or ways, though they are mere men; while this archangel dared not curse the worst devil, who is already condemned; but said no more than: "The Lord rebuke thee."

v. 10. *But these rail at whatsoever things they know not: and what they understand naturally, like the creatures without reason, in these things are they destroyed [corrupted].*

Such scoffers are they that they can do nothing but anathematize and curse, and deliver to Satan as his own not only kings and magistrates, but also God and his saints as is seen in the bull *"coenae Domini."* They know not that our salvation is founded upon faith and love, and they cannot stand it that we reject and condemn their works and we preach how Christ alone must help us with his works. Therefore they put under the ban and blaspheme all the Christian doctrines they do not know. But what they know through secular knowledge, namely, that the founding of masses and the like bring in money and accumulate treasures, they give themselves up completely to secular knowledge and thereby ruin themselves and everybody.

v. 11a. *Woe unto them! for they went in the way of Cain.*

Cain struck his brother dead, simply because he was more pious than himself. Jehovah had respect unto his brother's offering, but unto his own offering he had not respect. So now "the way of Cain" is to rely upon one's own works and scoff at the true good works; it is to circumvent and ruin those traveling on the right road, just as these very ones are doing.

v. 11b. *And ran riotously in the error of Balaam for hire.*

They should be established in the inner man, in the assurance of the divine grace; yet, they run abroad and scatter their energies in various kinds of outward good works here and there. They do it only for the sake of money, that they may fill their bellies, like the prophet Balaam, as we learned in 2 Peter 2:15.

v. 11c. *And perished in the gainsaying [rebellion] of Korah.*

An account of the rebellion of Korah and how he with his company were destroyed is given us in Numbers 16:1-34. Moses was desired and called by God to the end that he should lead his people out of Egypt; and his brother Aaron was also consecrated by God to the high priesthood. Now Korah was also of the same tribe and a relative of theirs, who wished to be great and become prominent. He joined to himself a party of 250 of the best and most prominent men among the people and raises such a rebellion and tumult that Moses and Aaron had to flee. And Moses fell upon his face and prayed that God might not accept their offering. He bade the congregation of the people to desert them, and he said to them, "Hereby ye shall know that Jehovah hath sent me to do all these works. If these men die the common death of all men, then Jehovah hath not sent me. But if Jehovah make a new thing, and the ground open its mouth, and swallow them up, and they go down alive into Sheol; then ye shall understand that these men have despised Jehovah. And it came to pass, as he made an end of speaking all these words, that the ground clave asunder that was under them; and the earth opened its mouth and swallowed them up; and their households, and all the men that appertained unto Korah, and all their goods, so they and all that appertained to them, went down alive into Sheol. And fire came forth from Jehovah, and devoured the two hundred and fifty men that offered the incense" (Num. 16:28-35).

This example Jude now cites and applies to these scoffers, who blame us for stirring up seditions when we preach against them, while they themselves are the cause of all the trouble and misery. For Christ is our Aaron and high priest, and we should let him alone rule. But the pope and bishops will not allow that. They have established themselves and wish to take the reins of government by force, having set themselves against Christ. These God punished by letting the earth swallow and cover them, so that they are drowned and swallowed by a worldly life and by pleasure, and they are now nothing but pure worldliness.

vv. 12-13. *These are they who are hidden rocks [spots] in your love-feasts when they feast with you, shepherds that without fear feed themselves; clouds without water, carried along by winds; autumn trees without fruit, twice dead, plucked up by the roots; wild waves of the sea, foaming out their own shame; wandering stars, for whom the blackness of darkness hath been reserved for ever.*

We have heard sufficient of this in Peter's epistles. All the world have reared their children to be priests and to have an easy life, and not to support themselves with their hands and daily labor. Neither dare they preach, but without care or worry they are to live in their luxury and keep in good spirits by feasting on the wealth of the poor people gathered by the sweat of their face. Likewise the people imagine that these idle fellows are the best part, the jewels of Christendom; while they are mere shame-spots and an abomination. They feast well, as the saying runs, "what is good belongs in the priests."

They are without care and fear, and they imagine that Satan does not wish to overthrow them. They feed the sheep not, but are wolves that devour the sheep. They are the "clouds" floating above in the air, they sit high in the church, as those who should preach, and yet they do not preach, but permit Satan to carry them hither and thither.

So also he says they are "autumn trees without fruit, twice dead." They have neither fruit nor leaves; they stand there alone bare like other trees; they make the claim and show as if they were Christian bishops, while neither the word nor the work of Christian bishops is there, but all is dead at the root.

Further they are like the "wild waves of the sea," that is, like the wind tosses and plays with the waves and billows upon the water, so they go just as the devil leads. They "foam out their own shame." Like a pot full of heat, they are so full of pollution that they run over and cannot retain control of themselves, but all must out.

They are "wandering stars," planets as they are called, that go backward and not in a steady, straight course. So these bishops have no regular course, their lives and teachings are mere error, in which they are misled and they misled all who follow them. Therefore "the blackness of darkness has been reserved for them forever."

Thus has Jude now appraised and painted our spiritual leaders, who under the name of Christ and Christianity introduce all kinds of profligacy and snatch to themselves all the wealth of the world and bring every person by their assumed authority into subjection to themselves. Now follows further:

vv. 14-15a. *And to these also Enoch, the seventh from Adam, prophesies, saying, Behold, the Lord came with ten thousands of his holy ones to execute judgment upon all.*

This saying of Enoch is found nowhere in the Scriptures, and therefore some of the fathers did not receive this epistle. However, that is not sufficient reason for rejecting a book of Scripture. For Paul in 2 Timothy 3:8 mentions two who withstood Moses, Jannes and Jambres, whose names cannot be found in the Scriptures. But be that as it may, we let it pass. It is nevertheless true that God, from the beginning of the world, has permitted his Word to be proclaimed to some, which promised to believers his grace and salvation, but threatened the unbelievers with judgment and condemnation, until after the ascension of Christ; when it began to be proclaimed publicly in all the world. But before the birth of Christ, God chose only a single line of descendants from Adam to Abraham, then to David and Mary the mother of Christ, who possessed his Word. Consequently the Gospel has always been preached in the world, but never so publicly as at present in these last times.

Thus also this father, Enoch, preached the word of God, which he without doubt had learned from his father Adam and had received from the Holy Spirit. For the Scriptures say of him in Genesis 5:24, that he led a godly life, and therefore God took him so that he was never seen again. Hence it is said that he will come again before the day of judgment. But that is not to be expected, unless it be understood that he will come spiritually; namely, that his preaching spoke of the day of judgment. For this passage in which he speaks of the last judgment sounds as though Enoch had the last judgment already before his eyes. "The Lord came with ten thousands of his holy ones," that is, with such a multitude as cannot be numbered. For that must be said only of the day of judgment when he shall come with all his holy ones to execute judgment. For heretofore he has not come with many thousand holy ones, but he came alone upon the earth; not to judge, but to bestow grace.

v. 15b. *And to convict all the ungodly of all their works of ungodliness which they have ungodly wrought.*

This passage Jude appropriately quotes, inasmuch as he is speaking of the false teachers to appear before the day of judgment. He concludes that at his second coming the Lord will overthrow the pope and his rule, since there is no help for them. For as long as the world stands there can be no end nor reformation of them. The passage cannot be understood of any others, than of our clergy, who woefully led all the world astray, seeing they cannot be worse. And if they were even worse, they would still have to hold on to the name of Christ, and in that name introduce all kinds of misery. Thus he refers this passage rightly to the last judgment, and names those whom the judgment will include. Therefore we conclude, that our young clerical gentlemen must expect the last judgment, be the time long or short.

v. 15c. *And of all the hard things which ungodly sinners have spoken against him.*

Here he at once speaks of their life and preaching and would say: They speak strongly and fiercely against the Lord who is to come, are bold and proud, and as Peter said, they mock and revile him. He speaks not of their sinful and shameful living, but of their godless character or state. But the "godless" are those who live without faith, although they lead outwardly an honorable life. The outward wicked deeds are indeed fruits of unbelief, but he is particularly called a godless character who outwardly appears beautiful, and yet his heart is full of unbelief. These very godless ones, he says, the Lord will punish because their preaching is shameless and presumptuous. For they remain ever headstrong, never allowing themselves to be swayed in the least. Hard as an anvil, they condemn and revile continually. Thus Enoch in this passage described precisely the state of things that shall exist in the world just before the day of judgment as we see now before our eyes. Further Jude says:

v. 16a. *These are murmurers, complainers, walking after their lusts, and their mouth speaketh great swelling words.*

When people protest against their doings as unjust and unreasonable, then there is nothing but murmuring and complaining. Likewise, if one should fail to give a bishop his right title, then they raise the cry of disobedience. Moreover they are a class you cannot restrain. For they assert how they have authority over body and soul, and that they have grasped in their own hands both the temporal and the spiritual power. They say no one can control them. Hence no one dare preach against them. They escape from paying all tax, tribute, and rent, so that no one dare touch their wealth. Besides, no one dare preach a word before they are asked first about it. And if one attack them even with the Scriptures, they reply: The exposition of the Scriptures must be left to them alone. Thus they live in all things as they wish, according to their own lusts. For they cannot charge us of that, as they gladly would if they could, seeing we have subjected ourselves both to the Gospel and to the civil authority; but they wish to be free from both and controlled by neither. And moreover, all their laws and claims are nothing but the fullness of mere high, proud, puffed-up words, which have nothing to back them.

v. 16b. *Showing respect of persons for the sake of advantage.*

That is the way of the papists; they judge all according to the person. In all the laws of the pope from beginning to end you do not find one instance that the bishop humbles himself to the priest, but the chaplain is under the priest, the priest under the bishop, and the bishop under the archbishop, and these under the patriarchs, and the patriarchs under the pope. And after that how each is to wear the robe, the tonsure and the cowl, and possess so many churches and benefices. Thus they have applied all their teaching to the externals and have carried on such a child's play and fool's work that they held it to be a great sin if anyone did not share their views. Therefore Jude puts it well, that they put a mask upon all their doings and have that alone before their eyes. Hence no one knows anything of faith, of love nor of the cross. Then the average person thus plays the monkey and the fool, and turns all his property over to them, as if they were devoting it to the true service of God; that is, they keep up a fine appearance, for the sake of their own advantage.

IV. How Several Admonitions Are Attached to This Picture (vv. 17-23b)

vv. 17-18. *But ye, beloved, remember ye the words which have been spoken before by the apostles of our Lord Jesus Christ; that they said to you, In the last time there shall be mockers, walking after their own ungodly lusts.*

This passage shows clearly that our epistle is not of Jude the apostle, for he does not count nor reckon himself among the other apostles, but he speaks of them as of those who preached long before his day. So, it is easy to conceive that another pious man wrote this epistle, who had read the epistles of Peter and taken this saying from him.

We indicated above who the "mockers" are, also who were "those walking after their own lusts." Not only after their fleshly lusts, but "after the lusts of their godless life" they lead, and they shape all according to their own pleasure, esteeming neither the civil authority nor the Word of God. They are neither under an external nor an internal government, neither under divine nor human control. They float about between heaven and earth in their lust, just as the devil leads them.

v. 19. *These are they who make separations [sects], sensual, having not the Spirit.*

Here he touches upon that of which Peter speaks in 2 Peter 2:1, how they secretly introduce destructive sects. For they are those who have separated themselves to divide the unity in the faith. They will not let the ordinary calling of a Christian answer, in which one serves the other, but they start new callings and offices, and pretend to serve God in them. However, they are sensual and brutish men and have no more understanding and spirit than a horse or an ass. They push ahead according to their natural reason and fleshly mind, and they have no Word of God according to which they govern themselves and live.

vv. 20-21a. *But ye, beloved, building up yourselves on your most holy faith, praying in the Holy Spirit, keep yourselves in the love of God.*

With these few words he comprehends the whole Christian life. Faith is laid as the foundation upon which we should build. But *building* means "to grow from day to day in the knowledge of God and of Jesus Christ," which takes place through the Holy Ghost. When we are thus built up, we should do nothing by which to merit anything and be saved; but we do all for the purpose of serving our neighbor. We are to be on our guard here, that we abide in love and not fall from it as the fools who advocate special works and a peculiar life, and thus draw the people from love.

v. 21b. *Looking for the mercy of our Lord Jesus Christ unto eternal life.*

This is the hope that is interested in the holy cross. Therefore, our life should be so ordered that it be nothing more than a constant longing and waiting for the future life, yet so, that such waiting be centered in the mercy of Christ. We must call upon him with the conviction that he helps us from this into the next life because of pure mercy and not because of our own work and merit.

vv. 22-23a. *And on some have mercy, who are in doubt; and some save, snatching them out of the fire.*

That is not expressed in elegant German, but Jude would say: Have mercy on some, save some; that is, let your life be so ordered, that you may have compassion on those who are wretched, blind, and hardened. Do not rejoice or delight thyself over them; but let them go, keep from them and have nothing to do with them. But the others, whom you can snatch out of the fire, "save." Deal kindly and gently with them as God has dealt with you; treat them not harshly nor rudely, but be disposed to them as to those who lie in the fire, whom you are to snatch out and rescue with all care, consideration, and diligence. If they will not allow themselves to be drawn out, then let them go and have mercy upon them—not as the pope and his inquisitors burn and destroy them with fire.

v. 23b. *Hating even the garment spotted by the flesh.*

True, we have received the Holy Spirit by faith and have become cleansed; but as long as we live here, the old garment of flesh and blood still clings continually to us and will not relax its hold. This is the spotted garment that we should lay off and withdraw from as long as we live.

V. The Conclusion of This Picture (vv. 24-25)

vv. 24-25. *Now unto him that is able to guard you from stumbling, and to set you before the presence of his glory without blemish in exceeding joy, to the only God our Savior, through Jesus Christ our Lord, be glory, majesty, dominion and power, before all time and now, and for evermore. Amen.*

These words conclude this epistle. Thus the apostles do: after they have written, taught, exhorted, and prophesied, they pray, express a wish, and give thanks. We have thus now seen in these epistles both what are true, Christian doctrine and life, and what are false, unchristian doctrine and life.